Mistress of Science

Mistress of Science

The Story of the Remarkable
Janet Taylor, Pioneer
of Sea Navigation

JOHN S. CROUCHER &
ROSALIND F. CROUCHER

AMBERLEY

Dedicated to those brave pioneers who
shaped the world of sea navigation

First published 2016

Amberley Publishing
The Hill, Stroud
Gloucestershire, GL5 4EP

www.amberley-books.com

British Library Cataloguing in Publication Data.
A catalogue record for this book is available from the British Library.

ISBN 978 1 4456 5985 5 (hardback)
ISBN 978 1 4456 5986 2 (ebook)

Typesetting and Origination by Amberley Publishing.
Printed in the UK.

Contents

*A science which cannot fail to elevate
and purify the heart*

Janet Taylor

Preface

St Helen Auckland is a village like so many others in England that have blurred into the environs of larger townships as they outgrow their beginnings, in this case Bishop Auckland, in County Durham. It can be found by driving north from London and following the alphabet of thoroughfares that mark out any journey by road in Britain: the M1 Northbound, counting in miles and numbered junctions, past Milton Keynes, Leicester, Sheffield, Leeds; the A1 north towards Newcastle-upon-Tyne; and onto the A86 and into the heartland of County Durham. The unwary traveller, without the benefit of satellite navigation, would probably drive right through it, only realising the mistake on reaching Toft Hill. Asking directions from locals evokes the sound of the wonderfully long-drawn-out 'o' of the north, when you learn of the correct 'rord' to take.

The parish church of St Helen Auckland, or 'St Helen's' as it is commonly known, is a curious mixture of original construction and renovations over nine centuries, but still bears the solid squareness of Norman churches. The path to the large front door bisects the graveyard, with mown grass and headstones sloping at various angles and in differing states of decay on each side. The monuments here, like in all churchyards, capture life in simple phrases. 'Poor Charles' reads one of the unassuming testimonials, saying everything necessary for its occasion. Behind the church you can find another simple epitaph: 'In memory of Janet Taylor. Born May 13th AD 1804. Died January 26th AD 1870.' In 2003 the grave was completely overrun with weeds, and the granite cross that once sat atop the plinth had been dislodged by tree roots and lay face down. Many of the surrounding graves were so worn that you could barely make out the tributes, let alone the inhabitants of these neglected resting places. Blackberries and weeds had wound their way into the grave plots and obscured the delineations of families and generations marked out in this burial ground. Although the tribute was modest, Janet's at least had survived longer than its neighbours, which were mainly made of sandstone and had badly eroded over the centuries.

Who would have thought that here, in this sadly neglected, nondescript burial plot, lay one of the most remarkable and talented women of the nineteenth century? An exceptional mathematician, astronomer, author, teacher, meteorologist, compass adjuster, instrument maker, inventor and businesswoman, Janet Taylor, born Jane Ann Ionn, made her mark as a brilliantly gifted scientist of her era, relentlessly burdened by a struggle to gain recognition in an overwhelmingly male-dominated field. Holding a position of leadership in numerous fields for over thirty years, she attracted the attention of royalty, engaging with the uppermost echelons of her profession and receiving the highest honours and gold medals from kings of Europe as well as the Pope. But almost all that remains to mark her achievement is a neglected gravesite in a small corner of the English countryside, 250 miles from London.

Janet's life was a constant struggle against the establishment, whether for money, which was an ongoing issue, or recognition for her achievements from males who refused to take her seriously. Today she would have been hailed as a genius and an entrepreneurial businesswoman, but 200 years ago she was expected, as a woman, to simply have lots of children and be a good wife. But have children she did – eight of them, along with three stepchildren. Her life was devoted to the benefit of others, notably the seamen who needed to navigate the oceans of the world and return home safely. In doing so she sacrificed a great deal, including her finances as in the end she died bankrupt and penniless.

To make matters worse, by the time of her death she was shunned by most of her children, save for corresponding with her son Deighton, who lived in Australia, and her stepdaughter Emily, whom she visited in Holland.

As if this weren't bad enough, much of the material written about Janet after her death assumed that all the work was done by her husband George and that she simply tagged along, taking over the business when he passed away. Nothing could be further from the truth. She was the brains and driving force behind every aspect of her multi-faceted organisation and her name is on every nautical instrument she produced, and she was the sole author of all the books published. George's role was to take charge of the operational side, that is, to make sure her wishes were carried out to the letter, and dealing with the people who could achieve this. In fact, she was loath to give him any credit at all, on one occasion referring to him as being in control of some small item of business 'nominally'. There is no doubt who was the boss and she would have been appalled that anyone would ever think otherwise.

One of her flagship inventions, the Mariner's Calculator that she patented in 1834, was ingenious and she was bitterly disappointed when it was rejected by the Admiralty as being impractical on the high seas. It was a brilliant device that she felt sure would replace a number of other instruments, but the verdict was that the average seaman would be too clumsy and perhaps even not bright enough to understand it. This was a watershed moment early in her career and led to the severe draining of her finances.

Only one of these instruments remains today and it is in private hands. And so we had the Mariner's Calculator reproduced from her original patent and tested by one of Britain's leading compass adjusters, Ron Robinson. His verdict as to whether she was fairly treated is outlined in the Epilogue and makes for fascinating reading.

As she had no assets other than a few personal possessions, Janet did not leave a will, nor was any personal diary found of her life. This book was pieced together with painstaking research from the many sources listed in the appendices, including letters that she penned, notes that she left and what she wrote in her publications. She was a religious woman, very much a product of her reverend father, and mentioned this in many of the prefaces to her works. There are gaps in specific events and narrative detail that we have reconstructed from fragments of the surviving records together with deductions based upon the experience of women of her time and place in history. Throughout the book the reader will also find interwoven a description of many of the historic happenings of the day. These provide a context for the world events that surrounded Janet, no doubt having an effect on not only her but the population at large.

In the journey, many people have participated – in libraries, archives, public records offices, and the myriad of places targeted by biographers and amateur sleuths – where the formal record keepers are known for their patience, interest and ready assistance. But there are always those who play an especially important role in reconstructing any story: those in the formal record places, but also the keepers, often unwittingly, of letters, diaries, a family bible, notes, photographs, anything that can add colour and movement to an otherwise bare narrative.

We would like to recognise a number of those people whose kind assistance has helped to make this book possible. On a rainy March weekend in Brittany, two of John's distant cousins, Elizabeth Soulsby and her younger sister Winifred Cameron, were kind enough to delve into the absorbing and marvellous family papers from Janet's long-deceased family and produced the rolled parchments and possessions of some of the main characters in this tale.

And then there were the many hours spent with Ron Robinson, master compass adjuster and raconteur extraordinaire, in Hamble in the south of England, with his knowledge and admiration for Janet, his ease with the subject born of a great mastery and love of a good conversation. Prominent among the others who deserve a particular mention is, of course, the late Ken Alger, who did his own initial scouting work, and his kind and generous wife Edna, who enabled his beginning discoveries to form the basis of this story. Special appreciation also goes to the community of St Helen Auckland, principally Father Robert McTeer, the incumbent of the parish, and Alyson Smith who, ably assisted by the wonderfully dedicated women and men of the parish, gave such a warm welcome. From time to time this marvellous group of people stop to remember an amazing woman who is buried in their church graveyard, and shared with the authors a toast to the memory of Janet Taylor on the 200th anniversary of her birth in May 2004.

Special thanks are due to Adrian Webb, historian at the UK Hydrographic Data Office in Taunton, Somerset, and Jenny Wraight of the Admiralty Library in London, now in Portsmouth, who both gave up their valuable time to assist by sifting through the hundreds of documents relevant for this research.

Other players of note included Simon Houfe for showing us the location of the Royal School for Embroidering Females in Ampthill, where Janet had spent some of her early years. The marvellously enthusiastic Anita Atkinson, through her excellent book on Wolsingham Grammar School, shed light on a number of important details. The Reverend Malcolm Goodall, incumbent at St Mary and St Stephen in Wolsingham, where Janet's father the Reverend Peter Ionn had been a curate for thirty-two years, was most welcoming and then, after his retirement, Fred Shepheard, churchwarden of the parish, and his wife Margaret, to whom we were able to present a copy of the portrait of Peter Ionn.

In Australia, the tracing of Janet's story also led to the Henning family, who were the recipients of a pastel portrait of Janet that had been passed through several generations of their family. When Julie Henning learned of the significance of the portrait, knowing that she herself was dying, she ensured that her children would give it to John and restore it to the bloodline of the Ionns. In 2008 they unselfishly fulfilled their mother's wish. It is the only known portrait of Janet.

Much appreciation goes to Dr Gloria Clifton, Emeritus Curator of the National Maritime Museum and Royal Observatory, Greenwich, for her interest, advice and efforts in providing valuable information on the instruments made by Janet. Acknowledgement also goes to Fay Watts McKenzie-Edmonds for the most useful information she supplied and to Bec Lorrimer for her excellent photography of some of the images included in this book.

Thanks also go to Annie Campbell and Alex Bennett at Amberley Publishing for believing in Janet's story and enabling us to bring it to life.

Together we have breathed life into the historical remnants to create this book, in tribute to the life of the remarkable Janet Taylor.

John S. Croucher
Rosalind F. Croucher

I

Wolsingham Beginnings

Jane Ann Ionn was born on 13 May 1804 in Wolsingham, a small village in County Durham, the sixth child of the Reverend Peter Ionn and Jane Deighton, who was the daughter of a country gentleman.

This was a time when Britain had been at war with France since 1793, and in the same month that Jane Ann was born, the diminutive French general Napoleon Bonaparte was made Emperor of France. For thirty of the forty years up to the end of the Napoleonic wars in 1815, Britain was involved in battles that were, for the most part, fought at sea. At the same time British merchant ships were also sailing to the far reaches of the globe. Britain had lost the American colonies after they declared independence in 1776, and turned her eyes on transportation of convicts. This led to the settlement of Australia in the southern hemisphere and on the other side of the world. The merchant fleet doubled to meet the demand in trade and transportation to the southern oceans. At the time of Jane Ann's birth, seafaring was a national industry and one family in six was reliant upon the ocean in some way for their survival.

But while Britannia ruled the waves, it was an uneasy reign as the sea could turn without warning. The dangers were often hidden and ships could founder in the blink of an eye. To make matters worse, navigation charts were often rough and incomplete. Too often serious compass errors were not fully understood, and the increasing use of iron on ships from 1810 only made the circumstances more serious. The problems were compounded by the poor standard of education of seamen in nautical matters. All of this led to the inevitable consequence of a substantial loss of ships and many lives. These were typified by 343 British ships being stranded or wrecked in 1816; in 1817 it was 362; and 409 the following year. As a result, an average of 763 seamen were dying at sea each year, resulting in an ominous state of affairs that showed no signs of abating.

This carnage had been going on for decades, one of the more notable disasters being the devastating loss of the convoy of ships led by HMS *Apollo*. The *Apollo*, a new frigate accompanied by HMS *Carysfort*, set sail from Cork on 26 March 1804 with sixty-nine merchant ships. They were heading for the West Indies, but on Sunday 1 April gale-force winds appeared without warning, with very heavy seas. Captain John Dixon thought that they were about 100 miles west of Portugal, and the fleet dutifully followed his lead. It was at 3.30 a.m. the next morning that the *Apollo* ran aground about nine miles south of Cape Mondego on the coast of Portugal, not at all where they thought they were, and the vessel was thrown again and again onto the rocks in the heavy seas. The captain and the crew, most stark naked, clung to whatever they could lay their hands on, with Dixon issuing orders as best he could in the dreadful conditions.

In an act of desperation they endeavoured to use the few remaining of the thirty-six guns, those few that had not disappeared into the sea, to warn the other ships, travelling closely behind. But visibility was so bad that these warning shots were too late to save them. As morning dawned Captain Dixon saw to his horror that at least thirty other ships of the convoy had also struck the rocks, some sinking before his eyes with the loss of the entire crew. As the shore was tantalisingly close, many tried to save themselves by swimming toward the coast, but were drowned in the roiling seas, while many others died of exposure while waiting for rescue. Dead bodies drifted onto the shore with other wreckage from the ships scattered over ten miles of beach. The *Carysfort* had shifted course on the evening of 1 April without waiting for the signal from *Apollo*, and a number of vessels in the convoy followed her to safety. Eleven days before Jane Ann was born, *The Times* carried a report of the disaster and a list of the dead, including the brave but unfortunate Captain Dixon.

Who or what was to blame for such a disaster? In such fierce weather the *Apollo* was reliant upon her wildly inaccurate compass, distorted by a load of additional iron on board. A series of small errors in heading were compounded over the days at sea, eventually adding up to many miles off course.

Sadly the catastrophe was far from an isolated one. Many remembered only too well the tragic sinking of the fleet of naval ships in 1707, over a century years before, under the command of Rear Admiral Sir Cloudesley Shovell. Sailing in convoy, like the ships with the *Apollo*, over 800 men were lost. They were not in battle, but heading home to England in the belief that they were sailing in the right direction, but they were not. In fact, the fleet was rapidly approaching the hazardous rocks of the Isles of Scilly some twenty-five miles south-west of the actual Channel entrance at Land's End. The entire crew, including Rear Admiral Shovell himself, perished as his ship, *Association*, disintegrated under the might of the elements. Aware of the tragedy too late, the following ship, *St George*, struck the same reef but somehow managed to suffer only a glancing blow, losing only part of her stern gallery. Fate wasn't as kind to the remaining ships and they were all smashed to pieces under the savage impact. None of their crews survived. The sinking of Shovell's fleet was to prove the major catalyst to the final solving of the elusive problem of the determination of longitude, through the award of prizes by the Board of Longitude, entrusted with finding a solution.

While the sea had its dangers, these great disasters prompted many scientists, mathematicians, teachers and instrument makers to find solutions, providing enormous employment prospects for young men as Britain depended on the sea in support of her growing empire. Such opportunities reached into the heart of many villages throughout England, particularly those where the principal occupation for young men was to go down the mines. One such village was Wolsingham, where Jane Ann was born. To appreciate why she embarked upon a life to assist mariners, it is necessary to go back to her village and learn more of Jane Ann's early years.

One of the townships in the picturesque area known as Weardale, Wolsingham lies on the north bank of the valley of the River Wear, which flows eastwards to Bishop Auckland, then to the city of Durham itself before finally reaching the sea at Sunderland. The people of the community worked almost exclusively as crop farmers or in the manufacturing activities of the area, making linen and woollen cloth, or in the lead, coal and limestone works that developed around the resources of the region. At the time of Jane Ann's birth, however, it was lead mining that dominated; and the Durham valleys, with Weardale at the centre, became known as the 'Lead Dales'.

Like so many other villages scattered across the English countryside, the life of Wolsingham centred on the parish church and the market. Letters arrived promptly at nine o'clock every morning by 'horse post' and were despatched every afternoon at ten minutes to three. The market was always on Tuesdays with the rhythm of the year, and of life, being marked by the seasons, by the births, deaths and marriages of the people. In this close and interconnected society, children were named after their parents and grandparents with the gravestones in the churchyard of the parish church of St Mary and St Stephen weaving the names, one into the other, in the tapestry of village kinship. Common among these were Allinson, Coulson, Thomson, Chester, Dixon and Deighton, all intermingling across generations and back again, with the recurring forenames of ancestors bearing witness to the familiarity and comfort of a small community.

The church had its own story to tell. The first timber structure, built for the Prince Bishops during the Weardale hunt in the twelfth century, was eventually replaced by a stone church that was built as if in chapters, each one recording its own age. The latest incarnation invokes memories of its past and things of the region, with its square Norman tower, still so evident today, marking the beginning of its present history from the thirteenth century. Crenulations were added to the tower during Tudor times, as they were to so many of the churches dotted across the landscape, and a lead roof, then clerestory windows in the 1700s as the wealth of the region grew. The dedication of the church to St Mary and St Stephen also spoke of its history, linking the Anglo-Saxons and the Normans in the names of their saints. And, like so many other young men and women of Wolsingham, it was at this parish church of St Mary and St Stephen that Jane Ann's parents, Peter Ionn and Jane Deighton, met.

Peter Ionn was born on 8 March 1762, the only child of Matthew Ionn and Elizabeth Chester. When he was six years old, the family moved to the town of Penrith where he attended the Free Grammar School, which was open to all boys of the parish. The headmaster, John Cowper, was a self-declared 'philomath', a lover of learning who found himself caught up in the contemporary fascination with topics such as mathematics and astronomy. Geometry, algebra, astronomy and navigation were all normal fare in schools, particularly in England's north-east where, during the 1700s, 40 per cent of British ships were built.

For many young men, the possibility for advancement away from the confines of the north-east and the mines to pursue a life in seafaring or in the trade enterprises of the East India Company was very attractive. From its beginnings as a commercial trading operation under a Royal Charter by Queen Elizabeth I in 1600, the British East India Company grew into a major quasi-colonial power in its own right. For a schoolmaster in eighteenth-century north-east England, the presence of seafaring and the career possibilities it offered were pervasive, and so it drove the curriculum.

The master was appointed by the bishop. His first responsibility was 'to instruct his scholars in the ground of religion', next 'in the plainest and most familiar sort teach them grammar, and the Latin and Greek tongues', and finally to inform them 'in good nurture and manners which are of themselves an ornament to religion and good teaching'. These principles were fairly universal for all such schools of the day.

Cowper's influence made a lasting impression on young Peter who would himself ultimately become a schoolmaster. His first posting was at South Shields, a town at the mouth of the River Tyne, followed by the position as master of the Free Grammar School at Wolsingham. In April 1783 he became the sole teacher of about forty boys, about one-third of whom were boarders, covering all stages of education. With only half of the class enrolled as paying students, the remainder being 'charity', the master had to be

> well reported for his knowledge, religion and life ... a lover and forward embracer of God's truth, a man ... diligent and painful in his own studies, of a sober and amiable carriage towards all men, able to maintain the place of a schoolmaster with dignity and gravity, given to diligent reading of God's word.

For his efforts Peter was paid the sum of £40 each year, not a large sum by any means, even for the times. In addition to the schoolhouse itself, he was entitled to reside in a dwelling house, garden (or 'garth'), along with over twenty acres of land on both sides of the River Wear.

By all accounts and despite his youth, Peter soon earned the respect and admiration of his pupils in the role as the new Master. Evidence of this is provided by a former student William Nicholson who wrote the following article in the 1840s on his experience at the school in those early years. Nicholson's family had been associated with the Church of St Mary and St Stephen and parish life in Wolsingham for over 100 years.

RECOLLECTIONS OF MY YOUTH

> I am an old inhabitant and a native of the town of Wolsingham and my memory serves me for more than half a century. I was schooled at the Free Grammar School. I remember well the headmaster the Reverend Peter Ionn and a jolly old boy he was, a good man for all that, we liked him as most school boys like those who are set over them, to instruct and thrash them, for flogging was part of the Master's privilege at the time I am speaking of. We had a capital school, 7 a.m. was the hour for school, mind before breakfast, that meal was almost swallowed whole as we only had from 8 to 9 allowed for both breakfast and play. We had no school bell or Church clock either, but a big lad or the assistant – The Usher I think we called him – cried out at the top of his voice 'All in, all in' when there was a general rush for the school door.

Mind, we were a strong force, 14 or 15 boarders, a score of pay and as many charity cases, not a few nearly men. How unlike the present day with scarcely a dozen puny lads, and what a noise about national Education! Well, when we were all settled in our seats our Reverend Master, whom we had learnt to fear if not love, took off his hat and we all went down on our knees while he read prayers, which we all repeated 'sotto voce' after him.

We boys who had not got our tasks off had to stand behind the door as punishment, which I am sorry to say was often the writer's lot, and so the regular routine until twelve o'clock. How glad were we to hear our good Master pronounce the welcome, cheering and gladdening word, to our empty stomachs (Ettiprandium) whether it was Greek or Latin us low class chaps could not tell, but we set off helter skelter.

As soon after dinner as possible we were again at our games until two o'clock – to think of doing things at those times it almost makes one get young again – what games at marbles, what Tows were lost and won, at scabs, hey what feats were played on both sides, what shins were broken, what bathing, how near drowning!

The breaking up of school at Christmas was an event leaving a lasting impression on my mind. On the afternoon of that blessed day we attended in our Sunday jackets and best corduroy trousers, some with two pence, some with three pence, and some even with sixpence in the said corduroy pockets. We clubbed all our money and purchased gingerbread snaps and nuts. The sixpenny lads had some punch but we poorer fellows with the corduroy had only some warm ale.

Our Reverend Master made a little speech, he hoped we would behave ourselves properly during the holidays, that he would be sorry to hear any complaints; we were to be sure to attend Church and always to bow our heads to gentlemen and especially the Rector. You have holiday one month come Monday. We responded with 'Hip Hip Hurrah, Hip Hip Hurrah!'

A month and four days was a long time to look forward to – we thought it would never end. Yet alas it did end and then away to school again.

W. N.

The rector referred to in Nicholson's notes was William Wilson, who from time to time had to provide information about his parish and curate to the Lord Bishop of Durham. One set of early responses gives an additional insight into the day-to-day life that Peter might have led. Having the role of 'surrogate' meant that Peter was authorised to conduct sermons and perform other duties in the church if the Rector so wished.

For the next few years Peter fulfilled his contract according to the terms of the school's foundation in 1612 by teaching 'Latin, Writing and Arithmetic, plus Classics if required'. It was customary in the case of poorly endowed schools for the trustees to allow masters to extend their curriculum in order to attract paying pupils. By 1790 the school numbers had grown to fifty-five boys, of whom fifteen were boarders, twenty were fee-paying and twenty were 'charity'. One fortunate legacy of his own schooling was that Peter became one of a number of teachers in the north of England to include the subject of navigation as an extracurricular activity. No doubt this would also have been an attraction for some fee-paying customers as it would have assisted them in gaining employment in organisations such as the East India Company.

Peter Ionn was an impressive and ambitious man, also seeking ordination in the Church, although the documentation in support was altered, most likely by himself, to make him appear a year older than he really was.[1] The influence of his own schooling came to the fore in expanding the curriculum, with his interest in navigation sparked by John Cowper. Not only was navigation a personal passion, but it soon became a calculated addition to the schooling he offered.

In May 1785 Peter undertook an additional role as curate, requiring him to conduct a morning service 'with a Sermon after', as well as afternoon prayers, while on Wednesdays, Fridays and holy days he also held morning prayers at eleven o'clock. And at such times the boys of the school were also required to attend. These activities brought him into close contact with the parishioners, and it was through this role that he would meet his future wife.

In his role as curate, Peter was subject to regular 'visitations' by his superiors. An example of this took place on 30 June 1789 during the Easter Visitation by the Right Worshipful Samuel Dickens, Doctor in Divinity, Archdeacon of the Archdeaconry of Durham, accompanied by the Reverend Thomas Hayes, Clerk, Master of Arts, Commissary of Official of the Archdeacon. On such occasions the rector and the curate were summoned to give a report on the state of affairs at the church and in the parish. In some instances, those unfortunates accused of crimes against God were also made to appear and their sins highlighted. On this particular visit the Reverend Wilson excused himself so that Peter had to entertain the pair by himself. Fortunately, there were no sinners to present on this occasion.

In 1786 the school was demolished and rebuilt on the same site, partial funding being provided by the Reverend Egerton, the minister at St Mary and St Stephen's Church which was adjacent to it. Other financial aid came from Lord Crew. The church walls were demolished and reconstructed with today the building serving as the church and Masonic hall.

An old stone tablet that still remains in the wall of the old Grammar School reads:

> THIS GRAMMAR SCHOOL
> WAS BUILT BY BISHOP EGERTON
> TRUSTEES OF LORD CREW
> AND OTHERS IN 1786
> WHEN THE REVEREND PETER IONN
> WAS SCHOOLMASTER SUCCEEDED BY
> THE REVEREND PHILIP BROWNRIGG

In 1792 a smallpox epidemic passed through Wolsingham, which would have had an effect on the whole town. By 1799 the population of the parish had grown slowly to 1,745. One piece of information recorded at that time occurred on 6 August 1799, when a meeting of the Trustees of the Grammar School was held in the schoolhouse. At that meeting there were a number of rules and regulations that were passed and entered into the parish register. Also present was Peter Ionn, who bore witness to the motions that were carried. Records also show that just two weeks before, on 22 July, Mary Nicholson was executed at Durham for poisoning her mistress. However, before the hanging was complete, the rope broke and she fell to the ground. The unfortunate woman was hanged on the second attempt one hour later. In contrast, it was also recorded that a 102-year-old woman passed away on 1 September.

Jane Deighton was the daughter of a 'gentleman' and one of the more prominent men of the district, Seymour Deighton, and his wife Joyce, *née* Thompson. Born in Wolsingham on 20 January 1769, Jane was the second of four surviving children; her elder brother, William, was five years her senior and her younger sisters, Isabella and Joyce, were born in 1772 and 1776 respectively. A well-to-do man, Seymour held considerable power and influence in the neighbourhood, finding the time to be a farmer, malterer and 'general arbitrator amongst the people of Weardale'. A mark of the family's standing in the community was that the Deightons had their own pew in the church. After a brief courtship, Jane Deighton and Peter Ionn were married on 20 December 1788, when Peter was twenty-six years old and Jane nineteen.

Life for the newly-weds was typical for the time, revolving around the family, the school and the church. Peter's duties required him to have an open door to many of the visitors to the parish, along with the boys who were boarding in the school and a growing household of children of his own. There was never a shortage of constant comings and goings. In March 1790, the Ionns had the first of their eight children, a daughter Elizabeth, with the second child, William, born the following year. With the arrival of Isabella in 1795 and Joyce in 1797, Peter and Jane had made their own additions to the population of the community which, by the end of the century, had crept slowly to 1,834. In August 1802 they had their fifth child, Matthew Seymour (known as 'Seymour'); and two years later, on 13 May 1804, their sixth, Jane Ann, the subject of this story, was born. Two more children were to follow: Emeline in 1806 and Frederick Peter in March 1811. Records show that in this year the population of Wolsingham had only increased by 149 in the entire previous decade.

But tragedy struck the family when, two months after giving birth to Frederick, Jane died, aged forty-two – as one of the one in eleven women at the time who died as a result of complications associated with childbirth and post-partum septicaemia. Jane Deighton Ionn was laid to rest in the graveyard of Wolsingham parish church on the same day that her son Frederick Peter was baptised, 1 June. In doing so, she joined her father, Seymour Deighton, her grandparents William and Margaret Deighton, her father-in-law, Matthew Ionn, and all the others in this close, interconnected and loving village.

Peter Ionn, aged just forty-nine himself, was now left a widower with eight children. With his school full of pupils, the congregation and the population still expected him to play an active leadership role, although four of his offspring were under nine and then there was a two-month-old baby.

Jane Ann had only just celebrated her seventh birthday.

II

The Royal School for Embroidering Females

By all accounts, the boys in Peter Ionn's school enjoyed their tuition in navigation as well as other aspects of the mandated curriculum. Astronomy was central to this study, as position at sea, through the determination of latitude and longitude, depended on sophisticated mathematical calculations by reference to the known position of the sun, moon and other celestial bodies. Jane Ann, a young child with a keen intellect and a hunger for learning, thrived in such an environment.

From an early age Jane Ann had been intrigued by her father's library books. Although his income from the position as schoolmaster and curate was quite modest, Peter's marriage, combined with thoughtful and judicious acquisition of property, improved his standing over the years. He was also of scholastic bent and built up an impressive library – particularly in the fields of his interest, navigation and astronomy – that he used both in instructing his pupils and simply for the sake of just having the books. He collected works such as the treatise of geometry of the third-century BC Greek mathematician Euclid, *The Elements*, Robert Norman's treatise on magnetism, *Newe Atractive* (1581); William Barlowe's treatise on navigation, *The Navigator's Supply* (1597); Sir Isaac Newton's, *Principia* (1687); and, what would have been highly prized, Dr William Gilbert's *De Magnete* (1600). Highly elegant creations, such as the star chart of the northern skies produced by the Reverend John Flamsteed, the Astronomer Royal, were also greatly treasured. But perhaps his unique and most precious purchase was a simple tiny piece of 'lodestone', from a travelling vendor of all manner of things at one of the fair days in Wolsingham.

Lodestone is magnetic and has poles; when suspended, it will point north to south. It was perfect to demonstrate to his pupils its power and importance in the art of navigation – and how intriguing the magic of the dark-grey piece of 'leading' rock (from the Anglo-Saxon 'lode', meaning 'to lead'). It captured Jane Ann's imagination, and she was transfixed by the tricks of the magnetised needle stuck in a cork and floating in a bowl of water. For the able and curious child it provided endless hours of fascination as she coaxed it from its determination to point north, with iron pots and kitchen implements in invented games of what to scientists and navigators was known as 'magnetic deviation', caused by the distorting effect of iron in proximity to the compass.

Jane Ann crept in to the back of the classroom while her father was teaching the boys to listen and watch. But it was far from an easy time for her as the other pupils resented her presence and taunted her mercilessly when her father wasn't looking. Rarely, and out of frustration with the boys, Peter would look to her for an answer, but rather than such exercises showing the students how readily they could find the answers themselves, it simply created anger and embittered them against this strange child; this *girl*!

Learning to bear this, she managed to steel herself to ignore the taunting for the sake of the knowledge she was gaining from the lessons. Even as the very young child that she was, she understood that if she felt hurt, dispirited or discouraged by the nastiness of the boys, *she* would be the loser, not them. Having a keen sense that she was smarter than all of them and that this inflamed the situation perhaps more than anything, she was very careful in the ways she showed her intellect. These were lessons that she needed to remember for the whole of her life.

Peter Ionn well knew he had an enormously gifted child who plagued him with complex questions when out of earshot of the boys. Where the talents of his pupils were often wanting, their attention so easily drawn to the games of marbles and general horsing around, Jane Ann was developing a prodigious ability in mathematics. So much so that her father used her as his testing ground, even utilising an orange, peeled and segmented, to explain the functioning of the spherical geometry that explains longitude.

For each segment, imagine 15 degrees. The circle is 360 degrees. Each segment is an hour. There are 24 hours in a day. Know which segment you are eating and you know where you are!

It was so simple and yet deeply profound as she saw the problem of longitude summed up in an orange. And she would laugh at the simplicity of the explanation, which painted a vivid picture to explain the complexity of mathematics. This was her father's gift, a passion for the subject made more intense by the inspiration of the explanation.

She listened in wonder as her father patiently pointed out the constellations of the north in the clear nights of the Durham sky – Ursa Major, the Big Bear; Ursa Minor, the Little Bear; Pegasus, the Winged Horse; and Orion, the Hunter. They were old and familiar friends to the scholarly schoolmaster and he was warmed by this young girl's delight in his lessons as the pattern of the stars became imprinted upon her imaginings. He would point to Polaris, the Pole Star, the centre of the turning world and the guide to the north, and tell her that it would be her guide, a constant companion, and that it would always show her the way home. In his precocious daughter he found a kindred spirit.

Peter promised his late wife Jane that their daughters would be educated 'as well as the boys'. With her father being a successful farmer, Jane Ann's mother wanted to ensure that her girls were schooled appropriately for aspiring middle-class women, in reading, writing, arithmetic, embroidery, music, drawing and French. But even at a very young age Jane Ann's intelligence was there for all to see and her mother soon recognised that the lessons she could provide would not be enough to fill her interests or attention.

Jane Ann picked up what she could from her sisters and her tutors, but she learned most from her father, meticulously following all his lessons including Latin and Greek, along with both theoretical and applied mathematics. And she was brilliant at all of them, and just like her father was a true lover of learning with an insatiable thirst for knowledge. She devoured the lessons for the boys in the grammar school, ignoring their bullying, but, above all, she was her father's most important charge and a constant source of inspiration. Her two eldest sisters had to step into the role of household managers, and having to deal with a gifted younger sister, as well as all the other demands of the household and the other siblings, was also becoming increasingly difficult.

During the two years following his wife's passing, Peter did what he could to fill his daughter's hunger for learning, but it was not enough. He could teach her no more, but she deserved the chance to excel, and he was determined to provide that opportunity whatever the cost. And such an occasion finally arose when Jane Ann was just nine years old.

A scholarship became available to the daughters of clergymen, naval or military officers, 'orphans of gentlefolk', to improve their chances of good marriages through better education and accomplishments. The Member of Parliament for Durham City, Michael Angelo Taylor, proposed that Peter Ionn's family benefit in this way. There were five Ionn girls, and advancing one of them through the scholarship would surely help the widower. Elizabeth, now aged twenty-three, Isabella, eighteen, and Joyce, sixteen, may have been considered too old; Emeline was only five. Jane Ann, having just turned nine, was well below the minimum age of fourteen years. But here was a child prodigy who demonstrated an extraordinary gift for mathematics at such a young age. Queen Charlotte, the wife of George III, herself had heard about this remarkable child and specifically waived the age for admission, reportedly saying, 'Let her come – not to work at the tapestry, but at her figures; and let her be educated with the others until she is of age to take the place of one of them.'[2]

And so in the late summer of 1813, Jane Ann boarded the mail coach in Wolsingham market to travel a journey of some 230 miles to the royal town of Ampthill, Bedfordshire, about forty miles north of London, to attend school. At least five years younger than the other girls, she had been awarded a scholarship to attend a school sponsored personally by Queen Charlotte. It was quaintly known as the 'Royal School of Embroidering Females', due to the numerous complex and lavish tapestries made by the girls that were used by the queen in the refurbishment of Windsor Castle. It was essentially a finishing school, with an eye on 'improving' girls for marriage. They were given instruction in music, languages, poetry, drawing, dancing, mathematics and astronomy, the 'practical part of science'. But they were also taught embroidery, one of the domestic accomplishments of middle-class women and quite distinct from 'sewing' or common needlework. The queen, herself the mother of fifteen children, was a renowned admirer of female achievement and personally sponsored the school with £500 a year. Only four scholarships were awarded at the Ampthill school annually and the recipients had to be at least fourteen years old. What, then, was a nine-year-old girl doing there?

It is difficult to imagine just how daunting the trip to her new school must have been when Jane Ann boarded the coach in Wolsingham market. There were no motor vehicles, not even a train, with the first successful steam railway in England, the Liverpool to Manchester Railway, not opening for passengers until almost twenty years later. The journey was all by coach, first by mail coach for the connecting legs to the main south road to London, then by stage coach, on roads that the Romans saw fit to build as they stamped their mark of empire abroad. The segments of the journey, up to forty miles a day in summer, were punctuated by stopovers in coaching inns where the teams of six horses were changed. Establishments such as 'The Red Bull', 'The White Bull', 'The Cock', 'The Bear', 'The Swan's Arms', 'The White Rose', 'The Turk's Head', the names of the taverns depicted in pictures on signboards hanging over the door, merged into a patchwork of history and zoology as mile added to mile of the trip south.

It is not known for sure who accompanied her on this trip. Perhaps it was one of her older sisters, or even her older brother, William, who had recently completed his articles of clerkship with his uncle George Dixon in Bishop Auckland. Jane Ann would have travelled as an 'insider', those that were seated inside the coach, while the 'outsiders', poorer and generally rougher clientele, sat on the roof and next to the driver.

To a nine-year-old girl, to be an 'outsider' may have seemed much more fun, but she had to be content with watching the soles of the feet of the roof-bound passengers as she peered out of her window to catch a glimpse of both the changing countryside and the imagined excitement of seeing it all from the roof. But for many, even the thick leather braces that cushioned some of the jolting were not enough to stem the queasiness brought on by the shaking and bouncing of the coach, drawn by the big, strong Cleveland bays and German coach horses. After a week of travelling like this, Jane Ann was delivered into the care of Mrs Nancy Pawsey, the proprietress of the Royal School for Embroidering Females, at No. 105 Dunstable Street, Ampthill.

Queen Charlotte took a great personal interest in the school that she sponsored and visited it often, making an effort to memorise as many girls' names she could, calling them her 'protégées'. She did so with the thick German accent of her youth – she had grown up as a young princess in the duchy of Mecklenburg-Strelitz. For the queen, now in her early seventies and very plump after fifteen pregnancies, these visits provided a permissible outlet for the passion and energy of such an intelligent and committed woman. Her public life was otherwise immensely circumscribed by the expectations of court, along with the great difficulties created by the mental illness of her beloved husband, George III, and the scandals that surrounded her son George, Prince of Wales. The queen's beautiful blue-grey eyes and genuine warmth always put the girls quickly at ease.

School days at Ampthill, especially for one so young, provided an interesting challenge and experience. Although there were no pupils near her own age at the school, Jane Ann was treated with much kindness and affection, fitting quickly into the role of their adopted 'younger sister'. Her preoccupation with 'figures' provided great amusement but her mathematical precociousness proved to be most useful in completing their own arithmetic exercises. Whereas the older boys at her father's school had been a constant torment, at Queen Charlotte's school, while the girls considered her odd, they readily turned it to their own advantage – and entertainment – but without the nastiness of the boys in Wolsingham. While the older girls drew elegant watercolours of bowls of fruit and worked their, Jane Ann turned her produce into imagined globes of the earth, each with segments of 15 degrees, and saw in the landscapes and the tapestries their geometric forms and mathematical maps. She was singularly preoccupied with her own view of the universe.

Her letters home to Wolsingham, and to her father, were filled with these new world experiences. She was especially delighted to report that she lived in 'an ant infested hill', the meaning of 'Ampthill' in Anglo-Saxon. The local market took place on Thursdays, not Tuesdays as it was in Wolsingham, but it was a relentless carnival of all manner of things, with cattle and goods pouring into the town centre. Looking out the windows of the school in Dunstable Street, the main access to the stalls, the sights and smells provided great entertainment and an immense distraction. Amongst this kaleidoscope of images were the recruiting parties for fighting men, still seeking willing, and often unwilling, volunteers for His Majesty's wars. Led by a piper, a drummer and a sergeant in their bright red jackets, they fought for attention above the braying cattle and competing vendors of all wares. The brave Admiral Horatio Nelson had beaten the French in his great sea victory in the Battle of Trafalgar in 1805, giving up his life in the process, but the war against Napoleon still needed the fighting men of England to do their duty. The cries of the vendors would have reminded Jane Ann of home, although nothing was quite like the calls of 'Old Joe', the pieman of Wolsingham, whose entreaties for the fare baked by his wife could be heard two miles away across the dales.

There were even stronger echoes of home in St Andrew's, the church the girls attended, with its Norman tower adorned with Tudor crenulations, bearing a striking resemblance to the church of St Mary and St Stephen in Wolsingham. It also honoured its leading citizens and curiously had a cannonball in its yard, the very one that killed one of its own most eminent men, Richard Nicholls. The monument to Nicholls was located in the memorial pediment on the north side of the altar. The worthy Richard, as a dutiful naval man, had captured New Amsterdam from the Dutch in the Americas in 1664. The British flotilla accepted the surrender of the Dutch and renamed the city in honour of James, Duke of York, who had been granted the Atlantic coast of America by his older brother, Charles II. It was then that 'New Amsterdam' became 'New York', in honour of the duke. Richard was killed in a later battle in 1672, and his body, and his cannonball, were brought home to Ampthill. The girls noted the history lesson told by his memorial, like that in so many other churches across the country, but, for Jane Ann, it was the cannonball that held the most fascination, intriguing as it was with the mathematical and physical properties of a large, heavy metal sphere, in sharp contrast to the pots and pans of her compass games back in Wolsingham.

There were other historical lessons to be found in the grounds of Ampthill Castle, with its cross commemorating Katherine of Aragon, the first wife of Henry VIII. Katherine lived in the castle from 1531 until her husband was able to secure the annulment of their marriage in 1533. An 'annulment' it was, notwithstanding over twenty years of marriage to the king, and precipitating his marriage to Anne Boleyn, along with the establishment of the Church of England. During Katherine's time in Ampthill she introduced lace-making to the town, and in turn they recognised the contributions of their rejected queen, erecting a cross in the park of the castle with an inscription commemorating 'the mournful refuge of an injured Queen' in 1770. It was through visits to such sites that the girls of Mrs Pawsey's school learned, and remembered, to a greater or lesser extent, their lessons in English history. But it was the poignant rhyming on the gravestone in the churchyard of St Andrew's, like that on the grave of Mary Boughton, who died in 1745, that provided the rhythm of their walk back to Dunstable Street after Sunday service:

Wife and Mother kind and Dear
Called on God and was Sincear
He gave her hope and faith withall
That did support until His call
The which Affliction long was tryd
In patence Lived in peace She Dyd.

Everyone at Jane Ann's school shared joyously in the great national celebrations when Napoleon was finally defeated at the Battle of Waterloo in June 1815; and then in May the following year when the queen's granddaughter, also named Charlotte, married, just two days before Jane Ann turned twelve. By this time King George III was incapable of ruling, being both blind and mentally deranged. Indeed, his son, George, the Prince of Wales, had been serving in his place as Prince Regent from 1811. Back in the period when he did have his senses, however, George had sought to lock into place strict control on the matter of succession to the throne in the form of the Royal Marriages Act of 1772, making it illegal for any member of the royal family under the age of twenty-five to marry without the consent of the ruling monarch, and, if over this age, without secure approval of their marriage by the monarch or by Parliament.

The aim was to ensure that his sons would marry Protestant princesses, but the Prince of Wales married twice: the first time in 1785 in secret, and without approval under this Act, to the Catholic widow Maria Fitzherbert. The second marriage, in 1795, was to his first cousin, Princess Caroline Amelia Elizabeth of Brunswick-Wolfenbüttel (Caroline's mother was George III's sister and therefore the pair were first cousins). This time the prince sought and was granted approval. Although the prince had eleven children by his illegal but happy first marriage, he had only one by his disastrous and ill-fated second union. Only when Princess Charlotte was born was there a legitimate heir to the throne, a matter of considerable relief to the prince's long-suffering mother.

But the joys of the nation from the princess's marriage soon turned to a pall of gloom when the twenty-one-year-old Princess Charlotte died on 6 November 1817. She had had a difficult pregnancy after two earlier miscarriages and was treated with the accepted remedy of the day, bleeding, which only exacerbated her weakened state. After enduring a fifty-hour labour, the princess gave birth to a stillborn nine-pound boy and, following a post-partum haemorrhage, she passed away. For Jane Ann, the massive outpouring of public grief overshadowed the personal pain in the memory of her own dear mother's death four years earlier.

And then, when the much-loved and admired Queen Charlotte died on 17 November 1818, the Royal School for Embroidering Females suddenly faced a most uncertain future. The Prince Regent was estranged from his wife, Princess Caroline, and there was no one willing to take on the late queen's charitable role. The Prince Regent's brothers were singularly preoccupied with doing their part in securing the Hanoverian succession by contracting legitimate marriages, putting aside their long-standing mistresses or non-approved wives and marrying Protestant princesses, and all the while focusing upon the production of legitimate heirs to the throne.

Jane Ann had now been at the school for five years and had just turned fourteen. For a little while the school continued to struggle on but, without ongoing support from the royal family, it was effectively doomed and soon disbanded. Jane Ann had lost one home and now she was to lose another. In spite of this misfortune, through the intervention and good auspices of family connections, she was placed in a boarding school for girls, conducted by Mr and Mrs Stables, at Hendon, near the village of Hampstead, just outside London. This was an environment that not only allowed a continuation of her own studies, but enabled her to provide some assistance as a tutor in the school. On one level it was simply the next chapter in her life that would 'complete' her formal education. For Jane Ann, still a young woman, it was a small joy when her younger sister, Emeline, just two years her junior, also joined her at the school. Emeline remembered their mother less well than Jane Ann, as she had been only five when she died, but she had also missed her older sister. And for Jane Ann, when joined by Emeline, her heart ached for her childhood, for their father and his tender lessons after their mother died, and she was overwhelmed with a sense of 'home'.

Barely twelve months had passed when, on 29 January 1820, the nation's attention was again firmly directed towards the crown with the passing of George III, the last nine years of his life having been spent away from the public eye with the recurrence of his mental illness. His eldest son, the problematic, dissolute, profligate and rebellious George IV, was now properly king, not 'playing at King' as he had described his position as Prince Regent. But in the year leading up to his coronation, the country was much distracted by the scandals of the king's attempts to disentangle himself from his disastrous marriage to his cousin Caroline by having her not only divorced but also tried for high treason. Queen Caroline had been separated from her husband since very early in the marriage, reputedly having consummated the marriage only once, resulting in the birth of Princess Charlotte. In 1813 Caroline left England to live on the Continent, while the Prince of Wales, as he was then, characteristically continued to engage in his notorious dalliances and liaisons.

As time went on his resolve to be rid of Caroline increased and he engaged agents to spy on his wife and provide him the evidence he needed. As the alleged adultery with her servant, Bergami, occurred abroad, she could not be tried with high treason. But there were other factors at play, with the king's own conduct involving multiple adulterous relationships, along with his prior marriage to Mrs Fitzherbert, making a divorce from Caroline impossible under ecclesiastical law. His only recourse was to seek to punish her through a bill 'of pains and penalties' in Parliament – a special legislative act to inflict a punishment, less than death, for her allegedly traitorous actions, without having to establish the latter in court.

The 'trial of Queen Caroline' polarised the public and not surprisingly delayed the coronation, from which George also excluded her. While the king was condemned for his own behaviour, the queen was portrayed as the innocent and persecuted victim. Even those who did not regard the queen as completely blameless took a charitable view and found the parliamentary proceedings appalling and, given his own transgressions, the king could scarcely complain. A view quietly expressed in many middle- and upper-class houses was that even if she had misbehaved herself and so could hardly be regarded as a heroine, his decadent behaviour was far worse, so why should she be blamed?

For Jane Ann, having turned sixteen in May 1820, life was not greatly occupied by these matters, but more the completion of her education after Queen Charlotte's school had closed. Like so many other intelligent girls of her education, aptitude and 'station', she also became a teacher. With her father's assistance and influence, she readily obtained a position as governess to the family of Reverend John Thomas Huntley, Vicar of Kimbolton in Huntingdonshire.

Kimbolton was a market town very much like Wolsingham, boasting a population of around 1,500 people and nestling amongst sloping hills and woodlands on the River Kym, sixty-two miles north-west of London. The church of St Andrew's, at the western end of the High Street, was a little grander than the parish church in Wolsingham, with clerestory windows, a spire and six bells. And at the eastern end of the High Street was Kimbolton Castle, the seat of the Duke of Manchester. Market day here was Friday, but the noisiest was 11 December each year, when cattle and hogs snorted their way all down the High Street to the Market Place.

Jane Ann settled into Reverend Huntley's household easily, intrigued by his passion for gardening, especially his orchids.[3] In her new role, she could now pass on the lessons she had learned herself to young charges of her own, in English, French, Latin and arithmetic. In selecting subjects for the drawing classes she bypassed the landscapes of the surrounding countryside, replacing them with the patterns of the stars. Constellations became a vehicle for recounting fables of Greek mythology, of English composition, a lesson in drawing and astronomy as well as a moral tale or two.

She regaled her young charges with accounts of the vanity of Cassiopeia, the Ethiopian queen, who considered herself more beautiful than anyone on Earth and in Heaven. The sea nymphs, of unsurpassed beauty, insulted by the queen's claim, decided upon a little revenge. Enlisting the help of Poseidon, the Greek god of the sea, they planned to punish Cassiopeia for her overweening vanity. (A vanity, Jane Ann thought, shared by the king, and expressed most potently in his lavish and indulgent coronation on 19 July 1821.) Poseidon's sea monster began to flood the land. The devastation could only be stopped by the offering of her daughter, Andromeda, as a sacrifice to the demon. Chained to a rock, she was rescued by the intervention of the hero, Perseus. After her death, Cassiopeia was transformed into the constellation that bears her name, reminding all of the dangers of such vanity. Jane Ann's pupils were transfixed by the eloquence and passion with which their young mistress delivered the narrative. They were terrified of the sea monster, but captivated by the saga. It was an interest she had no difficulty in sustaining when, like her father, she used fruit and vegetables in aid of her astronomy and geometry lessons. In doing so she cleverly succeeded in showing the relationship of the sun, moon and the earth, making an otherwise difficult concept seem so natural. It was this uncanny ability that would later change the lives of generations of seamen.

Although life in Kimbolton was somewhat removed from the great disruptions in London during the months of the trial of Queen Caroline, not a soul was untouched by the highly publicised concerns of the day. Immense crowds gathered over the summer months, the trial commencing on 17 August. Petitions and addresses with many signatories were presented in great sympathy for the queen, including one from British seamen on 13 September, and her supporters singled themselves out by wearing white 'favours' – ribbons made into bows. Ever present was the shadow of the revolutionary mobs of Paris streets when such disquiet spilled into the streets of London. When the government announced on 10 November that it had dropped the bill, people were said to have gone mad with enthusiasm for the queen. Guns and cannons were fired, church bells rang all over town and in the evening there were lights everywhere. Great bonfires were lit and fireworks set off in St Giles; even the ships on the River Thames set lights on their mast-heads. The clamour and noise echoed throughout the country and the effusive throng spilled out of London and caught up the outlying towns in its convulsions. By any account it was a memorable and monumental event.

While Jane Ann had been busily engaged in Kimbolton, her father was expanding his own responsibilities by adding to his portfolio, and his income, the cures of the parishes of Esh and Sately, adjoining parishes to Wolsingham. Notwithstanding his willingness to undertake the additional workload, shortly afterwards Peter died unexpectedly on 2 May 1821, aged fifty-nine, when Jane Ann was only days shy of her seventeenth birthday. He had presided over hundreds of baptisms, marriages and burials almost to the day he died. He had been her champion and mentor, but she had left him in 1813 and in the intervening eight years had not returned home, although always vowing to do so.

Now it was too late.

III

Joining the Family Business

The Reverend Peter Ionn was laid to rest in the graveyard of the parish church of St Mary and St Stephen of Wolsingham. Like so many others, he was buried in the very same grave as his wife and his father. He was well loved and well remembered. At the back of the church there is still a memorial plaque, dedicated by his pupils, which reads:

SACRED TO THE MEMORY OF
THE REV^D PETER IONN
LATE CURATE OF THIS PARISH
FOR 38 YEARS
HE WAS BORN AT GREAT STRICKLAND
IN THE COUNTY OF WESTMORLAND
AND DIED AT
WOLSINGHAM ON THE 10TH OF MAY AD 1821
IN THE 59TH YEAR OF HIS AGE
This monument was erected by his Scholars
in grateful remembrance of his care in
teaching them the principles of useful Knowledge,
and in training them up in the
paths of Religion and Virtue.

He was clever, had married well, and managed his fortunes judiciously. In fact, by the time of his death Peter Ionn had become a man of considerable property and achievement, and even quite wealthy. His assets had been boosted by property inherited from his wife, who had been left substantial assets by her father, Seymour Deighton, in 1793. In his will Peter specifically separated his bounty between William, his eldest son, and his other children. Through his education, William had already been advanced financial support when he married in 1818, and in helping his establishment in legal practice. Through his will, Peter sought to redress what he perceived as a paternal imbalance, permitting William to keep the 'furniture and plate' which he had borrowed in setting up house in Bishop Auckland, in addition to the 'remainder interest' in his father's house after allocations to his other children had been dutifully fulfilled.

To oversee the distribution of his assets he appointed his three older daughters, Elizabeth, now aged thirty-one, Isabella twenty-six and Joyce twenty-four, as executrices. This was a specific acknowledgement of the role of these women, especially Elizabeth, who had carefully overseen her father's household and, by necessity, stepped into the breach on her mother's death. Having risen so well to that task, she was now given the principal responsibility of executrix of her father's will, and in preference to William. All the unmarried children could stay in Peter's house until they married, and only after that could William inherit it. As Seymour was nineteen, Emeline fifteen and Frederick only ten, this looked like being some considerable time. Their father's books, papers, prints and manuscripts were to be disposed of, and the other Wolsingham properties were left to the children, apart from William. The net result was that each of them would receive several thousand pounds, a small fortune for the times.

This was a watershed in many respects for Jane Ann and her siblings. The money left to them by their father facilitated their launching of careers, making good marriages and advancing their status in life. Jane Ann was now seventeen, 'finished' at Queen Charlotte's school and had a handy inheritance to support her future. The expectation at this time in her life was to find a suitable husband, a task that should have been easy for a tall young woman of striking appearance, with piercing blue eyes and long, flowing hair. But she was no shrinking violet and had other ideas, never allowing herself a downward tilt of the head to affect demureness. She was determined to transcend the traditional marriage and would not contemplate doing so to a man she did not consider at least her equal in intelligence. This attitude only served to narrow the field considerably.

Acting in the role of children's governess turned out to be a useful occupation for Jane Ann, but after three years it was evident that her world could not be contained within the confines of Kimbolton. The universe of her imagination was full of the patterns of the stars and the complexities of a planet that was not entirely round and, very like the oranges her father used as his models, flattened at both ends. Notwithstanding the often mundane routine of her work in the vicarage, it still provided scope for expressing new ideas. Labouring by the light of the tallow candles in her small upstairs room in the late evening, she filled page after page with diagrams and equations that meant something only to her, and continued her exploration of the world.

In 1824 Seymour at last saw his share of his father's estate and drew upon his inherited entrepreneurial skills to purchase a business in London, a linen draper's shop at No. 44 Oxford Street. Although his father had wanted him to go into the Church, Seymour chose to be a linen draper and had been apprenticed to a first-class shop through the intervention and assistance of a former boarder in his father's school, Robert Taylor, himself a wealthy flax merchant in Holland. Seymour's inheritance now enabled him to set up on his own.

The brilliance of his younger unmarried sister, and her wizardry at figures, were also certainly not lost on him – and, like many bachelors, it was entirely appropriate for Jane Ann, now aged twenty, to live with him to assist him in his house. He even enlisted her support in setting up his business, providing her with an opportunity not only to escape Kimbolton and be with family again, but also to position her in the very heart of London.

Now, over ten years since their childhood days together in Wolsingham, Jane Ann was overjoyed to see her brother again. And it was even better when she learned he had also brought her a parcel from their sisters back home. Elizabeth, Isabella and Joyce recollected well the young Jane Ann's affection for their father's books and how she had lovingly pored over their pages with him on many an evening. They also remembered how torn their father had been when she boarded the coach that took her away from home when only nine, recalling vividly her childhood preoccupations with magnetised needles, and oblivious to the activities of a busy household that was endeavouring to function around her. The parcel contained his favourite books and, to her great delight, the tiny piece of precious lodestone, gently wrapped in silk and in a small wooden box their father had made especially for it. The three sisters had been charged under the will to give his books and papers 'to such of his children as they thought proper' and there was really only one sensible choice: their inquisitive and very able young sister.

Back in Wolsingham, in May of the previous year, Elizabeth, now aged thirty-three, had married George Dixon, a Quaker chemist and wine and spirit merchant (not to be confused with their aunt Joyce Deighton's late husband, but probably a cousin, given the interconnectedness of the Durham community). In November 1824, her twenty-seven-year-old sister Joyce followed with her marriage to the Reverend Matthew Chester, also in Wolsingham. With the rapid growth of their brother Seymour's business, it would have been a sensible and logical opportunity for the remaining unmarried sisters, Isabella, now twenty-nine, and Emeline, nearly nineteen, to travel south and become part of the family team in London. Soon enough, the establishment became even more crowded, with Jane Ann, Emeline, Isabella and Seymour all living and working at No. 44 Oxford Street. It seemed just like old times.

Household tasks were duly assigned, with the eldest of the sisters, Isabella, assuming responsibility for housekeeping – as she had done for her father with sister Elizabeth after their mother died – taking Emeline under her wing, while Jane Ann continued to help develop Seymour's business and worked on her own ideas in any spare time. The large dining table began to resemble that in their Wolsingham home, with Jane Ann's calculations becoming more and more complicated and occupying an even larger space, while Isabella and Emeline were able to spread out some of the fine cloth from their brother's business to make dresses in the latest fashion for themselves. All the while, copious pots of tea seemed to fill every space.

The rhythm of their lives, focused around Sunday services, had echoes of their Wolsingham childhood. Their parish church of St Giles in the Fields, an outstandingly beautiful building, built in the Palladian style in 1734, was in contradiction with its neighbourhood. It stood majestically among a jumble of the nether regions of humanity: prostitutes, thieves, poor labourers, vagrants and transients, stuffed into decaying, stinking tenements, dubbed the 'rookeries' and filling the streets and lanes between the church in St Giles' Circus and Great Russell Street. Everything was mould, dirt and decrepitude; and yet in all of this was the simple beauty of St Giles.

It would have been easy for anyone just to keep to the high side of Oxford Street, avoiding the rookeries below, and wander easily into St George Bloomsbury, designed by a pupil and assistant of the great Sir Christopher Wren, and keep the stench, not to mention the reality, at arm's length. But St Giles had a magic about it in the midst of the squalor of the Rookeries. It was a real parish, connected to a real humankind in all its wretchedness. Peter Ionn had very much admired this church and all its symbolism, revering the great men who also worshipped and were buried here, connected as equals before God in this solemn place. The Ten Commandments, painted in gold behind the altar, preached their edicts to the living as well as the deceased parishioners lying in the adjoining graveyard of the church – the likes of the poet Andrew Marvell, Luke Hansard, printer to the House of Commons, Thomas Earnshaw, watch and chronometer maker, and George Chapman, the translator of Homer. St Giles was also the last church on the route to the gallows at Tyburn, at the corner of Edgeware and Bayswater Roads. The churchwardens paid for the condemned to have a drink at the Angel, the neighbouring public house, before the unfortunate souls 'went on the wagon' and were carted off to be hanged. It was a church with a proud and sad history, with roots deep in the message of forgiveness, redemption and salvation. And it was to this elegant place of worship that the Ionn siblings made their way each Sunday morning.

Following the line of one of the old Roman military roads, Oxford Street was a typical example of busy, mercantile nineteenth-century London. It was noisy, bustling, and the heart of burgeoning middle-class commerce. In addition to a multitude of linen drapers, all competing with Seymour's business, were watchmakers, coach makers, tea dealers, hatters, furriers, corset makers, bonnet makers and gun makers, amongst many other speciality retailers. There were also booksellers. And while the window displays of countless bonnets and other assorted merchandise attracted Emeline's attention, Isabella focused more on the new line of featherbeds with the eternal optimism that she would soon find a suitable husband. But it was the bookshops, above all else, that captured the attention of Jane Ann.

Her father's library had provided an enormous reservoir of knowledge, but they also provoked in her an expanding list of unanswered questions. In teaching navigation to the boys in the grammar school in Wolsingham, Peter Ionn had endeavoured to show his charges the manner in which the pattern of the sun and the moon could be used in aid of finding your location, particularly at sea. Jane Ann spent much of her own time unravelling this for herself. Whenever confused and muddled in thinking through the practical equations such calculations required, she inevitably returned to the simplicity of her father's example of the orange.

It was on one of the walks along Oxford Street late in 1824 that a volume in a window display caught her eye, a newly published work entitled *Treatise on Navigation and Nautical Astronomy* by Edward Riddle. The author's name matched its subject, and she would have smiled as she remembered the challenges of trigonometry for her father's pupils. Riddle was the highly regarded master of the Royal Hospital School at Greenwich, where he taught the sons of officers and men of the Royal Navy and of officers and seamen of the Merchant Service. He was also well known as a regular contributor to the *Ladies' Diary or Woman's Almanack*. This included puzzles and questions for its readers, based on some of the astronomical and mathematical fascinations of the age. One volume would pose questions, while the next would provide answers submitted by readers. Quaintly, both the puzzle and the solution were often in verse.

As an avid reader of the magazine, Jane Ann immediately recognised the name from his enigmas and seized upon the book. It consumed her, but above all it made sense with its sheer *practicality*. It also made the connections for her between the orange and the seas in a meaningful way and further served to remind her of her father. She found herself craving an even deeper understanding of the subject, and to expand her knowledge, an ability to connect the stars, and more especially the moon, to the seas. Her childish games with compasses now took on a far more serious dimension. Kitchen inventions now included a device to measure the inclination of the sun and the moon, effectively creating her own crude quadrant. And as she came to understand it herself, she grasped the true lesson of her father to make the complex simple. His words to her as a little girl during their walks in the dales on moonlit nights continued to resonate: find the Pole Star and she would find her way home.

Her sisters, and the needs of an expanding family concern, drew her back to earth, at least for a time. Isabella, now aged twenty-nine, was still intent upon finding a husband as soon as possible, while Emeline, at eighteen, was soaking up the atmosphere of London with its colour, pace, liveliness, indeed everything she adored. Meanwhile, Seymour still required the full attention of all of his family in a city loaded with excellent business opportunities, but crammed with fierce competition. Together they got on with building their venture, while Jane Ann used her leisure hours to continue her work on navigational trigonometry.

During the ensuing years, Seymour became acutely aware of his precocious sister's mathematical abilities and well remembered how their father's lessons kept her enthralled but held no interest whatsoever for him. But his gregarious spirit and sound head for business gave him the foresight to use her aptitude to advantage. Furthermore, she had become a curiosity to his many friends and customers, among them a naval officer whom he had regaled with tales of his clever sibling, her kitchen tricks and peculiar fascination with navigation. This officer, enormously sceptical and affronted at the very thought that a mere young woman would have such claimed abilities, was determined to expose her. On his next visit to the store he revealed some of the difficulties he had experienced with a complex navigational problem that he had long given up trying to solve. After listening politely and intently, and after several minutes seemingly lost in thought, Jane Ann astounded him by pointing out the errors in the mathematical techniques he had been pursuing, and demonstrated how to solve it properly. Whatever the impact on the young officer, it marked an epiphany for her. It was also the catalyst to write a book of her own.

Becoming an expert on determining a ship's longitude by the lunar distance method for her own education and amusement was one thing, but she was also getting older with no marriage prospect even remotely in sight – and by age twenty, girls who were not at least engaged were potentially doomed to spinsterhood. In May 1829 she turned twenty-five, the very same year that Isabella finally found a husband; on 19 February she married the flax merchant Robert Taylor at All Saints Church, Marylebone. The couple promptly went to live in the Flemish city of Antwerp, then part of the United Kingdom of the Netherlands, where Robert was based.

Isabella's marriage had certainly been a joyous occasion. At thirty-three years of age she had spent much of the previous eighteen years since her mother's death sharing, with her older sister Elizabeth, the responsibilities of being a surrogate mother to her brood of five younger brothers and sisters. It seemed entirely appropriate that all those living in London would be witnesses to the wedding, including the youngest, eighteen-year-old Frederick Peter who was now also living full-time at Oxford Street and apprenticed to his older brother.

Isabella's marriage gave Seymour reason to speculate what would now become of Jane Ann. As her nearest brother, there was an implicit assumption that he would shoulder the responsibility for 'doing something' about finding her a husband. If his business had eventually managed to bring marriage to Isabella, might not the same be true for Jane Ann? Moreover, a marriage for Jane Ann presented an excellent opportunity to consolidate the family fortunes and provide heirs, the next generation advancing the prosperity of their forbears. Daughters and sisters were ideal for marrying and breeding to facilitate these goals, as women of this era could expect to have, on average, six children. And ensuring that the women were more marriageable was part of the business.

An eye-catching, intelligent and accomplished young woman of means should have presented an attractive marriage prospect, but there was considerable doubt she would ever bring herself to perform her part of such a matrimonial 'bargain'. It ran against her principles to spend her life playing the role of the deferential wife who managed the household, saw to her husband's and children's needs and provided offspring to continue the family tradition. In any case, she was now obsessed with the idea of writing her book on navigation, already drafting copious notes that might come in handy. But what man could ever take her seriously or view her as an 'obedient' wife?

Despite her private views on her place in the world, Jane Ann was troubled by the thought of marriage. Like all young men and women she loved the idea of romance, and, although well understanding the implications and responsibilities for women of her position and standing, had also seen its consequences. The demands, and the effects, of pregnancy were undeniable. Her mother had died. Princess Charlotte had died. But married women were considered *respectable* and this alone enabled them to fulfil their destiny. And yet by marrying, a woman could also lose everything. If she wrote her book, and was successful, any income earned would belong to her husband; it was conflicts such as these that continually plagued her thoughts. Her mother had already been dead for nineteen years, and her beloved father was also long gone.

For Jane Ann the choice was now stark: she *had* to marry or be condemned to the role of a 'maiden aunt' to all the children of her siblings. Masking her anxieties, she simply continued with her writing and research, trusting to fate, faith or her brother's good judgement to bring a fitting contender her way. A suitable candidate for her aspirations was just what she needed, not idealistic love to distract her from her writings and her calling. She had become very much her own person, with an air of independence and a focus on the idea of communicating her ideas to seafarers as an author and even as a teacher. To convey the simple beauty of her father's lessons to others, to simplify the complex and impenetrable writings into practical understanding, and therefore common wisdom. To show the world in an orange and to guide mariners on their way home had now become her challenge and burning desire.

Sitting in church, the words of Andrew Marvell echoed in her head:[4]

But at my back I always hear
Time's wing'd chariot hurrying near;
And yonder all before us lie
Deserts of vast eternity.

She shuddered.

IV

Marriage

George Taylor Jane was born on 20 March 1792 in London, the son of Bennett Jane and Rebecca Taylor, and baptised at the Barbican Meeting Place by John Towers, a leading Dissenting Minister. Protestant groups that had broken away from the Established Church of England, Dissenters were allowed this one liberty at the time of George's birth – to be baptised by their own ministers. Like many Dissenters, the Janes were middle-class and committed to the advancement of their family through a broad liberal education, for both boys and girls, in their own schools; and they were supporters of the Whigs, the more radical side of politics. While their religious beliefs put them at odds with the Church of England, they were also loyal to the Crown and encouraged their son, George, to enter the Navy and serve his country during the great struggles with Napoleon. This he duly did, reaching the rank of lieutenant by the conclusion of the war in June 1815, at which time he was twenty-three years old. And like many such naval men at the end of those hostilities, he then returned to civilian life, getting married and finding another suitable occupation.

Despite his service for his country, George was precluded as a Dissenter from holding public office, this being conditional upon being a practising member of the Church of England. And so he pursued a civilian career in business. Gregarious and industrious, his facility for dealing with men had been honed at sea and led him to do well in building a business as a wine and spirit merchant as well as running public houses. His migration into such endeavours came quite easily – and brewing and all associated enterprises was major business in London in the nineteenth century. The vast establishments of the breweries were a wonder in themselves and directions through London were regularly given in terms of public houses, as in this direction of the way to Aldgate:

> Go straight on till you come to the Three Turks, then to turn to the right and cross over at the Dog and Duck, and go on again till you come to the Bear and the Bottle, then to turn the corner at the Jolly Old Cocks, and after passing the Veteran, the Guy Fawkes, and the Iron Duke, to take the first turn to the right which will bring you into it.[5]

By the beginning of 1829, the now thirty-seven-year-old George had built a thriving business as a manager for the brewer Sir Henry Meux and was licensee of the Turk's Head Public House at 50 Haymarket, London. He was also the proud father of three children: his namesake, George Taylor (Jr), aged twelve, Emily Ann, aged eleven, and Charles Frank, aged seven. But in April that year tragedy struck when George's wife Hannah (*née* Gooch) passed away and, in a similar vein to Peter Ionn before him, he was a widower with three young children to take care of. Sir Henry suggested to George that he might go abroad for a while to think on other things – a trip to the Netherlands, perhaps, to see the great breweries in Antwerp, might be just what he needed.[6]

It was then that fate conspired to bring George Taylor Jane and Jane Ann Ionn together. Not long after Isabella's marriage, and as the autumn chill of 1829 hit London, their brother Seymour realised that his business, begun with such excitement and enthusiasm, was now failing. He had no choice but to leave London and when an opportunity opened for him in Hastings, he quickly seized it. By necessity, his siblings also had to go elsewhere. A position of governess for Emeline was readily found, with the family of the barrister George Hutton Wilkinson at Harperly Park, County Durham – a fine estate that Wilkinson had fortuitously inherited by marriage. Younger brother Frederick Peter was placed in a shop in Newcastle to continue learning the drapery trade. As for Jane Ann, she went to Antwerp where Isabella was living and looking forward to the birth of her first child. And it was in Antwerp that she would meet George Taylor Jane.

Jane Ann was on her way back to Isabella's from an English bookshop with a stack of books balanced precariously in her arms when it started to rain. The streets were damp from a recent shower and she stumbled, her precious bundle spilling all over the pavement around her. As it happened, George had just finished his meal at a nearby inn and emerged in time to see her trying to gather up her belongings. Although he was unperturbed, indeed quite at home, in the inclement weather, he was taken aback at the sight of a young woman desperately scrambling to gather her scattered belongings. He also noticed some of the English titles of the books.

'Sun beyond sun, and world to world unseen, measureless distance unconceiv'd by thought,' he quoted out loud after spying David Mallett's poetry amongst the tumble of books. In spite of her misfortune, she quickly looked up, quite taken aback at the deep baritone voice reciting English words that were close to her heart. Gazing directly into the craggy face of George, her first thought was that such a look could only be acquired at sea.

At once he raised his hat, introduced himself and offered assistance. He was rather intrigued by the titles being retrieved from the muddy pavement, noticing a mixture of the popular books of the day and a volume on sea navigation. As the heavens looked about to open up again, George asked whether she had far to go, even offering to fetch her a cab. She thanked him politely but declined, saying that it was only a short walk. But almost before the words were out the rain began teeming down once more and this time she had no choice but to accept his offer to hold her umbrella over her for the walk home. In ordinary circumstances she would have thought this rather 'forward', as she had not met him before, but this time she was happy to accept it as a simple gesture of kindness from her fellow countryman. In any case, it was not a time for formality as the alternative was to get drenched, along with her books. So George awkwardly sheltered both her and her books by holding the umbrella aloft. His chivalry in escorting her home also meant he became rather waterlogged himself in consequence.

Jane Ann felt obliged to invite her new acquaintance in to meet her sister and at least to offer him a cup of tea in appreciation of his gallantry and disregard for his own welfare in the wet. As are most protective siblings, Isabella was a little wary of this stranger, although grateful that he had come to the rescue. George sat by the fire in a futile attempt to dry out his saturated coat while they all drank their tea. The difficulty of the moment was somewhat relieved by the arrival of Isabella's husband Robert and, after an awkward start, eventually he and George managed to strike up a respectful, if somewhat strained conversation. George was bursting to find out why Jane Ann was acquiring books on navigation, but the revelation that she was writing her own book on the subject took him completely by surprise. Although the visit was brief, he was intrigued in a way that made him realise there was much more to this lady than even he had first thought. As they made their parting gestures, George asked if he might take the liberty of visiting again as he had found their conversation both fascinating and distracting, diverting his mind away from his recent bereavement (a fact he had revealed as they spoke). For her part, Isabella had been pleasantly struck by his congeniality, quick wit and, above all, kindness to her sister. The knowledge that he was a widower added another reason for her wanting to know more about him.

Over the next few months George took every opportunity for regular visits to Isabella's, ones that Jane Ann welcomed and increasingly looked forward to as here was a man of practical experience in the very field of her interest. Moreover, she quizzed him mercilessly on his time at sea and of the problems that occupied her in navigation. And although he could provide no help with mathematical solutions, when he spoke of the stars in the night sky at sea, images of her father played on her mind. Isabella was also delighted to see George's evident interest in her sister. Having only married at thirty-three herself, and now pregnant with her first child, she didn't want her sister to have to wait so long. And Jane Ann was such an odd one and bound to be rejected by men given her peculiar notions and occupations, she mused. Would he really see her as a possible match? Would her incessant questions eventually drive him away?

As it happened, for his part George wasn't the slightest bit deterred by Jane Ann's obvious intellect and strange obsessions with all things nautical. On the contrary, he found them rather stimulating. His education at a school run by the Independents put girls on a par with boys and, although it changed none of the awkwardness of dealing with the opposite sex, it made him far more accepting of clever and educated women. His conversations with Jane Ann seemed perfectly natural, or at least not as strange as they otherwise might have been.

On one of his visits Isabella learned of his upbringing outside the Anglican faith and was somewhat aghast, their father having admonished them on many occasions to 'keep to the Established Church' and rejecting any erosion of the Church by dissenting doctrines and sects. But, as George explained almost defensively, he had not maintained the religious affiliation of his parents, and his own three children had all been baptised in accordance with Anglican rites and not at the Barbican Chapel, as he had been. To him, his early education was merely a way to explain his current interest and acceptance of an outspoken woman like Jane Ann.

No sooner had George left that same afternoon when the two sisters became engaged in a long and heated conversation, the forerunner of many over the following week. Having initially viewed George as a potential suitor for her sister, suddenly it was all thrown into disarray. To marry a Dissenter would have left their father horrified; she had no doubt that it would have been out of the question. And yet it was a fact that George had been baptised and educated as a Dissenter, a rejecter of the Established Church, and as such would not have been welcome in their father's house. Just what were they to do? George had certainly not declared himself in the sense of proposing marriage and so there was nothing lost if they were not to allow any further visits. And as she was a guest in her older sister's household, Jane Ann was obliged to do as was required of her. But upon retreating to her room she was utterly confused.

The prospect of shutting the door on George made her feelings come sharply into focus. Suddenly she realised not only how much she sorely missed their conversations, but also how much she longed for the man himself – Dissenter or not. Her growing affection for him had gradually coloured their meetings and their conversations, since here was a man she could truly speak to. He was someone she not only respected but actually liked, and she was now acutely aware of the ever growing warmth between them. Where she had initially regarded him rather like a benign uncle, the more they spoke, the years between them seemed to melt and a bond of an entirely other kind began to grow.

George was also deeply affected by this evident change of heart at Isabella's. The abruptness of it also made him suddenly and acutely aware of the genuine feelings he now felt, not to mention that his children also needed a new mother. Here was an intelligent, lively and attractive young woman, full of purpose and energy and, as if to confirm his view, she was also entirely unlike his late wife, Hannah. With Jane Ann, rather than being reminded of things past, he had become invigorated and renewed. That he also wanted her as his wife was no longer in question and, being twenty-five, she certainly didn't need anyone's permission if he asked her to marry him. But he was sensible enough to realise that ostracising her family would only set up heartbreak and enduring trouble. He needed to win both Jane Ann and Isabella.

First, he wrote to Isabella, acknowledging her position as elder sister and role of mother to her younger siblings. Of course she was concerned. This spoke of the depth of her love and caring for her family, and he wrote how admirable he found this. He, too, respected family, but why should he be punished for his baptism? This was certainly not of his doing and so why should he be held responsible for it? 'Judge me by my actions,' he pleaded. His children were baptised as Anglicans at St Pancras Old Church. This was something for which he *could* be held accountable and here the choice was for the rites of her father's church. Surely this demonstrated his true leanings? He then spoke of Jane Ann. The accident of his birth and early education – yes, by Dissenters – had only led him to a far greater understanding of her abilities and inclinations than others may have had, indeed might *ever* have. Didn't Jane Ann deserve this? Wouldn't this have been what their father truly wanted: someone who appreciated the intelligence and true worth of his children?

He poured out his heart as he declared that not only was he accepting of her interests, but thought her idea of a book was a splendid one, and to be encouraged, not dismissed, as he was sure many men, indeed *most* men, would do so. Being a seaman he knew what was required in the way of assistance and he genuinely felt that he could, in his own way, help her. It was true that he had three children already, but was this so unusual? Many men were widowers and, after all, so was their own father. His children needed another mother, he needed a wife, and Jane Ann needed him. In short, he implied, although not in so many words, that she could not find another man like him. George left no doubt of the extent of importance he placed on the family bonds between Jane Ann and her sister. In a bold move, he vowed that he would not speak to Jane Ann until he had Isabella's acceptance of him, and that he anxiously awaited her reply. If she were to allow him to resume his visits, he would then ask Jane Ann to marry him, but begged her to keep this a secret so that he might put it to Jane Ann himself.

Isabella found herself reluctantly moved by his words. She could not simply ignore his letter. She knew she *could*, but she chose not to. Judge him by his own actions, he had pleaded. This was a powerful argument. How could she deny Jane Ann a chance of happiness? Her sister was quite confronting and increasingly so as she matured and gained further confidence in her views and, indeed, her mission to write a book. Personally she was also less inclined to resist such pleas as her own pregnancy advanced. She was well aware that her older brother William would need to be persuaded, but if she supported the relationship, there was little doubt that she would be able to bring him round. While her younger brother Seymour had taken almost the guardian role in recent years, he had problems enough of his own to worry about at the moment, after his business had failed. If William, the solicitor, were presented the matter as a legal one needing resolution, that would sort him out too, she reflected. As soon as she realised she was thinking in such terms, Isabella knew she could not stand in the way. She wrote to George and said that he may visit again, but that her sister's decision was entirely her own to make.

As it happened, Jane Ann had already decided for herself that she could indeed marry George Taylor Jane and was enormously grateful for this welcome, if not surprising, change of heart in her sister. She also accepted Isabella's suggestion that she should protect her limited fortune, a 'moderate competence' in the language of the time, in some way. William, practising as a solicitor in Bishop Auckland, advised setting up a trust. On marriage, husband and wife became one person, but in property terms the 'one person' would be George. Without the protection of a trust and the intervention of Chancery, any goods and chattels, even including her clothes, would become his property. In effect, by marrying she would lose her entire capacity to act as an individual.

George accepted William's proposal for a trust with good grace, as he had done well in business himself and certainly was not marrying Jane Ann for her money. If securing her inheritance through a trust was a means to pacify her family to some extent, then he was glad of it. Trouble with her family was the last thing he now wanted. For her part, Jane Ann had very clear ideas as to what she wanted to do with any money that was hers from her father; she wanted to open a school and to teach in his footsteps – only this would be a school of navigation. She wanted to write, publish and do everything in her power to help young men find their way at sea.

And so, on 30 January 1830, in the chill of a European winter, George and Jane Ann were married at the British Embassy in The Hague by the Reverend John Hay, Chaplain of the English Church at Rotterdam. Although Isabella had desperately wanted to be present, it proved impossible as she had only just given birth to her first child on 1 January – a midwinter daughter, whom out of affection for her sibling she named 'Jane Ann'. At the age of thirty-four she was quite old to be giving birth, especially as this was her first child. She was still full of trepidation and didn't dare to travel, especially over the necessary eighty miles in January, the dead of winter.

Just how much their own marriage was a new start for both George and Jane Ann is reflected in the fact that they both changed their names. They even agreed to take 'Taylor' as their marital surname, this being George's mother's maiden name. Jane Ann also curiously changed her given name from 'Jane Ann' to 'Janet'. It was fortunate that at this time this could be done simply, requiring no formality other than a commitment by both and then the adoption of the new names. While a certain fluidity in names, particularly in relation to spelling, was quite usual, such a decided shift by a couple on marriage tells another story.[7] It is one of equality and commitment to starting an entirely new chapter in life, serving to distance George from his Dissenting roots and his former married life to Hannah, while marking for Jane Ann a new identity as 'Mrs Janet Taylor'. This would be the name by which she would be known for the rest of her life. It was a symbolic baptism for them both.

After their honeymoon in Holland, the couple returned to London and set up residence at No. 6 East Street, Red Lion Square, a short distance from Oxford Street.

Her marriage had provided Janet with a ready-made family, even before she had even begun to think of the possibility of children of her own. Well aware that this could be a trying time for his new bride, George soon arranged for his housekeeper, the widowed Mrs Sara Marton, to stay with them at East Street. She knew his children well, and was utterly dependable and unfailingly loyal to her employer. Mrs Marton's husband, Samuel, had served in the Navy with George, who had taken him under his wing in civilian life, eventually enlisting him in his wine and spirit business. In consequence, when Samuel knew he was dying, George made him a promise to look after Sara if she needed help. As a result she became George's live-in housekeeper with his first wife, Hannah, in St Pancras, helping her with their children. When Hannah herself became gravely ill, it was Mrs Marton who nursed her until she passed away in April 1829 at the age of thirty-three. Hannah had been like a younger sister, almost a daughter to her, and the circumstances brought back the grief of the loss of her husband; this made her all the more committed to George and the children.

And so when George announced his intention to remarry, and only six months after Hannah's death at that, Mrs Marton could barely disguise her strong disapproval. But she also was painfully aware of the reality of life for women, for children, and for the widowed fathers. Women died; children died, sometimes more often than even the men. It was a widowed father's duty to his children, and indeed to his late wife, to find a 'suitable' new wife and mother as soon as practicable. So Sara Marton buried her pain and saw to making the household a good one and the children as happy and secure as they could be. She didn't know quite what to make of Janet, quickly summing her up as an odd character to say the least. But of necessity she begrudgingly held her tongue and her judgment, for the sake of George and the children, while taking on whatever responsibilities he saw fit for her.

George's sons, George Jr and Charles, now aged fourteen and nine, were away at school when the newly-weds returned from Holland after their marriage. Emily, now thirteen, had been attending a day school for girls nearby and was under the expert care of Mrs Marton. The young girl was delighted to see her father and her stepmother on their return. This proved a pivotal moment, so much so that when Mrs Marton saw how much Emily had warmed to Janet, it eased her acceptance of the new 'Mrs Taylor', although she still found the change of names unfathomable.

And yet, while she trusted and respected George completely, his new wife would have to earn it.

For the couple it was the beginning of not only a marriage, but also a business partnership. Janet was keen to publish her thoughts, the projects that she had been working on while still living with Seymour. So many plans, and so much to do. She knew that someone like Mrs Marton was necessary but still felt uncomfortable, indeed wary, of her established role and presence in the household. Assuming the position of the new head of the domestic sphere was quite trying as Mrs Marton was clearly chagrined by her now diminished capacity. Sensing the growing tension, George revealed to his wife the promise he had made to a dead comrade. It was sad, even romantic, and she admired him for his loyalty, but romance and reality are sometimes uneasy bedfellows.

Janet was not Hannah, whom she now regarded as part of the past and not in any way 'relevant' in her life or aspirations. But Hannah was still very real in the eyes of the suspicious housekeeper and this was the first 'difficulty' that had to be managed. Janet had to learn how to be the head of the domestic household while her thoughts were constantly on other matters, things of which Mrs Marton would have no inkling and with which she certainly had no sympathy. But she at least tried to build a bridge of understanding, confiding in Mrs Marton of her childhood in Durham, of her mother's death and of her love for her late father. This went a long way to easing the tension. She also decided quickly that Mrs Marton's loyalty to George, and to his late wife, was important to the family and it simply had to be accommodated. An uneasy truce prevailed, without anyone actually ever speaking of it.

On the business side of things George quickly warmed to the idea of developing an enterprise around the nautical community. His wide experience and understanding of the needs of the average mariner were a distinct advantage, and although his wife's aspirations were grander, they were still somewhat amorphous and ill-defined. Janet's ambition was clear in her own mind, but his was much more of a practical appreciation of what was needed to get it off the ground. Teaching was one thing, even laudable, but the backbone and money-earner would need to be the sale of the essential tools for the mariner, such as sextants, octants, telescopes, charts and anything else that could be produced. At this stage he had a list in his mind, but that was all.

Janet's head was full of possibilities, all directed towards the sea and sea navigation. Her fixation was to help the mariner find his way upon the seas, and of course to make it home safely. This was to be her guiding principle and her driving force in all her work in the years to come. It was fashioned early by her father's side beneath the panorama of the heavens in the clear skies of County Durham, and throughout her life she had acquired the knowledge and the passion to put this dream into reality. She would go much further than mere teaching. It was a fierce determination to find the clearest way to make the complex simple – the world in an orange.

At the kitchen table in her brother Seymour's household before her marriage, she had worked out the basic premise for her own work. It was quite straightforward, and crystal clear, at least to her. Others before her had got it wrong, or perhaps, not *right* enough. She was a perfectionist in a field where a slight laxity of formula could lead to shipwreck and loss of life; in short, catastrophe. Accuracy was everything. The first task at hand was to work on the basic formulas of her premise from which the more complex notions would follow. The key principle was a recognition that the earth was not a perfect sphere, but rather it was flattened at opposite ends, at the poles. It was *spheroidal*, not spherical, 'oblate spheroid' to be precise, the earth's axis at the poles being thirty-four miles shorter than that at the equator. This had to be translated in a way that would make sense to the simplest navigator. It had to be not only correct, but easy to implement, otherwise it would never be used or understood. Now married, she set about making her passion a reality.

George was fiercely encouraging in her endeavour. It intrigued him, even amused him, to see her so occupied. Indeed, he had never seen anything quite like it before. His life had been largely a world of men; but it suited him to have a wife so sure of herself and, essentially, 'occupied' with matters apart from him. Not only was he sympathetic to her lofty aims, his sound business sense and maturity would initially be a great asset. Feeling this was the wisest course to follow, he was content to indulge, even foster, his new wife's interests and to provide her an anchor in the real (and often rough) business world of seafaring men. As a bonus, it was obvious from the outset that Emily simply adored her new stepmother. For a man of the sea and the land, a man of men and business, the prospect of marriage and partnership in all senses with his wife was as exciting for George as it was daunting.

As the spring of 1831 turned into summer, England celebrated the first anniversary of William IV's accession to the throne. After the disruptive and polarising reign of his older brother, the dissolute George IV, a year of relative royal calm under the rather elderly but affable William, now sixty-four, was a blessing. In contrast to the vanities and self-indulgence of George IV, William was a straightforward and uncomplicated man who promoted an image of himself as a humble sailor, preferring plain food and simple living. Where there was much to lampoon in George, the main thing said of William was that he had a pointy head, like a pineapple or coconut, and was nicknamed 'Silly Billy' or 'Sailor William'; and that he sought to look after his many illegitimate children – the FitzClarences as they were called (or, less politely, 'Les Bâtards'). William was the third son of George III and Queen Charlotte and never expected to be king. But like his brothers, when George IV's only legitimate child, Princess Charlotte, died, he performed his royal duty by abandoning his mistress, Mrs Dorothy Jordan, with whom he had ten children. William married Adelaide of Saxe-Meiningen, a Protestant princess, in July 1818, who was not only half his age but reportedly 'the plainest woman in her dominions'.

William's brothers, the dukes of Kent, Cambridge and Cumberland, also married and, it was said at the time, joined in a 'race for the heir to the throne':

> Yoics! the Royal sport's begun!
> I' faith, but it is glorious fun,
> For hot and hard each Royal pair
> Are at it hunting for the heir.[8]

Adelaide had done what was expected of her and borne William two daughters, but both died in early childhood, and their subsequent twin sons were also stillborn. Notwithstanding such desperate disappointments, Adelaide was tolerant and accepted her elderly husband's illegitimate children as part of their household, thus ensuring at least that peace reigned at home. When George IV passed away in 1830 with no surviving legitimate children, William, as the next surviving son of George III (Frederick, Duke of York had died in 1827), ascended the throne at the age of sixty-four, the first monarch to do so at such an age.[9] He was to reign for seven years. While not a man of particular talents, he was acknowledged as one with 'a warm heart, and it was an English heart'.

On 1 August 1831 the king and queen opened the new London Bridge and the Taylors, like so many other Londoners, turned out to participate in the festivities. George, Janet, Emily, Mrs Marton and the boys, home from school for the summer, all donned their Sunday best and made their way down to the Thames to share the sights. As they strolled down towards the river they could hear the cheering of the crowds as the royal barge approached the steps on the Tower side of the Thames. There were other decorated barges and vessels of all kinds painting a rich tapestry on the water, and the music of the bands filled the summer air. This was quite a day. Old London Bridge had done its duty, but it had long outlived its ability to serve the city. By the first decade of the nineteenth century it had seen, and felt, the 90,000 people, 800 wagons, 2,000 carts and drays, and many more that crossed it every day.

What a story the old bridge could tell. At the heart of London's life and commerce, it had stood through many sovereigns, outliving the Plantagenets, Lancastrians, Yorks, Tudors and Stuarts and seeing the Hanoverians onto the throne. It had also been there when Magna Carta was sealed in 1215 and was still there at the Battle of Waterloo, some 600 years later. After serving London truly and well, the city now celebrated her retirement, and the opening of the new bridge to carry on the role of connecting London's north and south banks. In 1826 a level made from the wood of the old bridge was used by the Lord Mayor of London, William Thomson, to align the final keystone of its replacement. Its predecessor would eventually be dismantled, and, piecemeal, find its way into relics of one kind or another in the strange afterlife of unpicked civic structures. But its guardians of the north and south banks – the 'giant wardens' as Charles Dickens called them – would remain, although a little askew of the new bridge, in the churches of St Magnus the Martyr on the north side, and Southwark Cathedral on the south.

The partying continued long into the evening, with the royals and their guests celebrating in an enormous marquee that had been erected along the bridge, with flags of many nations displayed along its length. A highlight of the day, not just for the neighbourhood but for all of London, was Mr Charles Green, the celebrated balloonist, who marked the opening of the new bridge with an ascent in his famous balloon, his 192nd voyage. Janet wondered just how much of the world you could see from such a perspective – would it make things clearer, or just more confused?

The coronation was held on 8 September. Appropriately, plain William had a rather plain coronation, with a minimum of fuss and expense – in distinct contrast to that of his older brother, George IV. (The cost of William IV's was £43,159; George IV's was £238,000.) He would even have been happy without one. It was so cheap an event that it was dubbed the 'Penny Coronation'. Nonetheless, significant crowds gathered for the event, even cheering 'King Billy' while craning to get a glimpse of his oddly shaped head, on which sat no new crown, but only his great-grandfather George I's old state crown with padding stuffed in to make it fit.

But all too soon the summer disappeared into the oncoming winter, and after a particularly warm October, George and Janet approached the birth of their first child with the usual excitement and trepidation. On 30 December 1831, exactly eleven months after their wedding, they welcomed Herbert Peter Taylor into the world. For their first wedding anniversary George arranged for a portrait to be painted of his wife, in pastels, this being very much the fashion of the day for the quick and easy family portrait. It was simple, striking and fresh, capturing his wife in the bloom of early motherhood and with eyes full of aspiration and imagination.

And so George Taylor greeted the new year as the proud father of four children, the husband of Janet Taylor and the companion in a business partnership that was about to launch itself on the seafaring world. His role would oscillate between broker, agent and go-between, but always the supporter and peacemaker. As his wife's star rose in the firmament, his greatest challenge would be to find the place and role that suited him best, maintaining his position as the formal head of the household, without compromising it, and at the same time doing his best for his, and her, growing business, since, after all, he was a practical man.

In the chill of the evening of late January 1832, George sat next to his wife as she nursed their newborn son. A wave of quiet contentment washed over him. Although the household was full of childish chatter and activity, it was also the place of plans for a 'Nautical Academy' and she had been busy with all manner of studious writings as well as getting ready for the new school and the baby. His wife was busy, so much so that sleep seemed to be an unknown luxury for her. But he could not help feeling proud, if even a little amused, at her preoccupations. Perhaps the child would steady her, he thought forlornly, more in hope than expectation, especially for Mrs Marton's sake, as his housekeeper found Janet's writings not only strange but a wasteful exertion.

The candlelight glowed softly over Janet and tiny Herbert. George leaned back in his chair and opened the book of Mallett's poems that had been instrumental in their meeting. Finding the poem that they had loved independently and which, in many ways, had brought them together, he read aloud:

> Sun beyond sun, and world to world unseen,
> Measureless distance, unconceiv'd by thought!
> Awful their order; each the central fire
> Of his surrounding stars, whose whirling speed,
> Solemn and silent, through the pathless void,
> Nor change, nor errour knows. But, their ways,
> By reason, bold adventurer, unexplor'd,
> Instructed can declare!

V

Setting Up the Business

The shipping trade in the Port of London in the early nineteenth century was enormous. Tea, china, cotton and pepper came from the West Indies; rum, coffee, sugar and cocoa from the East Indies; tobacco, corn, rice and oil arrived from North America; and hemp, tallow, iron and linen from Europe. Nine million oranges each year and 12,000 tons of raisins were just some of the commodities to be unloaded at the height of the waterborne trade. The banks of the Thames were filled with the clutter, chaos and general confusion of ceaseless commercial activity, streaming to and from the factories and warehouses that crept as close to the water as they dared. The river itself was like a forest, with mast upon mast of ships, beginning downstream of London Bridge, the farthest point upriver navigable by large ships. The forest was dense and layered, in a seemingly orderly yet chaotic way. Ships were moored side by side, all in their assigned place – each upon the next, one upon the other, like sardines, adjacent to the huge privately constructed docks.

Among the more prominent were the West India Company Dock in the area known as the 'Isle of Dogs', downriver from the Tower towards Greenwich; London Dock at Wapping; the East India Dock further downriver at Blackwall; and Greenland and Surrey Docks at Rotherhithe, on the opposite, southern bank. Typical of the transformation of the river banks was St Katharine Docks, which had opened in 1827. A hospital, a medieval church and hundreds of houses were demolished to make room for them. Tea, rubber, wool, marble, sugar, tallow, and ivory were unloaded at the quays and stored in six-storey warehouses, the liturgy of former centuries in the chapel of St Katharine replaced by tallies of goods and produce. All were part of the transformation of the commercial heart of London in the largest privately funded enterprise in its history.

The new docks were built like fortresses to protect them against the petty thieving that was part and parcel of the scale of the commercial traffic of the time. But it was also the memory of war with France and the ravages of it on ships and upon people – conflicts that scarred generations – that drove the construction of the docks, guarding their ships on artificial harbours cut into the bank, gated by locks, within high walls. The moats of the castles of old were replicated on the waters of the Thames, their aspiration expressed in the foundation stone of the West India Dock which read, 'An Undertaking which, under the Favour of God, shall contribute Stability, Increase and Ornament, to British Commerce.'

At the water level were found all the smaller craft that darted like insects across the surface, at least 8,000 of them by the end of the eighteenth century (some estimated it was five times this amount), receiving, delivering and despatching, upstream and down. This is where the boatmen plied their trade: the watermen carrying passengers on wherries, the watergoing taxis of the Thames, from the myriad watermen's stairs; and the lightermen ferrying goods on barges and lighters to and from the ships and the warehouses. Their bible was the tide and its patterns were learned by rote. With only the strength of their arms on the oars of the heavily laden lighters, they needed the tide's assistance to get their loads upriver. The landing stages on the river's edge and the watermen's stairs that led like capillaries into its waters for passengers pulsated with its energy. The river was the centre of the circulation of commerce and the constant ebb and flow of goods and people, out and in, was like breathing. The order, the congestion, the busyness: this was the Thames of the early nineteenth century.

George and Janet spent many hours talking about the possibilities of their business that would one day embrace the Thames and the oceans beyond, and all the men who sailed upon them. It was an excited, exciting and bold vision. She wanted to write, to teach, to design, to solve things for seamen and navigators. His priority was to secure an income for his expanding family. It was a combination of vision and practicality and they laughed at themselves as they talked through their plans of their future. The booming maritime community around them was a place for anticipation and optimism.

But there was also risk. Janet was about to commit her entire inheritance to their plans, convinced of the rightness of her goals. As for George, his enthusiasm was still measured with caution, but he was sensible enough to allow her, indeed to encourage, the pursuit of her ambitions. He also appreciated the risk that they might lose everything. Despite his doubts, silence on the matter seemed the wisest course to follow, at least for the time being.

George set about finding suitable premises, not all at once but enough to start. A warehouse, perhaps, a space large enough to accommodate the manufacturing and storage facilities he knew they would need; and room for the tradesmen to work on the ideas that tumbled from Janet's active imagination. George liked Minories, a grand street leading down to the Tower of London, close to Trinity Square, the headquarters of Trinity House, the home of the Corporation of London, one of the pillars of the maritime establishment. The Tower itself sat on the edge of the Thames, between the Pool and London Bridge. George loved this part of the river and felt sure that this would be a good place for a business such as their contemplated venture. There were none other of the type yet in Minories; and he saw it as very much the future for their trade.

In the summer of 1831, before her pregnancy with Herbert had limited Janet's ability to travel freely, George showed her some of the alleys and byways that led towards the riverbanks brimming with the maritime character of the City. It was dirty, smelly and at times even dangerous, as all dockland areas of the world can be. There was an added cause for concern for George as the City, indeed the whole country, churned with agitation over the Reform Bill, introduced into the House of Commons on 1 March. This was to reconfigure the electoral landscape by creating new seats in the growing centres of population and eliminating the 'rotten boroughs', where a single landowner might nominate a Member of Parliament, such as the borough of Old Sarum, which was only a green mound, and Dunwich, which for centuries had lain beneath the North Sea.

In addition, many more households would be enfranchised: not the whole adult male population, but a much greater segment of the community than before. (Female suffrage had, of course, to wait until the next century.) Reform fever had been festering throughout the country the previous summer and autumn, with economic distress fuelling the pressure to reform the electorate. The 1831 Bill was passed in the Commons by a majority of a single vote, and after defeat in the Lords it got caught up in a general election, after which the new, strongly reformist government took it through the Commons again, this time with a solid majority. The turmoil of the times was underwritten by trepidation, fear of the mob and the memories of the horrors of the French Revolution at the end of the previous century.

Minories was certainly well placed for seafaring business, but a move there at this time would have been very costly. And so, in the meantime George settled on premises at No. 1 Fen Court, opening on to Fenchurch Street, that could be used to begin the teaching, and a warehouse in Cooper's Row, running into Trinity Square. Their living quarters would continue to be in East Street, Red Lion Square. But this was quite a way from the new business premises. They would need to install proper staff at Fen Court in preparation for the teaching side of their plans and rely upon transport, mainly by cab, to get them to and from there, not having a carriage of their own. When George travelled by himself he often caught the horse-drawn omnibuses, but with Janet in the last stage of her pregnancy in late 1831, they stuck to the hackney cabs: steady, reliable and ubiquitous, named for the London borough of Hackney (from the Old French 'haquenée', an ambling horse or nag), where the horses that pulled the carriages were raised.

Janet still endured an uneasy relationship with Mrs Marton. Although a truce of sorts remained, the birth of Herbert in December 1831 led to a different demeanour in Janet, one which Mrs Marton, and even George after a fashion, had not anticipated. For Janet it was as if nothing had changed; indeed having a child only seemed to make her more driven, using every available second to work on her writings. Mrs Marton, childless herself, could not comprehend this apparently selfish obsession, which is what it was from her point of view. And there were other worries. Cholera had hit London hard that bitterly cold winter, appearing in London from February 1832, and thousands were dying, but Janet seemed totally unconcerned about such matters.

For her part, Janet was able to set aside the tension that lay between them, recognising Mrs Marton's great value to the household. Janet knew she just had to make the best of a situation she considered less than ideal, as there was no prospect that George would replace her. Rising to the task, she decided to enlist Mrs Marton as her 'anchor' at No. 1 Fen Court. Once pupils began enrolling, Janet would need someone reliable to provide the solid backbone of the establishment. Appointing Mrs Marton in this role would provide her with a new focus, hopefully diverting her attentions away from matters concerning Janet's perceived deficiencies as a mother. Janet also enlisted Mrs Marton's assistance in finding several new servants for the East Street establishment. Mrs Marton would still be in charge, but they would need some extra help at home.

For some time George had been thinking that they would need a manservant in the household and to the rescue came Mrs Marton, who by chance had an acquaintance named Richard Tyley, a strapping twenty-four-year-old seeking a position in service in London. She was also aware that one of her young relatives, the fourteen-year-old Elizabeth Juggens, was also looking for employment. She was keen to assist, as Elizabeth's mother had been of great support to her when her Samuel died. Securing Elizabeth in the Taylor household seemed to provide a perfect opportunity.

It was also an exercise in 'bridge building' between Janet and Mrs Marton, and in quick time Richard and Elizabeth joined the Taylor household. By all accounts Richard and Mrs Marton divided their time between East Street and Fen Court, depending on the needs of both, while Janet and George were busily engaged planning their new business. Elizabeth meanwhile was installed at East Street where she would be a 'maid of all work' for Janet and nursemaid for young Herbert.

While Mrs Marton saw to the rearrangement of the household, George and Janet firmed up their ideas for their new business venture. While Janet would write the books that would be used in their navigation school, direct the teaching side of things and participate as much as she could personally, George's initial role would be to see to their publication, along with establishing the warehouse and supervising the men. By May 1832 things had become calmer in the City, with the great Reform Bill now law, and embarking upon a new business carried somewhat less risk, although there were of course still difficulties to overcome.

First, it was essential to operate from a shop, a retail face to the maritime world that would help to generate the necessary cash flow to maintain other aspects of the business, particularly during any developmental period of Janet's ideas in the instrument domain. The second issue was deciding what sort of merchandise they should stock, since revenue from the sales of these items was likely to be their main source of income for some time. And so George and Janet undertook some intelligence-gathering, forming their own lists and utilising his experience at sea. But things were constantly moving in the maritime world and it was essential to be progressive to be rewarded with success.

One establishment of obvious interest was that conducted by Robert Brettel Bate in Poultry, close to Mansion House, the official residence of the Lord Mayor of London and opposite the Royal Exchange. Bate was well known as a mathematical instrument maker to the Board of Excise, and from his premises at 20–21 Poultry he supplied instruments and books to the entire nautical community of Britain. From 25 September 1829 he had also become the Principal Agent for Admiralty charts. With an expansion of seagoing trade and exploration there was a parallel growth in demand for reliable sea charts. Appointment to this important role guaranteed a steady additional revenue source for Bate's business.

The oldest surviving sea chart is possibly the *Carta Pisana* (1275), dating from when the launching of the Crusades meant an increase in the sea traffic across the Mediterranean. Navigational techniques had developed through a mixture of observation, skill, science and, on some occasions, accident. The recording and passing on of the sum total of these experiences proved its foundation. Over the centuries mariners wrote down their experiences, meticulously recording prevailing winds, landmarks along the coastlines and of the sea bottom. These would be passed from one seaman to the next, recorded in rough notes with additions to each in turn, eventually being compiled as books, charts and maps.

The notes of mariners were collected in various ways. By the beginning of the sixteenth century the French were producing *Routiers*, which in English became 'rutters'. An example of an English manuscript of the fifteenth century gives directions like these:

> Berwick lieth south and north of Golden Stonys, the Thonde and Berwick haven lien west north west and east south east. And for Vanborugh to the poynt of the Thond the course lieth north and south.

Such rutters were the 'mud maps' of early navigators and, like Hansel's crumbs and pebbles for Gretel, they led the way. Embodying the collective experiences of mariners, they were the received wisdom in navigation. They described routes, prevailing winds, landmarks, things to look out for, things to avoid, anchorage points and any other information then available, like the nature of the bottom (sandy, rocky, etc.) by the things that stuck to the 'lead line' – a device for measuring the depth of the water, weighted with lead, but with a waxed end, to which bits of the seabed would stick ('sh' for shells; 'oz' for ooze; 'co' for coral, and so on).

The early nineteenth century witnessed a rapid rise of the large single chart, taking over from the books of charts and directions of earlier centuries. As charts and cartography extended their reach and the degree of detail, no longer could the world, or even parts of it, be contained in a single book. Each piece required its own map and so, by the end of the eighteenth century, mariners created a market demand for the development of single, loose charts. The magnifying glass on the world was now continually increasing, with a thirst for more detail, more accuracy, and a scale that revealed everything, or as much of the terrain of the coastlines and beneath the seas of the world that one could see. This was, above all, and perhaps the least of all stated, the age of cartography. With an expansion of seagoing trade and exploration, there was a parallel growth in demand for good charts. They were personal 'treasures', selected and bought by the individual mariner, and they were as personal as his navigational instruments.

Before the Admiralty actively developed its chart-making activities in 1815 on the conclusion of the war with France, chartselling lay in the hands of private individuals. Even after this time, merchant seamen were still reliant on commercial publishers. These non-Admiralty charts were known as 'bluebacks', the unbound versions of the charts in the formerly bound pilot books. They contained the same information on large sheets, usually using a Mercator projection, a cylindrical projection of the earth developed by the great Flemish cartographer Gerardus Mercator in the late sixteenth century but not embraced fully by the nautical community until almost two centuries later.

The charts were a snapshot, a small-scale chart, for the passage along a recognised route across the seas and tracks were often annotated on them, indicating the sailing directions of collective previous mariners. Large-scale charts accompanied them and local pilot books to assist the mariner into port, in much the same way as the street directories of today which include different scales for different purposes.

After the Admiralty started printing its own charts, there were two parallel sources. The Admiralty charts were sold through appointed agents, and the 'bluebacks' by others. In 1825 the Admiralty issued a list of seven official chartsellers in its 'Admiralty Chart Catalogue'. Since 1829, when the Lords of the Admiralty appointed Bate as their first Principal Agent, all corrections had to be funnelled through him.

The demand for sea charts precipitated a constant stream of seamen to Bate's shop, carrying armfuls of sea-worn charts with their notes for amendment, acquiring new charts and the latest navigational books and instruments. The Taylors recognised that for their business chartselling would need to be a critical foundation plank, first with the bluebacks, and then as a sub-agent for Admiralty charts from February 1830. But it was only one aspect of their planned enterprise.

By the end of 1832, George and Janet had worked out broadly what their business would comprise. Plans for teaching were in progress and George had found appropriate premises. So now, Janet had to complete her planned treatise on navigation, *Luni-Solar and Horary Tables*, for her students, for this to fall into place. But how would she manage to do this? She had been married not quite two years. She had a baby who would turn one on 30 December and had relationships to build with her stepchildren. There were also two premises to oversee and servants to organise. How would she find the mental space necessary for the exacting and precise work required to produce her book?

Janet coped by focusing her energy and drive into every available moment, becoming accustomed to finding a space amongst the hive of activity around her. As she learned as a child, a corner of the kitchen would suffice; so long as she had a flat place, a quill and paper, she could blank out the world around her and make a world in her figures. In such a household, this kind of survival technique served her well. As her responsibilities to others increased – as mother, as stepmother, as head of the domestic sphere and, she anticipated, soon as teacher – her ability to imagine this quarantined space amongst the surrounding turmoil became her anchor. Her plans, ideas and inventions kept tumbling around in her imaginings, providing comfort, even when she had to leave them there for a while to deal with more mundane matters, until she could recover her 'corner in the kitchen'.

At East Street she designated the study, usually a male domain, as hers. The servants were somewhat taken aback, but this quickly became established as 'the norm' in the Taylor household. But Janet needed far more than just a physical space in which to work. She had to draw upon all her intelligence and capacity to quarantine a space in her mind that was reserved for her scientific work. It was exhausting, but also exhilarating. Janet had to establish a truce of sorts, or at least an understanding, with Mrs Marton, and thankfully Elizabeth Juggens proved to be a good worker and an excellent nurse for baby Herbert. In the new year she planned to search for a teacher to help her, but in the meantime she had to focus on completing the book. She just had to get it done, and that meant disappearing into a quiet space whenever she could, not thinking about her own physical well-being or her fatigue. Not only did her work need to be finished, but her reputation and the future of their enterprise would depend on it.

VI

Authoress

In July 1833, at the age of twenty-nine, Janet published her first book, *Luni-Solar and Horary Tables*. She was also heavily pregnant with her second child, due three months later. Finishing the book was both a labour of love and one of frustration as the previous eighteen months up to the publication had been testing ones. On top of everything else she had to manage, in March her older sister Elizabeth had passed away aged forty-two, the same age as their mother had been when she had died. Elizabeth had stepped into their mother's place as the eldest daughter when she was twenty, and so Janet really knew her more as an aunt than a sister. Her pregnancy at the time of Elizabeth's death brought back the pain of the loss of her mother – and the anxiety surrounding the perils of childbirth.

What kind of a book was it, her *Luni-Solar and Horary Tables*? The volume consisted of sixty pages of mathematical calculations, examples and formulas and 233 pages of tables. It comprised tables of the moon and sun at particular times and in specific places, fashioned in the style of a number of other such works. In conventional style it began with mathematical calculations, examples and formulas, with the remaining sections devoted to tables for the determination of latitudes, amplitudes and similar subject material. Such tables were of vital importance to navigators, representing one of the earliest, most familiar and still the most reliable ways of calculating longitude. It fitted into the genre of navigational books designed to assist in the calculation of latitude and longitude by the 'lunar method' of astronomical observation.

Latitude and longitude are a function of the shape of the earth. Position is calculated by two coordinates at right angles to each other: latitude (parallels north and south of the equator) and longitude (lines running from pole to pole parallel to the 'prime meridian', which for British mariners, was a line running through the Greenwich Observatory, London). Determining latitude and longitude requires very sophisticated mathematics and astronomy, by reference to fixed points: the moon, the sun and other known celestial reference points, such as Polaris, the 'North Star'.

The North Star is conspicuous in the northern hemisphere, the most famous star in the constellation known as Ursa Minor ('Little Bear'). It is the closest point towards which the axis of the Earth is directed and is approximately the position of the north celestial pole. The various constellations make a circuit round Polaris as a pivot, taking twenty-four hours to complete their anti-clockwise circuit. Because of its brightness it can easily be seen, and if you can see Polaris you can tell which way is north. By measuring the angle of Polaris above the horizon, mariners eventually were also able to calculate their latitude. It was, and remains, a very useful star for navigators.

Polaris, and the movement of the constellations around it, were the foundations of celestial navigation. Over the centuries, arithmetic calculations to estimate position relative to a star (the fixed point) by measuring the angle of elevation (altitude) of the star from the observer (apex) and the earth (horizon) were made by astronomers and compiled into tables. The first official tables of this kind in England were produced from 1767 as the *Nautical Almanac*. Star charts were also produced. In the seventeenth century the Reverend John Flamsteed, the first Astronomer Royal of the Greenwich Observatory, and other northern astronomers produced star charts of the northern skies, while Edmond Halley, the second Astronomer Royal, produced a similar chart of the southern skies. The sun was also recognised as providing essential clues to position at sea. Measuring the altitude of the sun at midday or Polaris at night in relation to other stars in Ursa Minor was the basis for calculating latitude.

How did mariners measure the altitude of celestial bodies? One of the earliest known devices was the astrolabe, thought to be one of the oldest scientific instruments used for this purpose in everyday survey work and calculations. Its origin dates back to 150 BC, when it was used by astronomers on land, and by the fifteenth century the Portuguese navigators were using it to explore the west coast of Africa. The astrolabe was a complex but expensive tool consisting of a disk of metal or wood with a circumference marked off in degrees. It was suspended by an attached ring, while pivoted at the centre of the disk was a movable pointer used to view distant objects. A typical astrolabe was only about six inches in diameter, although much larger and smaller ones were made.

For measuring the altitude of the sun, other devices used indirect or backwards observations, so that the shadow of the sun was used – the ingenious backstaff of the late sixteenth century – rather than the observer having to look directly into it, as had been the case with its predecessor the cross-staff. By the end of the seventeenth century, the quadrant, developed by John Davis a century before, had become the principal instrument of English mariners for taking observations at sea.

The disastrous sinking of the fleet commanded by Sir Cloudesley Shovell in October 1707 precipitated the solving of the elusive problem of the determination of longitude. A petition signed by the 'Captains of Her Majesty's Ships, Merchants of London, and Commanders of Merchant Men' was presented to the British Parliament in 1714, demanding that the government address the issue of the calculation of longitude. They insisted that a research fund be established, with a fortune being offered as a reward for the individual who could solve the problem. The situation had indeed become desperate, as the increasing number of vessels also brought a corresponding growth in the loss of ships and lives, and so in 1714 Parliament, under the Longitude Act, created the Board of Longitude, and offered three levels of prizes for the discovery of a 'practicable and useful' method for the determination of a ship's longitude at sea.

The huge rewards proved a huge fillip to invention and saw a rapid increase in the number of navigational instruments developed to assist in the determination of longitude – like John Hadley's improved version of the quadrant called a 'reflecting octant' for the accurate measurement of lunar distances, the first account of which was given in 1731 to the Royal Society, the eminent body of scientists established by Charles II in 1660. It represented an important step in the accuracy leading to the more precise sextant in which the arc was extended from 90 degrees to 120 degrees. With an improved degree of accuracy over the octant, it was used to measure the distance of the moon from the sun or star in order to find the longitude by lunar observation. Improvements in instruments were accompanied by accurate data on the positions of the moon, sun and various planets that were published as tables in the annual *Nautical Almanac*. These provided an essential companion for the mariners of the day.

For over twenty years, however, nobody really looked like they would win the Board of Longitude's major prize. Then, in 1736, John Harrison, a Yorkshire joiner, presented a strange-looking clock, or marine chronometer, claiming that it would solve the longitude problem. The idea of such a device was that it would be set constantly to Greenwich time and that by comparing local time with Greenwich time, longitude could be determined, each hour of difference representing 15 degrees of longitude. The board was very dubious of his 'sea clock' device, the 'H-1', which weighed seventy-five pounds. While the principle was undoubtedly correct, the board steadfastly refused to award the money, doubting the reliability of the instrument. Harrison, meanwhile, kept working and, over the next twenty-two years, improved his invention with versions 'H-2', 'H-3' and finally 'H-4', which looked like a large pocketwatch of just over five inches in diameter.

His H-4 is arguably the most famous timepiece ever made and was later tested on the ship HMS *Deptford* at Portsmouth on 18 November 1761 for a voyage to Jamaica. The destination was reached on 21 January 1762 when, after allowing for its computed rate, was only slow by five seconds or 1.25 degrees of longitude. The Board of Longitude, however, had a feeling that the accuracy of H-4 was a matter of compensatory errors or sheer coincidence and, to the board's great discredit, Harrison spent a good deal of his life trying to earn the reward to which he was rightly entitled. He ultimately did so by Act of Parliament in 1773, after a petition made on his behalf to King George III.

While chronometers gradually became the essential tool in the calculation of longitude, mariners still relied upon calculations based on the lunar method. Janet called the moon 'a lamp to guide the navigator by night'. All mariners had to understand the method and this is where books like Janet's were the foundation. What she did was to bring the principle of the earth as an oblate sphere directly into the calculation of latitude and the 'clearing' of the calculation from the effect of refraction by the atmosphere and parallax (the difference between the position of the celestial body as seen from the centre of the earth and from a point on its surface). In her own words:

> A knowledge of this enables us to find the breadth of any degree of Latitude, without the trouble of traversing the Globe for the purpose of making observations, as many of our Navigators and Astronomers have done, otherwise the contemplations of Sir Isaac Newton, in his library, where he made his calculations, would have but little benefited that science to which his sublime genius was devoted, and into whose interminable recesses it dived to an extent before unknown.

'Most of the former solutions,' she contended, were 'grounded on approximated method.' Her plan, by contrast, was 'mathematically exact and concise'. New tables were included according to the principle of the spheroidal shape of the earth. The science had been acknowledged before, but there had been no 'satisfactory improvements' yet made in the tables, which were then 'before the Public in their imperfect state'. Her goal was to make things simpler to the ordinary seaman – and to rectify this imperfection. She sought 'to supersede the beaten track of former Authors', otherwise she would not have bothered:

> For, surely when our shelves groan with such a cargo of accumulated books, it would be an offence unpardonable, to think of adding to the number, without at least the redeeming supposition of increasing the stock of knowledge also.

Having finally worked out her formulas, Janet was soon able to delegate the labour of the required calculation to others for her luni-solar table, under her personal direction although at first uneasily, while she assumed the role of supervisor at No. 1 Fen Court, where she began to take pupils, with the aim of developing her 'Nautical Academy' within a short time. While many of the tables were 'stereotyped' and replicated from other places, as was the custom of the day, she had no option but to engage the services of assistants to undertake the massive amount of trigonometric calculation necessary to produce the additional tables according to her formulas. In addition, her aim was to craft practical examples in an effort to explain and simplify the steps that a mariner had to use. It was the inclusion of these explanatory additions that particularly distinguished one volume of such tables from another. Janet sought to explain things in simple language and simple analogies, as in her explanation of refraction:

> Place a piece of silver in a basin, and stand at a distance from it. Fix your eye steadily on some remarkable part of it. Then let another person gradually pour water on it, until it is covered. The piece will appear to change its first or true place, (the latter called its apparent place,) and the angle the elevation of the piece makes with the eye is called the Refraction. This also decreases according to the elevation of the eye on the horizontal line of the true place of the piece, or according to the elevation of that true place, until the eye is immediately over the piece or the piece over the eye: likewise, on putting a rod obliquely into smooth water, the part immersed will appear higher than that which is out of the water; raise the rod to make any angle you please with the surface, and you will observe that the part immersed will gradually become straighter, until by putting it in perpendicularly, both parts of the rod form a straight line, in which there will be no refraction. When you form an angle with that part of the rod in the water, draw an imaginary

line from your hand, making a straight line with the part of the water. The angle this line makes with the part immersed, is the refraction of the angle it makes with the surface of the water.

And this of longitude, spoken of in terms of a ship sailing along a meridian:

During the elapsed time, a ship generally makes a difference of Longitude, unless she sail on a meridian, in which case she increases the elapsed time, at the rate of 1 hour to every 15° of Longitude if it be West; but if she sail Easterly, she decreases it at the same rate.

She had to use language of this nature, although the picture of her father's orange was the one she had in mind.

Meanwhile, the more Janet thought about the tables, the more the kinds of tools that were necessary became clearer to her. Her larger project was to find expression in three forms: the book of tables according to her new formula, accompanied by a text of principles explaining more fully the premise upon which the tables were based, and a new instrument that would make everything simple, combining the means of making observations with the power of giving solutions to all the problems in nautical astronomy. It was an ambitious enterprise.

As spring neared its end in 1833, George had become very anxious about the completion of the book as they had planned to take in the first pupils at the end of the summer. But Janet was meticulous, totally consumed with checking the work performed by her assistants. She had a voracious need to verify everything, spending countless hours poring over the thousands of numbers and calculations. These involved seriously complex mathematics, long before the benefit of calculators. And still she kept finding mistakes and with every new reading even more errors were found. All the while George was hurrying her, pleading with her to stop the obsession with checking; saying this was enough. But every evening she headed, once more, to her study – *her* study – candle in hand, while the children and her husband slept soundly all the while.

She was a perfectionist while he was the pragmatist; and she was pregnant. Pregnancy had its own timetable and agenda, but George wanted her simply to get the book finished: for the sake of the students, for herself and before the baby arrived. They were both aware that it would be hard for her to take on the teaching now, even any of it for a while, with the infant due in a matter of weeks. So she needed this book to be finished more than ever, not just for the pupils, but also for the teacher she was to enlist and to be sure that he would be following her methods.

While her assistants were busying themselves with the calculations, Janet was able to focus her intellectual energies upon another project: the design of a radical instrument she had in mind: an all-in-one tool, indeed a universal 'calculator'. Like her games around magnetic properties as a child, this idea started from a simple proposition – to simplify, combine, make easy – and grew from there. It would be, for her, the manifestation of her ideas in practical form: an elegant but simple tool, that did everything for the navigator in one. The formula and the instrument were the kinds of lofty, yet practical, ideas that filled her head as her body swelled inevitably towards the birth of her second child.

As this was her first book, Janet thought long and hard about what she would say in her opening pages, especially the important dedication and the preface. The dedication was the easy part, as she knew she would acknowledge her early benefactor, Queen Charlotte, the mother of the reigning king, William IV. The scholarship that she had won as a nine-year-old eased her path in gaining a hearing from the king, himself having served as an officer in the Royal Navy. Indeed, so taken was he with Janet's enterprise and obvious intelligence, he suggested to her that she might lend her services as a reader to his fourteen-year-old niece, and likely heir to the throne, the Princess Alexandrina Victoria. Janet was overwhelmed at the prospect of such an engagement but, given her pregnancy and her other plans, it was just not possible and she respectfully declined. William understood her predicament and was most willing for her to dedicate the book as requested:

With much anxiety I launch this Volume into a criticising world, and would claim for it Your Majesty's support and protection, hoping that the practical knowledge you possess of a science, it may be tend to benefit, and your feelings of interest in that class of your subjects, who form the strongest bulwark to your dominions, may elicit some portion of Your Majesty's attention to its humble merits, and ensure it a kindly reception at the hands of those who may be inclined to condemn unheard, the humble efforts of one, whose sex would seem hitherto to have been an effectual barrier against the pursuit of the more abstruse branches of literature.

Whatever be the merit of the present Work, the talent from which it has sprung was fostered by the benevolence, and under the immediate patronage of your Illustrious and Revered Mother; therefore, with feelings of the deepest gratitude and respect, I now presume to Dedicate to your Majesty, the following pages; and subscribe myself,

Your Majesty's Most Humble, Most Devoted, And Faithful Subject,
JANET TAYLOR

The preface, however, was proving a much harder proposition. It was here that a writer, especially a new one, introduced themselves to the reading public. But this was also a specialist area and must seize the attention of the practitioners of that field. She worked over and over in her mind just what she would say. She also found that she could think through things much more clearly while she walked, the late stages of pregnancy making sitting for long periods exceedingly uncomfortable.

On many occasions George had witnessed the way his wife worked, with her constant pacing, talking aloud and even debating with herself. But he had reached a certain understanding, or patience at least, with these characteristics and his principal concern, outside the home, was for her safety. He had introduced her to the magic and intrigue of the streets near the Thames, and saw how it fired her imagination. While this was undoubtedly good for their business aspirations, he was uncertain about it where her safety was concerned. At least while they lived at East Street, Red Lion Square, they were in less perilous territory, but even then, he was reluctant for her to go walking alone. He was much happier and relieved once they had engaged Richard Tyley in the household and very grateful to Mrs Marton for her enterprise in seeking him out. Janet's walks now were usually accompanied by Richard if George himself were not able to participate, and also her stepdaughter Emily when she was not at school.

With the brawny Richard in tow, George was even able to accept her occasional excursions down to the Thames. It was here, he knew, that she found great inspiration among the masts of the ships where she imagined herself into the universe of the mariner. The twists and turns of the planet on its axis, its rhythm, its shape, and its relationship to the fixed points in the heavens around it would all be played out in the planisphere of her imaginings. Even on such journeys through the docklands of London, with their smell and chaos overflowing in the early summer heat, her mind kept focused upon her goals, far larger, and far more important than the jumble and stench of the immediate world around her.

It was during this summer of 1833 that Janet became acutely aware of herself as a woman in a man's world. While her childhood in her father's school had led her not to be so conscious of her gender, her swelling belly marked her as a woman so clearly in a universe that was so clearly a man's one. And then there were the figureheads, the carved figures on the bowsprits of the ships, big-breasted women proudly protecting the ships in the Thames. Oliver Cromwell had replaced Henry VIII's lions with a figure of himself trampling upon his enemies, but, after the Restoration of Charles II in 1660, these were suitably disposed of by being sawn off and burned. Like Guy Fawkes, these symbols of a former era were sent to the fire. Seamen were superstitious and much of this became focused on the figurehead, embodying as it did the spirit of a ship. The merchant ships loved their women both voluptuous and naked as this was the way to calm a storm at sea, so it was believed. While women were considered bad luck at sea, a naked woman was believed to help the mariner see at night and ward off the devils in the storms. But they only seemed to taunt Janet.

In the face of the masculinity of maritime London, she was conscious that gender was something that had to be acknowledged in her preface, even using it to her advantage if she could. After careful deliberation she wrote:

> When a new writer obtrudes himself upon the Public in the capacity of Reformer of long-established usages – and this too in a department the most important of all science, whether we regard the deep calculations it involves, or the momentous interests which endear it to the public – something like an apology may be deemed requisite on his part to qualify an undertaking, which may otherwise seem presumptuous.
>
> If then, this may be applicable in the case of the strongest or stronger sex, how much more indispensable is it that the female – with all the disadvantages of a confined school, and the prejudices additionally which attach to any efforts that would seem to court publicity in the way of literary innovation – should bespeak indulgence at the hands of a criticising world, for the bold but well-meant intention, which has prompted the following attempt.

Being raised essentially motherless, Janet had, by necessity, developed her own reference points. At Queen Charlotte's school the other pupils had let her 'do her own thing' and her siblings found her simply amusing and so they, too, left her largely to her own devices. George was patient and helpful; but he was focused upon setting up the business, and not upon the detail of her writing. It meant she had to find the right 'pitch' herself, acknowledging what her gender meant, while never once allowing it to affect her or having to apologise for being a 'Reformer of the long-established usages'. Indeed, her gender could be used for leverage, a way of explaining her 'well-meant intention' and to deflect 'prejudices'. This was an elegant move, designed to be deferential, but determined and undeterred. It was also somewhat naive.

Her argument was that established 'usages' or techniques had been successful in navigation *despite* the errors that they contained. Although being careful not to denigrate those before her who designed them, declaring they did as well as they could with the information available at the time, it came across as an ironically 'patronising' remark:

> It is no part my wish to traduce the laudable exertions of those who have preceded me on this head; they did as much as the lights of their day, no doubt had warranted.

Janet likened herself to Lynceus, one of the Argonauts of Greek legend who was able to see through trees, walls and underground, in her detection of errors 'in a system which was known to "work well"'. Why should she volunteer her zeal, she asked, in such circumstances. Her answer was straightforward:

> If it has 'worked well' *in spite* of those errors, it is the more likely to work better when released from their operation.

It was to this outcome that her 'humble efforts' were 'most studiously applied':

> Regardless of the obloquy which some may choose to lavish upon the rashness of the design, and looking for my reward in the profitable results alone, which accrue to the community, from the successful prosecution hereafter, at the hands of a more experienced head-piece, of the abstruse investigation which I shall at least have originated. Or, if I shall have failed in this issue of my fondly cherished hopes, why, then let me seek shelter in the conscious disinterestedness of the view which propelled my speculation.

If there were any mistakes in her calculations (and there *were*, she felt sure, as this was common enough at the time with books of such complex detail), then these were trivial as the method was everything. George had badgered her to get the book out quickly and argued, incorrectly as it turned out, that surely she would not be condemned for merely mechanical errors. He encouraged her to say something by acknowledging the errors and that practitioners should not to be too fussed about them. The method itself would shine through. And so she confessed, almost as a postscript, in spite of her own sense of better judgment, but hoped that they would be 'trivial in nature':

> Being obliged to hurry the publication of my Work, for the use of some friends, I am under the necessity of omitting several Exercises in the

Practical Problems, and likewise in the Use of the Tables, both of which will be further illustrated in the next Edition.

Some errors may have crept into the calculations, from the multiplicity of entries, &c., these, I trust, will claim the indulgence of the public; for the system on which I have worked being mathematically correct, and founded on sound principles, any slight oversight in the figures can be of little moment, and very easily rectified.

The 'friends' to which she referred were her pupils and also customers of the business in time; it was a customary euphemism.

With the publication in July 1833, Janet pinned her pennant to the mast. She was firmly convinced that her method was right and that other techniques were merely an approximation of her correct one. And she was not afraid to say so, a characteristic that Janet was to carry and display throughout her life. This represented far more than just another contribution to the growing library of possibilities of the early nineteenth-century mariner. It was, for her, another birth, and a tribute to her father. It was also a symbol, or a symptom, of her future. When the book was finally published in July, Janet was exhausted.

The first review, in the *United Service Journal*, arrived just one week after the birth of Henry Frederick ('Frederick' as he was to be known) on 5 October:

> Though this book has been handed to us too recently to admit of a full investigation of its claims, we have examined it sufficiently to recommend it a berth in the mathematical library of every navigator. Indeed, when it is announced that a lady, soaring above petty pursuits and frivolity, has drilled her mind to the difficult and responsible labour of clearing away all obstacles from the *paths* of the ocean, we are sure that the attempt will be received with as much gratification as surprise, and that the name of Miss Janet Taylor will be respectfully mentioned in many a floating castle.

Although the commentary on her work was somewhat superficial, it was nevertheless heartening. It went on to recommend that sailors should purchase a copy of her book. In fact, it even suggested further that had she produced such a fine work several years earlier it would have received a grant from 'the poor departed Board of Longitude', whose awards for finding the best method of determining longitude had prompted many contributions, including the work of Harrison.

The review also clearly identified her as a woman – 'Miss Taylor'. Janet was somewhat taken aback by this designation. 'Mrs' meant something.

It was respectable and she had earned it, promptly vowing to be emphatically 'Mrs Taylor' in all subsequent writings and that would be as the world would know her.

Another judgement appeared in the 1833 edition of the colourfully named *The Literary Gazette; and Journal of Belle Lettres, Arts, Sciences etc.* that, among other things, reviewed new publications. It was generally favourable, emphasising that it was the work of a woman. After a brief mention of another science writer, Mrs Mary Somerville, it read, in part:

> We now have our attention directed to a volume on a subject connected with the same science by another lady, both of which prove that peculiar habits of thinking, with all the disadvantages of a confined course of education, form no barriers to extensive excursions amidst the intricate mazes of mathematical calculations. Such works, and from such writers, give a character to the literature of the age in which we live, and place their respective authors in the foremost ranks of astronomical science.
>
> The nature of this work will not admit of our giving an analysis: it must, therefore, be sufficient for us to say, that this treatise on navigation cannot fail to be useful for those whom it is intended. We merely assure the enterprising writer that she has no occasion to apprehend any prejudice to the results of her labour from the work being from the pen of a female; on the contrary, we dare venture to affirm that this circumstance will rather be a recommendation to the seaman – that his vessel will be guided in its course over the trackless ocean by the genius of this fair countrywoman.

The review was encouraging, although clearly not a scientific one, rather focusing inordinately on her gender. But Janet was painfully aware that selling her book to the nautical community would not be easy without the proper backing of the establishment. This meant endorsement by the 'big three': the East India Company, the Admiralty, and the Corporation of Trinity House. The East India Company was the major provider of survey charts used on British merchant ships. The Admiralty saw to the Navy, and, in 1795, established its own Hydrographic Office. The Corporation of Trinity House, first incorporated by Royal Charter in 1514, was the general lighthouse authority for Britain and responsible for the examination and licensing of pilots. It was absolutely critical to gain the endorsement and approval of one or more of these bodies; and she well knew it. As a first step, the week before the review came out, on 29 September 1833, Janet sent her book to an examining board at Trinity

House. But her book was compared unfavourably, and probably unfairly, with those of the very experienced author Thomas Lynn:

> Mrs Taylor is entitled to the thanks of nautical men for her concise method of clearing a lunar distance; and, although with some exception, they consider the tables inferior for ready and minute calculations to those published by Mr Lynn and others, they beg to recommend that as many copies be purchased for the use of the Corporation as the Court shall see fit to direct.
>
> Ordered that our thanks be returned to Mrs Taylor for the communication of her work and that she be requested to supply six copies thereof for our use.

To a young aspiring author this was a setback of some moment, but she was not to be deterred now. Besides, there were other pressing matters to attend to. Trinity House had not heard the last of her, by any means.

VII

Inventor

While recovering from the birth of Frederick on 5 October 1833, Janet instructed her workers in the development of the prototype of an instrument she thought would revolutionise the nautical world. She called it the 'Mariner's Calculator', and in March 1834 Mrs Janet Taylor of East Street, Red Lion Square, Middlesex, lodged an application for a British patent for it, claiming 'improvements in instruments for measuring angles and distances, applicable to nautical and other purposes'. The application, No. 658, was granted in September 1834. Between 1617 and 1852, the year after the Great Exhibition, only seventy-nine patents were awarded in the category 'Compasses and Nautical Instruments'. The patents were awarded to renowned leaders in the field such as John Hadley in 1734, for his quadrant, and Edward Troughton in 1788, for a method of framing for nautical instruments. But only one of these was to a woman, just one: to Mrs Janet Taylor, aged thirty. What led Janet upon such a path?

Making the calculations easier and more accessible was one thing, as she had done with *Luni-Solar and Horary Tables*, but designing an instrument that could combine a number of functions, *that* would be an astounding contribution to the maritime world. While Janet continued to work from her study in East Street, it was the warehouse at No. 8 Cooper's Row, Trinity Square that proved an ideal place for the workers engaged in the painstaking work of developing the prototype of her invention, making necessary minor alterations in accordance with her instructions. Janet often worked late into the winter nights to complete it as soon as possible. She was utterly driven in her goal.

It was an intriguingly clever concept, combining an instrument of double reflection, like a sextant, with a mechanical means of solving spherical triangles, the essence of calculating longitude. It was in the shape of an open sphere and in the instructions that accompanied her design Janet claimed that it removed the necessity of performing tedious mathematical and trigonometric calculations. It was ingenious and she was convinced that 'the mariner will find it of essential service':

To find the true Time
To find the true Altitude
To fine the true Azimuth
To find the Latitude by double Latitudes and elapsed Time
To clear a Lunar Distance
To find a Lunar Distance, as in the Nautical Almanac
To find the Distance between any two Places
To find the Bearing of One from the Other
To find the differences of Longitude

She even went so far as to make the bold but naive claim that her invention would solve 'all problems in Nautical Astronomy'.

Janet was convinced that the concept was sound, at least in theory, but also knew that her own testing ground for her model was a limited one. It must work at sea, on rocking and unstable vessels, to do what she imagined it could. George privately had lingering doubts. He wondered how a navigator could manage such a complicated contraption (in his eyes at least) on the ocean, with rough sailors' hands, but he humoured her and made no effort to dampen her enthusiasm, even though it meant using a significant part of her inheritance to invest in the project. George could not help but admire her tenacity. And he wanted peace, even with the grave financial risk it carried.

Notwithstanding her confidence in the rightness of her invention, it was with some trepidation that Janet delivered a prototype of her new device to the Admiralty for assessment, at the same time ensuring that her idea was protected by applying for a patent, while she anxiously waited for the Admiralty's verdict.

The Admiralty settled upon giving the Mariner's Calculator to their own Hydrographer, Captain Francis Beaufort, for assessment. Beaufort had had a long naval career, beginning at the age of fourteen in 1787, rising to the rank of captain in 1810. He saw much active service, collecting an assortment of wounds, so much so that he ended up with a 'wound pension'. As commander of the *Fredericksteen* in the Eastern Mediterranean, he not only managed to survey the coast of Karamania in Asia Minor but suppressed some of the fiercest Mainote pirates infesting the coast of Africa. His surveys and account of his explorations between

1810 and 1812 attracted great interest when published, and for the next sixteen years after his return to England Beaufort was engaged in the preparation of charts taken from his surveys. They were of such fine quality that they were engraved directly from his drawings as sent to the Hydrographic Office. In 1829 Beaufort was appointed the Admiralty's Hydrographer, a position he was to hold with great acclaim for the next twenty-six years.

While Janet waited on the assessment of her instrument, she continued to produce more books and also confidently promoted her invention, describing herself as 'Janet Taylor, Inventor of the Mariner's Calculator', securing permission to dedicate it to King William's wife, Queen Adelaide. By late May 1834 she was becoming impatient and wrote to Captain George Elliott, Secretary to the Admiralty, declaring that she was 'deeply anxious' as to the fate of her instrument. 'Forgive my intrusion', she wrote, pleading her object 'being the furtherance of science' as her excuse. She urged him to put to the Admiralty, if he thought proper, that she had 'arranged all of the elementary points of navigation in as simple a manner that which was once nearly unattainable to a sailor'. She had just turned thirty a few weeks earlier, on 4 May, and it gave her an added sense of authority to press her viewpoint. At least, she hoped it might.

Despite her seeming bravado, Janet was still very much feeling her way in the nautical community, in business and in the world of men. Here she was, the daughter of a country curate and married to a former naval lieutenant (and a Dissenter) who had run public houses. One of his attractions for her was that he always seemed completely at ease while at times displaying a roughness (albeit gentle), making him a difficult target on which to take out her frustrations. So in dealing with the revered men of the Admiralty she had great difficulty in deciding exactly what to say and when to say it. She wrote with timidity because she was not quite sure if she was intruding at all, and thought it safer to adopt a style of deference. She was confident in her ideas, but the nuance in writing, even in speaking, for a woman, in a world of men, provided a real dilemma. Deference was undoubtedly a habit of women, but it also spoke of class. How should she disentangle one from the other? For now, she stuck to deference: 'Forgive my intrusion.'

Captain Beaufort was a man of high reputation and esteem, and a worthy one, in ordinary circumstances, to undertake an assessment of the Mariner's Calculator. On this occasion, however, the timing could not have been worse. What Janet did not know was that Beaufort was in the throes of a great personal crisis. His wife of over twenty-one years, Alicia, was dying. In the late summer of 1832 she had found a lump in her breast and it foretold a slow, painful and certain death. The only analgesic available was laudanum, a mixture of opium and alcohol that induced a deep sleep, as well as hallucinations. A woman of great religious faith, Alicia bore her suffering with great dignity, even calmness, until she passed away on 27 August 1834. It was agonising, and her husband was greatly affected. In the midst of this great upheaval in his life, Beaufort delivered his report to the Admiralty, as noted in the Admiralty Minute Book of 2 May 1834:

> Three of the problems proposed by Mrs Janet Taylor have been worked with the Mariner's Calculator, and the results obtained have ill agreed with the truth. Perhaps this may have arisen from the imperfect construction of the instrument, to which she alludes, but if it were well made and the results accurate, the difficulty which the clumsy fingers of seamen would find in small measurements with compasses and the impracticability of measuring circular arcs would always render it objectionable. Even if the Instrument performed all that is stated it is not worthy of their Lordships patronage from the mischievous tendency which it evidently has of inducing a slovenly and empirical mode of working observations and leaving the operator totally in the dark as to the reason of his proceeding. The union of the quadrant with the calculator only renders the Instrument more complex and the free use of the latter would prevent the former even remaining in adjustment.

Captain Elliott was able to reply to Janet, including the report of Beaufort's judgment. By the time Patent No. 658 for 'The Mariner's Calculator' was formally granted on 27 September, however, its fate had effectively been sealed. Without the Admiralty's backing, there was little chance that the other two organisations would support it and it was clear to Janet that it now had no future.

Janet was desperately disappointed. Perhaps George had been right all along in having his doubts. To make matters worse, its development had severely drained her funds and she now had no choice but to abandon it. There were to be no accolades and no celebration when the patent was granted. In her heart she felt that she had been wronged. The fact that her name sat in the register of patents for 'Compasses and Nautical Instruments' alongside men like John Hadley in 1734, was cold comfort.

VIII

More Books

With the dismissal of the Mariner's Calculator, the reputation and reception of Janet's books became more important than ever, serving to draw attention to her Nautical Academy. While waiting for the patent to be confirmed, and for the Admiralty to deliver their judgment, in July 1834 Janet produced a revised version of her first book, *Luni-Solar and Horary Tables*, as a first edition of a new work – a common practice of the time – under the simpler title of *Lunar Tables*. At the same time she busied herself with an expanded companion text, *The Principles of Navigation Simplified*. The preface to this text, like that of her first book in 1833, was to prove important in revealing her mind.

She explained her remorse in simply producing a set of tables in her first book without including a comprehensive enough explanation of how they should be used. To rectify this she had now added about 130 pages of geometrical and trigonometric examples along with theorems and various types of sailing such as traverse, plane and parallel. Her assertiveness did not desert her, however, and she was again critical of other authors who had contributed 'nothing new' to the field for years. She also poured scorn on the state of teaching in navigation. 'Can we wonder at the loss of life and property at sea,' she posed, 'when we look at the general education of the seamen who, with little time and few opportunities of diving deeply into science.' It also served as a timely bit of advertising for her Nautical Academy.

In addition to dedicating *Lunar Tables* to William IV, and the Mariner's Calculator to Queen Adelaide, once more, Janet secured permission to dedicate the volume to the Duchess of Kent:

TO HER ROYAL HIGHNESS
THE DUCHESS OF KENT

MADAM,

I feel assured from your general condescension, that you will not reject my humble offering, nor consider me presumptuous in placing this small volume before the public, under the protection of your Royal Highness. Its merits, I trust, will be found such as to render it an useful contribution to the Literature of the country, and thereby ensure it of the continued patronage of your Royal Highness; – for, my chief endeavour has been to benefit Science on a point to which the energies and abilities of some of the most scientific have been directed.

With great respect I subscribe myself,
Your Royal Highness's humble and faithful servant,

JANET TAYLOR

As the mother of Princess Alexandrina Victoria, the likely future heir to the throne, this dedication to the duchess is a particularly noteworthy addition. While Janet was unable to be a reader for the young princess, a suggestion that followed her meeting with King William and Queen Adelaide, the duchess agreed to allow the book to be dedicated to her.

The *Atlas Magazine* of August 1834 'rejoiced' in the 'much improved' form of the work of 'the fair and learned authoress' in the publication of her *Principles*. It also lauded the book 'as an invaluable present to the student and Nautical Astronomy'. As a book review, though rather shallow, it was better than nothing, particularly at a time when she had not had much encouragement. Janet had achieved royal patronage, but she still needed to secure strong endorsement of 'the big three'. In fact, the Trinity House assessment, even if she had acquired it, would not be enough of itself. The kind of backing she initially sought was the simple granting of permission by the body to dedicate her books to them. As an alternative, or even better in addition, perhaps they might also give her financial assistance. If just one of these bodies were to provide endorsement, of any kind, the others would surely follow.

Trinity House was again in her sights on 2 October 1834, almost exactly a year to the day after her first attempt, when she wrote again, this time enclosing further extracts of her *Lunar Tables* (the revised book). Much to her disappointment, it was sent to exactly the same committee that had been appointed when she had applied before, and the same group of men came up with exactly the same result:

> The consideration of the specimens of the Table was referred to the Committee previously appointed and her application in respect of the dedication of her work having been considered. Resolved, that this Court declines to accede thereto.

One feels Janet's irritation and frustration in her reaction, which was to try again just five weeks later. On 6 November 1834 she now enclosed a copy of the complete book, *Lunar Tables*. Not surprisingly, they were still unimpressed, and appeared somewhat irked by her repeated application. This time they merely noted her letter in their Minutes:

> A letter from Mrs Janet Taylor dated this day, accompanying a copy of her new Work upon the Lunars was laid before the Court and read.

They did not bother to reply, nor indeed to take any action at all. Although she had failed for the third time to gain their approval, they would be mistaken if they thought they had heard the last of Janet Taylor.

But the reviews were not all negative, including that in the *Atlas Magazine*. And then the October 1834 issue of *The Lady's Magazine and Museum of the Belle Lettres, Fine Arts, Music, Drama, etc.*, intriguingly subtitled as the 'Entertaining Companion for the Fair Sex, Appropriated Solely to Their Use and Amusement', included the following comment:

> This book is dedicated to the King, in a letter expressing gratitude for favours received in early life from his illustrious Mother; as being calculated especially to benefit seamen, it can be hardly fail to interest a naval monarch, but we trust it will be found extremely useful, which is perhaps the highest and, in fact, the sweetest fame.

All the information could have been gleaned from the flyleaf to the book and was typical of much non-scientific review writing of the time, where the reviewer may never even have read the book, let alone known anything of its subject matter. Such publications as *The Lady's Magazine* had wide appeal to a middle-class female audience, hungry for information and education otherwise unavailable to them. Despite this gendered focus, Janet had no hesitation in using the praise in her future advertising.

Of broader circulation was the report on her *Lunar Tables* in the December 1834 issue of the monthly *Metropolitan Magazine*, a regular publication in London since 1831. It highlighted one of her main strengths, namely the ability to simplify complex mathematical calculations for the ordinary seaman:

> Mrs Taylor has here simplified the means of obtaining the Longitude, in a manner that will be found highly serviceable in the Seaman's Education, which by necessity is frequently very limited, she has shown us all the tedious calculations, allowances and preparations hitherto commonly used may be dispensed with in the application of her 'Lunar Tables', calculated for the effect of *refraction* and *parallax*, which it is well understood, cause the error in the Angular Distance. We would therefore recommend these Tables to Sailors who will find that they give a very simple, easy and accurate method of working the Lunar Problem.
>
> We understand that it is Mrs Taylor's intention to open a Nautical Academy, and we most heartily wish her that success she so obviously deserves.

The mention of her Nautical Academy was very welcome as any encouragement of income streams was always greeted warmly in the Taylor household.

Another favourable review appeared in the January 1835 issue of the *United Service Journal*. While more important professionally, it drew largely on the review of her first book (*Luni-Solar and Horary Tables*) that was published in the same journal in October 1833. There was little more added to the original comments, except to again emphasise her gender.

> We have had occasion to notice the labours of this Lady in our former pages, for her ingenious application of a formula for correcting the difference between the perfect and oblate spheres, a minutia which had hitherto been neglected. We have to announce her further progress in improving the useful and national science of Navigation, by a Series of Tables which are to allow the observer to avoid the usual tedious preparations previous to clearing a 'Lunar Distance' from the effects of parallax error and refraction.
>
> Mrs Taylor's method appears, from the examples given, clear and short, and her book being more portable and less expensive than the plates of Margett's, will be more eligible for use.

This review also mentioned the Mariner's Calculator:

> Mrs Taylor also describes an instrument which she calls the 'Mariner's Calculator' and which is said to combine the means of making observations,

with the power of giving solutions to all the problems in nautical astronomy, without the use of a single calculation or log. From the description, it seems ingenious; but not having seen the instrument we must refer our readers to the work of the authoress 'for further particulars'.

So, it gave the impression of being 'ingenious'. But by now it was dead in the water.

The year of 1834 for Janet had been a testing one indeed. She had been so focused on her own work that she had barely noticed the goings on outside her door, let alone the 'Dreadful Conflagration' of 16 October upriver from the Taylors, when the Palace of Westminster, the site of the Houses of Parliament, was gutted. Much of both the Commons and Lords was destroyed. Janet had just written, for the second time, to Trinity House. Her son, Frederick, was just a year old. Herbert was not yet two. She had 'conflagrations' of her own to deal with.

The Thames was at low tide and the fire proved too much for the London Fire Engine Establishment, formed only the year before, and the soldiers and police who fought desperately alongside them to contain the blaze. There were twelve engines and sixty-four firemen, but the river from which they drew their water was too low. Fortunately, Westminster Hall, housing the Courts of Law, was saved, as were many of the books from the libraries. The fire was apparently started by the burning of long-discontinued wooden exchequer tally sticks in the stoves of the House of Lords. The heat set fire to the chimney flues. It was a devastating spectacle and it took years to rebuild, with the House of Commons not reopening until 1853. The smoke affected all the surrounding area and caused a great hullabaloo. But Janet displayed only passing interest.

She had now published three books. There was praise, but not the kind that would sustain future business endeavours. She had only a handful of expectant pupils. Janet had not secured endorsement or recognition, other than a modest purchase of her books by Trinity House. The Mariner's Calculator had not secured approval or endorsement. It had sorely depleted her inheritance and she was pregnant again, another baby, her third, due the coming February. And George's patience had been sorely tested. The books, and the Nautical Academy, simply had to succeed.

Janet needed the maritime 'establishment' to accept her, while George's requirements were peace in his household, a steady profit in their business and a wife who would sit by him of an evening and share the warmth of a fireside and a calm space at the end of the day. That time when the children were in bed and the affairs of the day had shut down for the night, where the pace changed and all the outside world was closed, respectfully, outside the door of the Taylor household.

Janet needed the quiet time too, but only so that she could continue with her work into the long hours. And that did her marriage no good at all.

IX

Taking On Her Critics

The new year of 1835 brought with it the challenge of fully establishing Janet Taylor's Nautical Academy at No. 1 Fen Court. It also saw the first professional consideration of the calculation method that was at the heart of her books, this time by the highly respected *Nautical Magazine*. Aware of its influence in the nautical community, she was understandably anxious that her mathematical techniques be greeted with approval by the maritime establishment. Although receiving favourable reviews in the *United Service Journal* was encouraging and others mostly from laymen were also heartening, the true test was to earn approving coverage in a technical publication that was read by the elite of the profession. The previous superficial reviews had little merit beyond advertising.

To be found worthy in the *Nautical Magazine* was a far cry from acceptance by *The Lady's Magazine*. And in January the *Nautical Magazine* published their review of her first book, *Luni-Solar and Horary Tables*. This was in fact a late review as the book that had been published in July 1833, with both the second edition and her *Principles of Navigation Simplified* having appeared in the meantime. The later books, however, developed upon her central premise: that the proper calculation of longitude by the lunar method had to take into account that the earth was spheroidal, not a perfect sphere.

Janet hastily turned to the review pages and began reading:

> The science of navigation is advanced in two ways. The first is by the labours of mathematicians, who may from time to time discover new methods of solution, or improve the old ones, or suggest entirely new problems: in this way much does not now seem likely to be done.

The other is by setting forth what is already known in such a manner as to make it either better understood, or more widely extended, that is, to raise the standard of practice: in this way, we think, much yet remains to be done, although this has always formed part of the avowed object of writers.

There is obviously an entire difference between the navigator and the mere worker of problems in navigation ...

Janet read this with a sense of foreboding, and bristled in sensing that she was put into the description of being a 'mere worker of problems in navigation'. It was all she could do to urge herself to read on.

... the latter indeed does as the rule tells him, but no more; and consequently when his observations do not agree, he knows not to which of them to attach the greater credit. The former, with perhaps no more science than the latter, learns by the exercise of reflection to time his observations properly, and to judge truly of their value. It is for this class, therefore, we think, that writers should study to adapt their works.

We are of opinion, that it is not spherical trigonometry nor the theory of logarithms and so forth, that constitutes the able navigator; in other words, that it is not his knowledge of the construction of the rules, but the judicious use he makes of them.

Her anticipation turned to dismay as she continued to read. It was over 3,000 words; and it was savage.

But it is not, as we observed, the working of the problem, but the application or use made of it, wherein lies the art of navigation; therefore it is not the number of problems, or the variety of their solutions, that the seaman wants, but useful information respecting them, and the reason why he is to prefer one mode of solution to another.

The advocates for this waste of time and labour justify it on the ground of general habits of accuracy, but we take leave to observe, that the exercise of the judgment, in discriminating between what is necessary and what is useless, and the consequent habit of perceiving the relative importance of accuracy in the data, and which no monotonous drudgery can ever teach, is a quality of a far higher order than performing to perfection in any such horse-in-a-mill routine. This disproportionate accuracy is, in general, inconsistency arising from want of thought; thus the stickler for minutes of a degree in working the ship's course, lumps, without scruple, courses and distances in his own watch by wholesale. As a particular example of degrees of accuracy, suppose the distance of the Lizard, found by logarithms, to be 50 miles; then, if the log. be wrong by unity in the seventh place, the error in distance will be two barleycorns. What a source of comfort must a table to 7 places be to a scrupulous computer! ...

'Waste of time'! 'Useless'! 'Disproportionate accuracy'! 'Two barleycorns'! By now she could hardly contain herself as the patronising condescension continued.

The work before us being the production of one of the fair sex, and, we believe, a first effort, disposed us to treat it, as in gallantry we were bound to do, with every indulgence ...

'Gallantry'! 'Indulgence'! It was unbearable.

But we are of opinion that Mrs. Taylor has ventured, on the present occasion, rather beyond her depth, and we hope, accordingly, that she will consider the remarks here offered, as a rope thrown to her in time; and we recommend her, when she publishes a second edition, to look well about her, not only by a diligent examination of the works of the day, but of those of many years ago. She would do well also to submit her next work to the scrutiny of some competent person, for, had this been done in the present case, it is impossible that such errors could have vitiated the work.

Janet's sense of injustice raged through her body. She was so angry at the unfairness of it all. Everyone in the household heard about it. They were used to her walking up and down as she mused and thought, talking aloud as she pondered upon her 'Principles', tossing around with an imagined audience just how to express things best. But this time she stormed. Up and down; up and down. Her voice was raised, speaking her furious protests to her faceless, nameless critic. True to form, Mrs Marton shook her head in disapproval, as did Elizabeth Juggens.

'Anonymous! What a coward!' Janet fumed. Everything else now paled into insignificance. This was no good, no good at all. It was demeaning, sarcastic – so much she had half-expected – but decrying her principle of spheroidal geometry? He was the one who had got it all wrong, not she. 'How *dare* he!' she ranted. All her attentions became firmly focused on showing that he was wrong.

It was not only the attack on her scientific method that stung, it was the condescension, the offhanded dismissal of her *as a woman*. And the timing was just woeful. Her academy had just opened its doors and the new editions of the *Tables* and her *Principles* were on the market. She didn't need this. Not ever but especially not now. She felt utterly crushed, not to mention that she was also eight months pregnant.

George held grave fears for her state of mind. The pregnancy had gone well so far, this being her third, but no birth was easy. He was concerned that such fury may be harmful not just to her, but also the unborn child. He pleaded with her to let her anger go. Those who knew anything about anything, he said, would not take much stock of such a review. He reminded her of the other good reviews, and their other plans – the charts; the teaching; and lots of other things they could sell.

But his words only seemed to fuel her rage. She was *right* and she knew it. How *dare* the reviewer be so condescending and so *wrong*? George soon realised that his pleas only made things worse as she wouldn't, and couldn't, let it go. Still fired up, she immediately set upon writing her reply.

Single-mindedly she focused upon her rejoinder. This had to be done right away, and before yet another child was upon her. She felt an overwhelming sense of the rightness of her argument. People were not only being taught poorly, they were also learning the wrong things. Why couldn't George see this too? If mariners didn't understand the importance or the magnitude of the errors that could result in not seeing the earth as spheroid and not spherical, they could founder upon rocks or other treacheries fifty miles or more off course. This was no small matter. But penning the words was crucial, they had to be just right to defend the veracity of her work.

The editor of the *Nautical Magazine* since 1832 was thirty-nine-year-old Lieutenant (later Rear-Admiral) Alexander Bridport Becher who had been the assistant to the Admiralty Hydrographer Francis Beaufort since 1823, a role he would have for forty-one years. As a matter of courtesy and protocol, Becher was obliged to afford Janet a right of reply to any possible criticisms. It came as no surprise that she was not going to let such 'peevish' remarks go unanswered. Declaring it as a matter of honour, she went on the attack. (How perspicacious was the reviewer in the *Nautical Magazine* when he spoke of her 'confident tone' and her 'zeal' – if he had known Janet better, he may well have foreseen that this could turn upon him.) Round One may have been his, but Round Two was about to begin.

Her response of just under 2,000 words was published in the February 1835 issue of the *Nautical Magazine*. Her opening salvo adressed the cowardly nature of the attack upon her:

> Had the writer of the article been more impartial, less captious, and treated the subject in a more experienced and manly manner, his remarks might have had some weight even with the 'novices and schoolboys' to whom be alludes, and would have elicited a different reply from me.

She was restrained, and responded to the charges squarely, throwing the reviewer's 'barleycorns' back at him:

> I am not, however, anxious to split either straws or 'barley-corns' with the writer, and think, if he will calmly read over the work, he will find that I have not cavilled so much at barley-corns as he has done. It is only a pity he does not extend his scrutiny to some other works on navigation which at present rank so high in public estimation considering himself called on to fulfil conscientiously the 'duty of his station'.
>
> Had he, as he professes, been well acquainted with his subject, and possessed a better knowledge of the works of some of our best writers on navigation, or even of the articles in the magazine in which he writes, he must have known more about spheroidal figure, and the necessity of corrections being applied accordingly, in more instances than the one to which he refers in his note.

To counter his assertions, she declared that every problem in her book had been worked out in two distinct ways, one assuming the earth to be a sphere (which 'sometimes may be accurate enough'); and the other assuming a spheroid, which she considered superior.

However, by quoting from the respected Scottish mathematics teacher and author Andrew Mackay (1760–1809), who had determined the latitude and longitude of Aberdeen in 1781, she claimed that, unless the geocentric latitude based on the *spheroid* assumption was used, then the error in calculating the longitude could be as much as fifty miles. And fifty miles at sea was a matter of life or death:

> If the reviewer had merely been actuated by his love of the science, or his anxiety to place before the public errors which might have endangered the welfare of a great portion of his fellow-men, it was incumbent on him, as holding so high a place in the estimation of the nautical world,

to have taken either the rule or the problem to which he objected, marked out each error as it arose, and thus have proved the fallacy of its principles; then, indeed, I might have thanked him for 'the rope' he has thrown out but at present, notwithstanding the warning contained in his review, I consider myself too firm in the system I have introduced, to seize even the end he has thrown across my shoulders. I cannot for a moment imagine that the two first pages of the article refer to me, as the writer may have observed that one rule pervades the whole work, and, that by the tables I have introduced the subject is rendered both concise and accurate; and, however much I may contend for nicety in their application of nautical astronomy, yet in the common course of navigation, I am no stickler for that 'disproportionate degree of accuracy' of which the reviewer complains. I am, however, surprised that a man professing so great an interest in the public weal, should promulgate an idea of the unimportance of a sailor understanding the fundamental principles in his art. I am of opinion, that, were the education of that class of men attended to as it ought to be, in schools established for that purpose, we should have fewer disasters at sea, and a more intelligent class of mariners.

But navigation has hitherto been too much mystified; the memory is taxed without the understanding being called into play, and thus the pupil becomes tired of rules, which, from not being properly demonstrated and explained, are easily forgotten. If the reviewer will take the trouble to examine impartially my work entitled 'Navigation Simplified', he may be more inclined to do me the justice to acknowledge that what I have done has 'combined the maximum of intelligence with the minimum of labour'.

Perhaps the only issue where she did agree with the reviewer was that she did indeed have the 'confident tone' mentioned in the review; and reiterated that her 'opinions will bear the strictest investigation'. To illustrate her contention, she went on to provide a numeric example that, if her method were not used, it would result in a significant error of 28', or about fifteen miles, in the calculation of the longitude. Other practical examples of why her method was correct were supplied and she challenged the reviewer to prove the alleged 'fallacy' of her principles. If he had been able to do so, she might have thanked him for 'the rope he has thrown', but as it stood, she would not even bother to 'seize the end' of it. Moreover, she was 'appalled' that a person writing in the public arena should feel that it was unimportant for a sailor to understand 'the fundamental principles of his art'. This, of course, gave her an opportunity to promote navigation schools such as her own Nautical Academy where, if more sailors attended and understood the principles of navigation a little better, there would be 'fewer disasters at sea'.

In a final swipe at the reviewer, Janet once again accused him of not bothering to take the time to give an impartial view of her work. On a more conciliatory note, she concluded her response by thanking the editor of the magazine for his 'kind and gentlemanly manner' in allowing her to use his forum for the right of reply to the criticism of her work. She had won Round Two, and just in time, too, as her third child, Seymour (named after his maternal grandfather), was born just days later on 19 February 1835.

The anonymous reviewer was clearly not amused. His own integrity and knowledge had now been called into question and he certainly was not going to let the likes of a mere pretentious woman get the last word. His fresh retort was unrelenting, even stronger than the original outburst, and was published in the very next issue of the *Nautical Magazine* in March 1835. He immediately went on the attack, declaring that her ideas could 'have the effect of misleading ignorant persons'; and if it were 'so conspicuous' an error, how could it have been 'so universally overlooked by preceding authors'? The patronising tone of the first review was again in full swing:

> We gave her an opportunity of tacitly reconsidering the effect of her work, but this she has rejected: she scorns our friendly hints; and, with a zeal worthy of a nobler cause she insists on the validity of her doctrine.

Followed by a direct swipe at her navigation teaching:

> In this country, where there is no tribunal of science to pass its imprimatur as an authority that a work published for the use of the seaman is fit to be placed in his hands, and as navigation is a matter by which he is to sink or swim, he is exposed to the most serious mischief by the ignorance of unqualified persons who volunteer to instruct him. This consideration, therefore, deepens the responsibility of those who write or review works on nautical science. We do not, indeed, affect to think that the work in question is got up with sufficient skill to obtain many disciples, even on a matter which appears at first very plausible, and certainly there is no chance of practical men adopting a more complicated calculation in preference to a simpler one, from mere attachment to theory.

And an incredulous dismissal of other reviews:

> We have been led into these observations from seeing some of our contemporaries take on themselves the responsibility of gravely pronouncing an eulogy on this very work, without waiting even to examine its claims. That examination we undertook, not only in justice to the author, but to our readers and perhaps to our national character. For if, through the indiscreet recommendation of a writer in an influential periodical a work containing erroneous doctrines should pass through successive editions, what opinion could foreigners entertain of the state of navigation in this country?

It was then down to specifics, firstly by refuting the notion that the blunders she made were merely 'typographical', citing several errors of fact and demonstrating through a numerical example that she was mistaken with her preoccupation of the spheroidal shape of the earth. Then it was back to the self-effacing comments that 'Mrs. Taylor has so mean an opinion of our humble attainments' that she dares suggest that the reviewer does not know what he is talking about. He finished by declaring:

> We have now concluded the remarks which the reply of Mrs. Taylor has rendered necessary. Whether they may induce her to consider our former review of her work in a more favourable light than she has done, or whether they may fail in leading her to revise her theory, we cannot say; but having taken up her work on strictly scientific ground, we have allowed no extraneous consideration to lead us from the candid and impartial review of its contents, that is demanded by works of the kind.

Round Three to him.

Janet fumed again, but she still had much more fight in her. Although drained from the birth of the child, and the fact that the baby was quite sickly from the outset, she managed to draw upon an inner strength in the face of the reviewer's condescension. This was a forum in which her gender was always going to be relevant, but she at least could say what she thought. That made it a slightly more level playing field, provided the editor played fair. So she enlisted him, writing privately to Lieutenant Becher and left him in no doubt that she was not going to let this go.

Becher was alarmed, as he had not expected the open verbal warfare between Janet and her reviewer. He greeted it with a measure of interest, indeed intrigue, as it provided a fascinating, if unseemly, spectacle for the readers. It was obvious that this woman was not to be ignored, and certainly not underestimated. After three instalments of the joust so far and clearly with many more promised, he was not sure what to do. His sense of gallantry was also brought into play and it was here that Janet's gender finally worked in her favour. Becher found it somewhat unchivalrous that the reviewer was being so trenchantly condescending and condemnatory. He felt moved to seek advice from Captain Francis Beaufort, the Admiralty Hydrographer, in whose department he also worked not just as his assistant but a respected hydrographer in his own right.

Beaufort had read the correspondence in the *Nautical Magazine* and it concerned him greatly. He had been the one, after all, to make the judgment on her Mariner's Calculator and was aware of how distracted he had been at the time in the midst of his wife Alicia's suffering. She had passed away on 27 August 1834. Beaufort still considered his judgment of the calculator fair, but was aware of just how hurtful it must have been. Recognising the passion that lay behind such innovations, he admired Janet's spirit. It was not a lunatic invention at all, indeed it was quite brilliant, but he just felt it would be unworkable at sea, and he had not the time, the energy (he was aged sixty), nor inclination, at that time, to test it further. So he felt somewhat responsible, and motivated, to give her at least some assistance, if not encouragement.

Having dismissed the Mariner's Calculator, Beaufort's curiosity of the inventor led to his making enquiries about Mrs Taylor, and he must have recognised some aspects of his own life in her. He, too, had been the child of a country clergyman, his father having been a parson in Ireland – and one of scholarly bent, with interests in astronomy, mapping and architecture. This was to find practical expression in his father's topographical map of Ireland, published in 1792. The interests of the father had whetted the appetite of the son and Beaufort developed a vast curiosity and profound love of physical observation, along with a burning desire to go to sea. As a young man he wrote in his journal in 1806, 'Everyone has a hobby or insanity. Mine I believe is taking bearings for charts and plans.' Beaufort recognised in Janet a tenacity that was all too familiar to him. He saw, as did Becher, that she had stood her ground and would not concede defeat. Making it clear that he would have no further episodes of the public brawling, Beaufort urged that a truce be arranged somehow. The first step was the mention of the birth of Seymour in the magazine:

> On the 19th inst., Mrs Janet Taylor, the celebrated authoress of 'Luni-Solar and Horary Tables, Navigation Simplified, &c.,' of a son, East Street, Red Lion Square.

It was not exactly the acceptance that she needed or deserved, but it was an acknowledgment of sorts. 'Celebrated authoress, indeed,' she thought. It was notable because the column in which the announcement appeared was normally strictly reserved for service personnel. It was perhaps somewhat backhanded, but it was something. By this time Beaufort also took the trouble of obtaining a copy of her formula for himself. He found her argument persuasive, but wondered if it were really worth all the effort and passion she had poured into it. He requested a face-to-face meeting to judge for himself.

It was a brief but significant occasion, bearing in mind that Janet was but half his age. After dispensing with the usual introductory pleasantries, he furrowed his brow and came straight to the point, pressing her to explain why it was all so important to her. She was taken aback at the Irish lilt in his voice, not being sure what to expect, perhaps a voice and accent more elevated, more upper-class, but certainly not so *Irish*. It was quite disarming, even quaint. It reminded her of the broader accents from her own childhood and immediately put her at ease in replying that it had been her father – as well as the Durham skies. Beaufort responded in kind, saying that it was his father too, along with the sea.

This instant rapport surprised them both: the elderly, serious and dignified Admiralty Hydrographer and the earnest, passionate and very determined young woman. She conveyed her sincerest sorrow that he had lost his wife the year before, sharing with him the precariousness of the new business she and George had begun, but also her commitment to an enterprise that had the mariners of the world at heart. Beaufort even suggested that she might revise, not abandon, her formula, while working on the abridging of the calculation of lunar distances. She should build on the work of Maskelyne, rather than emphasising too much the impact of the spheroidal aspect of the calculations. He invited her to send her revised work to him when she had completed this fresh approach and, somewhat flattered, she decided to take his advice and review her formulas.

The *Nautical Magazine* battle had been very wearing for Janet, but out of it, curiously, was to emerge a most respectful, even warm, relationship with Captain Beaufort. While her books had shown early promise, and generated some, although not prolific, sales – and despite the alarming review in the *Nautical Magazine* – they were certainly not enough to support a viable business on their own. The failure of the Mariner's Calculator had severely eroded her inheritance. It was essential that the academy succeed and that they should develop the other fledgling aspects of their business, such as chartselling and instrument retailing and manufacturing, if possible. But just as they thought the storm was over, another, more menacing one appeared on the horizon.

X

Overstepping the Mark

1834 had proven an unbelievably busy year for Janet, bringing many low points but finishing more positively with the meeting with Beaufort. But her recent good fortune was short-lived; in her haste to have her *Principles of Navigation Simplified* published, she had included one table without the permission from its author. Books like Janet's, by their very nature involving many tables of various kinds, often relied to a greater or lesser extent on the incorporation of tables of others. These were largely stereotyped, the real value in the work being the inclusion of commentary on how best to perform the calculations. But where tables were incorporated from established works, obtaining permission, or licensing the use from the author or owner was implicitly expected, even though matters of 'copyright' were still somewhat a developing area of the law of the time.[10]

The 'Table of Latitudes and Longitudes of the principal ports, harbours, capes of the world' in Janet's book had been taken directly from a rival navigation textbook, *A Complete Epitome of Practical Navigation* by John William Norie, a well-known and established author and teacher with his own Nautical Academy at 157 Leadenhall Street, in close proximity to Fen Court where Janet had also been teaching. The Leadenhall Street premises were decorated by the trade sign of the Wooden Midshipman, mounted on the wall outside the shop, later immortalised by Charles Dickens in the serialised *Dombey and Son* (1846–48) as the name of the nautical instrument shop kept by the character Sol Gills. Norie had been writing nautical books since 1797 and had been conducting his academy since 1800 and now, aged sixty-two, was very much the elder statesman of nautical writers and teachers. Janet had meant to seek his permission, indeed she thought she had, but she had been so consumed by the crisis with the Mariner's Calculator and her pregnancy. It was a critical detail she had overlooked, as well as being a major lapse of judgment.

Norie was well aware of the Taylors. They had been in his shop, just as they had been in Bate's, and there, too, Janet had made her presence known. He had naturally read her stoush in the *Nautical Magazine* and took personal slight at the comments by her of others in the field. It was impertinent to suggest that *he* and others like him had got it wrong. Who did she think she was?

Janet provided Norie with an unexpected avenue for putting her in her place and he promptly threatened legal action against her. If he sued successfully she would be ruined, with the only alternative being to agree to withdraw the book altogether. She was trapped and she knew it. The book had now been in circulation for a year and was proving to be a good seller. Although withdrawing it from sale and destroying remaining copies would have had serious financial implications, taking on the established Norie was an even bigger risk. She knew that pleading with him to overlook her indiscretion would have no effect and she didn't even make the effort. He was clearly adamant and undoubtedly within his rights, leaving no choice but to comply and withdraw it. She was devastated.

To make matters worse, she could not publish a revised edition of her book without including this vital table, making it necessary to find another source. News of Norie's intimidation spread quickly among the nautical community and Janet again turned to Lieutenant Becher for advice. But far from blaming her, it was actually Norie who felt the brunt of his peers for taking such a heavy-handed approach. There were many who felt he had gone too far and that he knew full well what the effect of his demands on the young author would be. Moreover, her spirited response in the *Nautical Magazine* had gained her a measure of sympathy for her willingness to take on her critics. Becher felt moved enough to consult Francis Beaufort and he in turn enlisted Captain Alexander Maconochie of the Royal Geographical Society and the chartseller John Arrowsmith (nephew of one of the founders of the Royal Geographical Society). The Arrowsmith family originated from the town of Winston, located only about twelve miles from Janet's native Wolsingham, a fact that almost certainly worked in Janet's favour as her team of rescuers put their collective thoughts together.

Between them, and drawing upon their various resources of tables and contacts, they managed to recreate the offending table from scratch, in an original and even more accurate 'Table of Latitudes and Longitudes of the Principal Ports, Harbours, Capes etc from the latest Observations, Surveys and Charts', from completely different sources. The reason for their involvement was most likely a combination of sympathy for her suffering at the hands of Norie, performing an act of gallantry to help a struggling newcomer (and a woman at that), whom they felt was being harshly treated. Here, it seems, Janet's gender was her ally. There was also a nice irony in the situation because, when compiling these new tables, it was discovered that Norie had made a number of crucial errors in his own table. When her next edition appeared, she wasted no time in pointing this out, together with a begrudging acknowledgment of her own shortcoming:

NOTE. – As I considered all authentic positions and Places were published for the benefit of the public, I unfortunately copied the Table of Latitudes and Longitudes in Mr Norie's 'Epitome' which he obliged me to suppress. For this however I thank him, for on comparing his Table with those works on the subject, which are recognised and used by Government, and which Capt. Beaufort and Lieut. Becher of the Admiralty, and Capt. Maconochie of the Royal Geographical Society subsequently lent me, (to whom I take this opportunity of returning my warmest thanks,).

I find it to differ from them most materially. For instance, the entire Coast of Africa, according to Capt. Owen's Survey, is wrong; several islands on the Eastern Coast which must be passed (if not touched) daily, by vessels to India, & are laid down from 1 to 5 degrees in error; some important points on the South and East Coasts of Italy are many miles from their true position; and it is with surprise I look at the east Coast of Greenland as laid down in 'the Epitome', where there are errors of from 2 to 10, and even 13 degrees. Indeed, discrepancies of this nature are too numerous to particularise in the brief space of a note: however, this may be a sufficient hint to the mariner.

Mr. Norie insisted that his Tables were constructed according to private authorities on which he founded great originality, but I find that, since the suppression of my Copies, he has edited his tables with some alterations in his boasted original positions; but I think there yet remains numerous instances in which originality prevails at the expense of accuracy.

To Mr. John Arrowsmith I am indebted for much useful information on this subject, as well as for the reference he has allowed me to make to his valuable Works.

The same defiant tone that had filled her response to her critic in the *Nautical Magazine* was again in evidence. Norie's attack had misfired badly, instead revealing rather that his own table had been shown wanting. This gave her vindication and she desperately wanted the nautical world to know that Norie had been outsmarted, along with acknowledging those who helped her. While her misuse of the Norie table was clearly a mistake, here she unwittingly erred again. In publicly attributing thanks to Beaufort and the others, she had overstepped an unwritten, although unstated, mark.

Beaufort and his colleagues had gone out of their way to assist her, but it was an act that still needed to sit alongside their position in the world of men. It was meant to be chivalrous, but also discreet. Janet just didn't appreciate this. Her upbringing was not one in which such nuances were seen or taught, resulting in a naivety in so many respects regarding the behaviour codes of men. In her mind she was simply profoundly grateful and considered it only fitting that she should record publicly their service. But 'fitting' it was not; and sadly it revealed a most unfortunate misjudgement.

In any case, with the troubles of the table seemingly behind her, Janet was keen to get the revised book out as soon as possible so as not to lose too much momentum caused by the withdrawal of the original edition. As was their custom, they sent the proof pages of the table to Beaufort, but the final copy, containing the acknowledgment, was not seen by him until December. When it finally did come to his attention, he exploded.

In the meantime, however, Beaufort continued to assist her where he could. The spat with Norie had proved very costly for the Taylors and meant that it was becoming even more urgent for Janet to secure strong sales of her books and, if possible, to obtain some kind of financial assistance. To achieve her goal, there was a realisation that she desperately needed to do something else. Should she revise her formula for clearing the lunar distance, or even change her whole approach? If she had convinced no one of the merits of her formulas, what good was that?

It didn't matter that she might have been correct, the key issue was that she had failed to convince the Admiralty, Trinity House or the East India Company. It turned out to be Beaufort that suggested the answer, encouraging her to review her approach and make her main focus an abridged method for solving lunar distances. This had the advantage of retaining her commitment to the earth as spheroidal, but also emphasised the utility of the abridged method she devised. After making the suggested adjustments, Janet sent her revised formula to Beaufort for consideration:

Dear Sir,
I forward to you the formula as you requested and I feel assured that it is needless in me to request you to be careful – on you and it rest all

my hopes. To you I appeal and trust the future welfare of myself and infant family, knowing your power to be extensive and your inclination to serve your fellow creatures great. Forgive me if I repeat that I trust more than my life in your hands in perfect confidence there your power to serve me will be exerted to the utmost and could I but trespass on you to shoulder fully the tremendous sacrifices I have made I have no doubts finally effectual.

With many thanks for the trouble you have taken about me.

I am and continue

Your obliged servant
Janet Taylor

Her fresh approach at clearing the lunar distance was considered far more impressive by Beaufort and he promptly sent her formulas to the Irish astronomer Dr Thomas Romney Robinson for approval. Robinson was a Professor of Astronomy and appointed to the Armagh Observatory, Northern Ireland, in 1823, a post he held for a record fifty-nine years, the longest for any observatory in the world. His reputation had been firmly established by publishing a number of classical works including *Determination of the Longitude of the Armagh Observatory* in 1830 and *On the dependence of a Clock's rate on the height of the Barometer* the following year. Beaufort knew Robinson not just by reputation, but as a colleague as they had worked together in 1832 on a committee to improve the standard of the annual *Nautical Almanac* published by the Admiralty. He proved an excellent choice, and without hesitation his judgment was undoubtedly in her favour.

With Robinson's endorsement, along with Beaufort's backing, it came as no real surprise the Admiralty now considered they could provide her with some assistance. On 22 June 1835 she received a brief note:

Tell Mrs Taylor that in consideration of services she has extended to seamen we have great pleasure in according to her request and have ordered the sum of £100 to be paid to her order for payment from scientific funds.

Beaufort had proved himself a true ally. This was no small sum, as £100 represented nearly three months' full salary for Beaufort himself. The grant also provided just the leverage she needed to secure a similar amount from the Elder Brethren of Trinity House. Not wishing to look churlish, even foolish by dismissing her request for a further, now fourth, time, they capitulated. It was one thing to reject an unknown Mrs Taylor, but quite another to dismiss Captain Beaufort, the Admiralty and Dr Robinson. Her perseverance had paid off and even the *Nautical Magazine* now congratulated her on achieving 'a handsome pecuniary award' from the Admiralty and the Elder Brethren for following their example.

Janet saw to it that Beaufort's role would not go unacknowledged and so shortly after receiving the grant from Trinity House, she put pen to paper:

My dear Sir,
Knowing that you will be gratified to hear that success is following my humble endeavours. I take the liberty of intruding myself again on you to mention that the Elder Brethren have followed the example you have set them and that today I received from them one hundred pounds.

Your interest in me was the first gleam of comfort which had visited me for many months. From that I date my presently good fortune which has increased the debt of gratitude I owe you – believe me I feel deeply my obligation.

Yours very gratefully
Janet Taylor

With two of the three major bodies won over, it was now time to focus her attention on the third and final one, the East India Company. Leverage worked again and a further grant of £100 was soon within her keeping.

There was no doubting her energy and zeal. And with a fresh £300 to work with, a rejuvenated Janet threw herself into completing the next edition of her book, the third edition of her *Lunar Tables*, now including dedications to the Admiralty, Trinity House and the East India Company. She had won them all, and this time the book was praised not only in England but in Europe and the United States of America. What set this edition apart from those previous was the inclusion of a new section on the use of the chronometer, in recognition of its growing importance. Although they provided the means for the accurate determination of longitude, chronometers were expensive, thus ensuring that the lunar technique remained in vogue, at least for the time being.

With the welcome change in fortune, George was at last able to secure premises in Minories and so, in August 1835, the family moved both their home from East Street in Red Lion Square and their business from Fen Court, Fenchurch Street, into No. 103 Minories, right in the heart of maritime London. The street was named after the abbey of the Minoresses of the Order of St Clare, which had stood on the site until the Dissolution of the Monasteries under Henry VIII in 1536. No. 103 was a four-storey building that had previously been rented by the tailor John Fox and was one door up from the corner of Hammet Street. It was only a short walk to Tower Bridge and St Katharine Docks on the River Thames and located in a bustling commercial neighbourhood filled with activity. Wagons laden with goods made their way to and from the great warehouses beside the docks, their teams of horses toiling up the broad sweep of Minories. It was an inspired move, as theirs was the only business of its kind in the immediate vicinity.

The Taylors' new next-door neighbours were David Richardson, a grocer at No. 102 (on the corner) and William Brown, a linen draper, at No. 104. The Richardsons also had a little boy, George, who was only a few months older than Frederick. By now the Taylor household comprised George's son Charles (now thirteen), and daughter Emily Ann (now seventeen), George and Janet's sons Herbert (aged four), Frederick (ten months) and the baby, Seymour. George Junior, now eighteen, no longer lived with them. And then there were also the servants, Mrs Marton, Richard Tyley and Elizabeth Juggens. The new quarters in Minories with many rooms were certainly large enough to expand the business. There was ample space for the shop on the ground floor and for pupils on the second level, while the family living quarters were located on the upper floors.

The move to Minories was both opportune and exciting, providing the chance for the business to grow as they had always envisaged. But it also required significant adjustments on the domestic front, as the rituals of the household were just like those of other London middle-class households. Janet was unquestionably in charge, although by this time she and Mrs Marton had found a respectable accommodation that allowed her mistress to make decisions and give directions about the vast range of daily household enquiries that had to be made or answered. In this era a servant's working day was long and arduous. While the house had piped water, the servants still had to carry water up the many flights of stairs for washing or bathing. In addition, London and its houses were perpetually dirty from the coal that provided warmth in winter and fuel for the kitchen, covering everything in a thick dust. The round of carrying, dusting, scrubbing and beating was both monotonous and relentless.

Sundays were for church and family and, after prayers with the servants, the Taylor family always made the short walk to the church of St Katherine Coleman, where they now worshipped. While they were in Red Lion Square they had continued to attend St Giles in the Fields, and both Frederick and Seymour were baptised there together on 21 April, two months after Seymour was born, but with the move to Minories they were in the parish of St Katherine and so the family now travelled there.

With the commanding fortress of the Tower of London and its moat on their left, they would pass the island of four-storey houses of Postern Row towards Trinity Square with its circular lawned garden in the middle. They walked past Trinity House, built late in the previous century, the headquarters for one of the bastions of the naval establishment to whom Janet directed some of her entreaties. Finally, they would make the right turn for the gentle stroll uphill towards Fenchurch Street where the church stood. The early eighteenth century church had been built on the foundations of an earlier sacred place, as had many across Europe; here it was a medieval building. As the Taylors went to worship, the simple peal of the two bells of St Katherine's rang in their ears, mingling with the bells that created the soundscape of London, as much as any town across Britain, including those of St Olave Hart Street, St Katherine Cree, St Botolph Aldgate, St Botolph Bishopgate and St Andrew Undershaft just a few blocks away. Sundays throughout Christendom were alive with bells.[11]

After morning service the family then returned for a large meal, such an occasion being the one time when George was very firmly head of the table. It seemed only then did Janet defer to him without question. It was also a time that was the closest to her childhood, when her siblings all sat up to table with their mother and father, said their prayers together, read aloud stories suitable for Sunday and entertained each other with playing the piano and singing. Janet respected the Sabbath, both out of the moral conventions of the age as well as her deeply held religious convictions and upbringing. Although overtly she did not 'work' on Sundays, her mind was always fixed very actively on what she would do the following day.

The good fortune offered by the move and the clearing of the Norie storms beckoned a time for celebration in the Taylor household. But it had to be put on hold when the youngest of the three children, Seymour, who had never been strong, became increasingly ill over the summer. And finally, on 25 October 1835, just as the autumn chill began to settle in London evenings and the smog of the city that accompanied it began to envelop the streets and their inhabitants, he died.

Life for young children in nineteenth-century England was a most precarious thing. They often clung to life by the barest thread, over half of them dying before they reached the age of five years. Indeed, around half of all the funerals in the City of London were for those who had not reached their tenth birthday. Death was part of 'the normal' for the young, and their mothers, at this time, as that preceding it. No matter how much child death was part of the usual rhythm of life, the death of your own child always was its own very personal agony. One did not become immune to pain such as this. It may have been expected, but it was never easy. As for Janet, on occasions it even made her question God's will, which had formed such a guiding principle for her.

Janet's response to her grief at Seymour's death was to throw herself even more deeply into her works. The light was getting poorer but she didn't notice. Straining by the thick yellow flame of the gaslight she could barely make out the figures while desperately trying to forget that she had just buried her son. As a result of her relentless endeavours, two more editions of *Lunar Tables* appeared in the ensuing months, with both being encouraged by more positive reviews. With Seymour's death, something inside her had also died and, although George did his best to ease her distress, he would never find the right words, if there were any, to ease the pain. He knew full well the ache of losing a loved one and when all else failed he suggested another child. Not a replacement, but new life in the household. And so, still with a heaviness of heart, she did fall pregnant again in the early months of the new year, 1836.

Her standing in the seafaring world was steadily growing, especially in the area of charts, as evidenced by a letter headed 'Danger in the eastern Seas' from Captain Thomas Macker of the barque *John Dennester*. In writing to the *Nautical Magazine* in their January 1836 edition, he declared, 'The following notice of a newly-discovered danger in Banks Strait, Van Diemans's land, we have received from Mrs Janet Taylor', and went on to describe a rock that she had uncovered off Swan Island in Banks Strait. The magazine said it was 'recorded for the immediate use of navigators, as cautions to them when in its vicinity'.

This was also a time that brought Janet's earlier misjudgement concerning Beaufort into focus. It was only on 18 December the previous year that the final copy of the republished book with her acknowledgment of, and gratitude for, Beaufort's intervention was received at the Hydrographic Office. Far from being pleased, he was deeply irritated, tearing the page from the book and firmly crossing through his name in black pen. Not only had his assistance and that of his fellow rescuers been intended as a discreet act of chivalry, as Hydrographer to the Royal Navy it would have been quite improper for Beaufort to be seen to be taking sides in a matter of this kind. Private expressions of thanks were fine and appropriate, indeed welcomed, but here Janet had not only thanked him *publicly*, but she had put the boot into Norie, who was, notwithstanding his attack on

Janet, still a leading and senior member of the nautical community. And Beaufort simply could not be seen as ridiculing him.

In January Janet sent a humble apology:

Dear Sir,

Before I sent you the proof sheets of my Table, I had had the opinion of a professional man who said I was *safe*, consequently without hesitation (as I can likewise prove the truth of all I am attested) the remark went to press, and, at the same time I am sorry to say, your name which I learn you object to. Believe me, Sir, gratitude and respect alone suggested the idea of offering you a slight compliment by publicly expressing my sense of obligation for your kindness.

On no other account would I have taken such a liberty and therefore I sincerely hope that as all law proceedings are out of the question, and consequently future inconvenience avoided, you will excuse that which now appears a liberty, but which I had intended to be otherwise interpreted.

I have had too much difficulty in making friends to hazard the losing them by so trivial an act and I am grieved that in this instance I should risk giving you offence and I hope this explanation will remove any degree of displeasure towards me.

I am, dear Sir,

Your obliged
Janet Taylor

She could not afford to lose such an important and revered ally as Beaufort, especially as within a few months she would need to appeal to him for help again.

The move to No. 103 Minories had been an inspired choice, but it had also brought great risk. Cashflow was an ever present issue. George and Janet had been banking on the sale of her books and the income from teaching to keep their stream of revenue and were now hoping for the infant chartselling arm of their business to provide a source of income. But for now it was sales of the books that were seen as the backbone and major contribution to their fortunes.

By Monday 2 May 1836, and having had no further word on the matter, she assumed that her apology had helped to assuage Beaufort's irritation and made the tentative step of seeking his intervention to secure sales of her books to the Navy. The Admiralty had kindly granted her £100 in June the previous year and allowed their move to Minories, but she needed an assurance of ongoing purchases. Without question, the buyer of greatest significance was the Navy itself:

Dear Sir,

Like the importunate widow, you will think I am determined to be heard for my much speaking, but I will be brief in my application, which I pray you listen to patiently. Can and will you assist me in obtaining an order for my Lunars in the Navy? Either for those vessels now commissioned or those to be commissioned of which we hear so much. I am presumptuous enough to think that I have given a fillip to Navigation which will be extensively and beneficially felt and altho' I am doing very well, yet no *negro* works harder than I am obliged to do and that without cessation. Another edition of my Lunars is in press, and I think a little of the money granted for the supply of the Navy might be hence employed in them giving me a gleam of sunshine to cheer me on my pilgrimage, particularly as it is in the furtherance of a scientific and useful object.

The Works of others may be more elaborate but I question much whether mine, before I have done, will not ultimately be found more generally useful. I do not mean as far as you Gentlemen of the Navy are concerned, but the Merchant men who daily leave our ports make up a *vast* portion in the seafaring community, and it has been to the improvement of their infamous system of education my chief attention has been directed, leaving our Colleges to furnish forth a *few* bright examples. If you cannot assist me in this matter, perhaps you could direct me to the right source where I might be successful in my suit, particularly if aided by the interest of friends.

Hoping you will pardon this trouble I am giving you.

I am and continue

Your obliged and grateful
Janet Taylor

Once again, however, Janet miscalculated. Beaufort greeted her letter with some annoyance. He also knew the parable, in which the widow was a nagger and irritated the poor judge to the extent that he awarded her the suit, but only selfishly for the sake of peace. Her persistence was not in question, but he felt affronted that she did not show him more respect than the judge to whom the 'importunate widow' made her pleas. She had gone too far, especially so soon after securing £100 to assist her. It was time to put a stop to it. But a few days later his attitude softened somewhat and he returned her letter with a gentler, but still firm, tone:

Madam

I am sorry that I cannot in any way lend myself to your request. There are two ways by which their Lordships could have afforded some assistance to your useful labours – 1. by the purchase of a certain number of copies of the book – and 2. by giving you a sum of money. The latter was adopted as most direct and most beneficial to you – and in accepting it I think you should have felt precluded from asking for the alternative in addition.

I am sorry thus to destroy your hopes but I have no alternative.

Janet was mortified as once again it seemed that she had managed to offend him. Her only recourse was to pay him a personal visit to try and make things right. As soon as she was ushered in, Beaufort saw that once again she was expecting a child. Janet was very contrite, expressing sorrow for any further offence she may, in her naivety, have given him. She was eternally grateful for his support and interventions on her behalf. She was not asking their lordships to purchase her books, but rather suggesting that the Navy may find them useful, as she understood the Admiralty supplied the Navy with such things.

Beaufort felt taken aback; perhaps he had misunderstood her intentions after all. It wasn't Admiralty money she was chasing, but rather simply some help with getting the Navy to adopt her books. He was also aware that she had lost a child not so long ago, so that seeing her pregnant again was quite disarming. He reminded himself that this young woman sitting before him was not only producing new editions of her books at an impressive rate, but had taken on chartselling *and* running a Nautical Academy. And apparently had not long ago moved their entire enterprise into costly new premises.

Being a man who admired talent, Beaufort recognised in Janet a kindred spirit. He now readily agreed to look into her request, wishing her well with the coming birth and the new edition of her book. He even went as far as to try and recover a little of the easy rapport that he had felt with her at their first meeting. Indeed he considered it his duty as both a senior naval representative and a gentleman. He recalled to her that he had recently read of a woman who by magnetism was able to communicate maternal care and attention to her children though separated from them. This made Janet smile and respond that, while she recognised how powerful a force magnetism was, it was not one that she thought could truly tend to children, notwithstanding however much mothers might wish it.

Beaufort's assistant, Becher, was puzzled to hear laughter from Beaufort's office. He had wondered about the tenor of the meeting in view of Beaufort's prior irritation, and his own experience of Mrs Taylor's tenacity, and was rather relieved to hear evident amusement emanating from the other room, and to see the calm as he saw her out. Now, with her relationship with Beaufort restored to a respectful, but easier state, Janet was able to concentrate on the important task of running a viable business operation.

Once they were settled in her new premises, Janet was at last able to launch the foreshadowed 'Nautical Academy' and before long it settled into a regular rhythm. For her head teacher, she had chosen James Griffin, 'a clever and able mathematician', as she described him in the preface of her second edition of *Lunar Tables*, published on 1 December 1835. In a letter to Beaufort in September 1836, Janet singled him out for special praise, as well as their method of instruction:

> The gentleman teaching for me is a good Geometer and Mathematician and possesses a knowledge of Navigation seldom to be met with, and so confident am I of his superior abilities on these points that I would not hesitate placing him on trial with the best and most clever man in the Kingdom as his competitor. Our method of tuition is likewise so superior to that usually adopted, and in consequence the progress of the Pupils so rapid and satisfactory, that our school room is free of access, and open to every investigation.
>
> A short time ago we had several youths with us, who, *in less than six weeks*, went through such a course of navigation as is seldom to be met with and we would willingly have challenged for them any examination. We are only anxious that our system of conveying instruction should undergo the strictest scrutiny and for this purpose *coach* and *freely* answer every enquiry on the subject of navigation. So highly are we spoken of and appreciated by all who know us that we, at this moment, have a gentleman studying with us who is himself preparing young men for Addiscombe,[12] and who came to us from the recommendation of a man who was formerly *prejudiced* against us in the highest degree.

She was most critical of the 'shameful manner' in which navigation had been, and continued to be, taught. In the same letter she wrote:

We know of numberless instances where men are teaching it without knowing anything but the application of rules, for which they cannot account nor even properly explain.

In the establishment of the Nautical Academy, she repeatedly demonstrated her frustration at what she perceived as critical issues in ensuring the safety of mariners. At least through an academy of her own the wrongs she alleged in the instruction of others could be rectified. In the chartselling business, however, she could not solve the frustrations that quickly began to spill over into the sales of Admiralty charts. Another storm was brewing in her world, but this time a new enemy appeared in the form of Robert Bate, the Principal Agent for Admiralty charts, and, with him, a battle that would continue until his death intervened.

XI

The Battle with Bate

London in the 1830s was fast becoming the largest city in the world and the nerve centre of Britain's sea-borne empire. To be a chartseller was a key part of any business that focused upon the maritime world, as sea charts were both the street directories and X-ray maps of the oceans, the recorded memories and experiences of seafarers past. They were the dividing line between fair sailing and disaster. The wider the reach of sailors across the oceans, the more prone they were to shipwreck on unknown or unfamiliar coastlines. George and Janet had hoped that their sales would provide a reliable income stream as being very much the 'bread and butter' of any nautical enterprise of the time. Being appointed sub-agent for Admiralty charts was an important indicator of status, on a par with the likes of John Norie, who was one of the first to be granted such a privilege.

In his position as Principal Agent for Admiralty charts, Robert Bate was allowed 40 per cent of the returns on sales, but he was not permitted to publish or sell any other charts. The Admiralty appointed various sub-agents under him, but all had to acquire their Admiralty charts through him, and had to direct any corrections to him as well. The *Nautical Magazine* was in the habit of publicising 'newly-discovered dangers to navigation' so that chart-owners could personally adjust their own charts, but any official corrections to Admiralty charts had to go through the Principal Agent. When something new was to be added or a correction made to an Admiralty chart, it was a requirement that the information had to be sent to Bate. On becoming a sub-agent, the threads of Janet Taylor's story and those of Bate's became inexorably entangled.

Robert Brettell Bate was a man of standing, having inherited 'bearings' that had been granted to his ancestor, Leonard Bate of York, in 1565. He was a younger son, educated well, and thought himself clever. He sought adulation, foreseeing a life of triumph and fame mapped out before him. But his life took an unexpected turn at the age of twenty-two when his youthful pastimes with his first cousin, then aged twenty-five, ended in her pregnancy. Their somewhat hasty marriage took place in February 1804, just three months before Janet herself was born. As a young man without capital, Bate was then forced, by dint of these circumstances, to move in with his widowed mother-in-law, Mary Sikes. While not exactly the kind of advancement he may have thought was his natural due, this unanticipated marriage proved fortuitous in many respects to further his ambitions. As luck would have it, he had married into the business.

Bate's deceased father-in-law, Bartholomew Sikes, had been an inventor of note, particularly in the field of gauging instruments, such as hydrometers and saccharometers, to measure the content of alcohol in different fluids, these being critical to the calculation of excise taxes. At the time of Bartholomew's death he had just successfully negotiated with the Excise Office to supply them with his improved hydrometer. Bate's marriage into the family saw his mother-in-law become his champion in seeking permission for him to continue this lucrative monopoly. It was, in effect, a licence to print money, as the Excise Act of 1813 had made Sikes's hydrometer the sole means to gauge the 'proof' of spirituous liquors.

This unexpected turn of events proved just the financial fillip Bate needed to bring his lifestyle into line with his ambitions. With his wife, daughter Mary and new son Bartholomew (named after his late father-in-law), the Bate family moved into No. 17 Poultry, a prestigious location close to Mansion House in the heart of the City. Although boasting a frontage of only eighteen feet, with a depth of thirty feet, it was four storeys high with an attic – a slice of building, staking a claim of territory in the upper echelons. Location and presence were important yardsticks of status and in this respect the Bates had arrived. Three more children were born there, and by 1824 their fortunes had improved to the extent that they were able to move to much expanded premises at Nos 20–21 Poultry.

Bate had expectations, but limited ability. He managed his affairs by seeking to keep everything in order within his domain. He was controlling and he brooked no opposition, having little time or patience for those who crossed him. Everything needed to be 'just so'. Mary's birth had caught him completely by surprise and although his forced marriage had catapulted him into good fortune, it engendered a deep resentment at the ensuing dependence on his wife. To make matters worse, he also wasn't expecting his second child, Bartholomew, to be born deaf and, while it was very much the natural order of things in marriages in the early nineteenth century, he certainly didn't count on another daughter, Anna Maria, to be born just a year after Bartholomew, followed by John, less than two years later.

To most, this would have been very normal, but for a man with a sense of where his place *should* be in the world, Bate's inability to determine his world overwhelmed him. As a result he tried to render what order he could by implementing strict rules and patterns of behaviour for himself and those around him, but at times it was all simply beyond him. His lack of power over his own universe, despite the outside trappings of wealth and standing, sent him at times into periods of prolonged depression, bitterly resentful that he had been forced to marry so young. His darkest thoughts were compounded by his dependence on the interventions of his powerful and domineering mother-in-law, first to win the excise trade for himself and then his own shortcomings whenever he turned his attentions to endeavouring to invent anything remotely original or imaginative. His only recourse was to opt out for a while, to retreat to Northumberland, accompanied by his doctor and his long-suffering cousin-wife Betty, where it was quiet, where there was family, and where he could recover his sense of mastery in his dominion once again.

His times in Northumberland were spent in fantasy, dreaming up plans of 'great things', of ways to make his name important for its own sake, to be recognised and lauded amongst his peers. While feeling that he should have a certain prominent place in the world, Bate was ill at ease in the company of others and kept to himself. He was also uneasy in himself, needing, but at the same time resenting, his strong and domineering mother-in-law whose connections brought him the fortune and prospects he craved.

By 1824, however, Bate had gained sufficient reputation of his own to be offered the preparation of weights and measures. This proved to be both a crucial test and a mark of his character. He was dogged in his application to his task, spending twelve hours a day on it, relentlessly putting all else aside to complete it. This was how he was to prove himself to the world in his own right and he managed to complete his assigned job with considerable acclaim. Except for his bill. He promptly invoiced the board for an outrageous weekly sum, reflecting a hugely inflated sense of his own worth.

It turned out that Bate was a good, solid technician. His weights and measures were well crafted and of high quality. He had a sound grasp of optical theory to the extent it supported his claim to be a spectacle-maker, so much so that he was soon appointed 'optician in ordinary' to George IV. It was a worthy but not glorious position, in that he had the privilege of supplying the royal household, but not necessarily the sovereign himself. But, unfortunately, he had reached the limit of his ability and imagination, since whenever he did venture upon bigger ideas they were either lame or verging on lunatic. For instance, one of his grand projects, dreamed up in one of his retreats to Northumberland, was a method to make lighthouse lamps visible on foggy nights by sending a jet of water perpendicularly into the air. His theory was that it would refract the light of the lighthouse to the summit of the jet, making it visible in foggy weather. So confident was he, he wrote to Beaufort about it, wanting to try it out.

As Principal Agent, Bate had developed an accord of some sort with the Hydrographer, and he wrote to him as 'his friend' about his lighthouse lamp ideas. Beaufort was respectful of Bate's claims to higher status, albeit that Bate was a younger son. Deference was a habit of centuries and occupied an unspoken universe of assumed entitlement and mannered responses; and Beaufort's background was closer to Janet's than to Bate's. But the lighthouse idea was as ridiculous as it was impractical.

By 1833 Bate had reached the stage where he was no longer interested in the detail and only concentrated on securing the business – and his fortune. It was in this respect that he was totally at odds with Janet. Her concern was *exactly* the detail, not only getting it right, but doing so in a timely fashion.

The curmudgeonly Bate certainly took his time whenever one of her orders arrived. His deliberate obstinacy irritated her no end, as did the seemingly glacial speed at which he attended to any necessary corrections to the charts, for which he was responsible. It was left to the *Nautical Magazine*, with which Bate was also closely involved, to publish corrections regularly, this being the only way that mariners could make authorised amendments to their own charts in a timely fashion. But what good was that to the man who was at sea with errors in his charts?

Seamen would invariably find their way to the Taylors' shop with news of any new sighting or information they thought relevant, including a lighthouse absent, or a new reef not yet shown in the charts. Sea captains would naturally request the latest versions and would share anything of note with Janet who in turn relayed the news to Beaufort:

Will you have the goodness to inform me, by my messenger, whether any surveys of the SW Coast of South America have been made within the last 18 months. A gentleman just returned from there called on me today for information on the subject. He has marked several great inaccuracies in the Charts now made of that Coast and should no surveys have been made within the time mentioned, he thinks it is his duty to report to you his observations.

Her mission was simple in that all she ever really wanted to do was to help the everyday seaman. It didn't take her long to realise that bureaucracy and inefficiency stood in her way, the chief difficulty being that everything had to go through Bate. She had been thwarted by him once too often. The solution was obvious: make the corrections herself. And so, in July 1836, she floated the idea with Beaufort.

Sir,

I have long been anxious to request your assistance and approval of a plan respecting your Charts which I will briefly state to you. I am solicitous they should become more generally known when I feel assured they will be appreciated. Dates you will not sanction my altering, but if you would have the kindness to cause a copy of any chart, when any recent corrections have been made on the coast, to be properly corrected for me in red ink, I would keep it as a copy and correct all that passed through my hands by it.

For instance the Channel Chart which is much liked, if I had one copy with all the buoys lighthouses etc added, which have been placed or erected since the survey was made, I would correct all copies I sold (and that is a great many considering the time I have been here and the obstacles with which I have to contend) which would prevent my hearing very unpleasant remarks respecting omissions which in many instances are very glaring. For example, the absence of the light on the South of the Goodwin Sand – likewise that on the Bull Humber and a variety of others I could name.

You need be under no apprehension about their being properly inserted, for they would be corrected entirely by myself I hope you will not consider this a vicious proposal, but will cause me to be informed, when any corrected copies are ready, that I may send for them. I understand there has been a reef discovered on the S. W. of Kangaroo: If this be the case, I should like to be informed for no ship ought to be allowed to leave this Port for Australia without notice of it, particularly if it be of the magnitude reported ... I will again repeat the request I made in the beginning to which I hope you will accede ... I consider that already I have made considerable head against my opponents and

with a little of your support in my *reasonable* demands I shall be enabled
to do still better. Hoping for a favourable reply.

I am Sir

Your obliged
Janet Taylor

Imaginative and practical, yes, but with the protocol of the day she never
stood a chance. Instead, as a compromise, Beaufort asked her to send to
the Admiralty what corrections she deemed necessary and they would
decide if they were worthy enough to incorporate into the amendments
to the official charts. This of course still respected Bate's position and so
her request really amounted to nothing. The mariner still had to wait for
the announcements of corrections in the *Nautical Magazine* or for the
amended charts to become available through Bate – the proper channel.

By the end of the third week of July, she had become so exasperated
with Bate's persistent delays that she even tried to work around him.
Writing at 4.00 p.m. on Friday 22 July 1836 to Beaufort's assistant
Lieutenant Becher, she pleaded for a substantial order of charts as soon
as he could supply them. Janet complained that it was 'little use' sending
it to Bate: they could not supply the number she needed and 'the time for
executing the order admits of no delay'.

Becher was alarmed, if not appalled, that not only had Janet sought to
bypass the Principal Agent, but, in addition, sought to have the charts at
the same discount given to Bate. He knew what Bate's reaction would be,
not to mention the protocols of the Admiralty sub-agencies. It was not
only quite outside the rules, but as soon as Becher raised her request with
Beaufort, he demanded to see her straight away.

There was a measure in the tone of the request that caused her great
worry. Although she had recovered some of the ground lost since their
first meeting after the embarrassments of the previous year, she was still
on tenterhooks. To have Beaufort's respect was vital to her operation
and ambition. But her fears were laid to rest when she discovered that he
actually just wanted her to keep him informed about problems with Bate,
as well as to reassure her that her information about problems with
the Admiralty charts were not being ignored. Once more, when he laid
eyes on her, Beaufort again found her advanced state of pregnancy quite
disarming. It seemed to him that she was pregnant more often than not.

But reporting on Bate's shortcomings was not at the heart of her
concerns. She had an obsession to ensure the charts were as right as
they could be – and practical. It was in this regard that she and Beaufort

were of a single mind. As a man to whom every detail was important and inaccuracies in their recording a great torment, he was earnestly concerned to have as much information from Janet, and others like her, as he could lay his hands on. Buoyed by the success of her meeting, within the week she was writing again; in her letter of 28 July she was not just complaining about Bate, but the errors to be found in the Admiralty Chart for the Bay of Biscay.[13] She also made some suggestions for improving its format:

Sir,

When I had the pleasure of seeing you last, I remember a remark made by you which induced me to address you now. You said the Chart of the Bay of Biscay was any thing but what you liked or approved. This I find generally the case, as Captains find the *half sheet* is very inconvenient. I will suggest a means of remedying this evil, which, I feel assured, will render the Chart very saleable and be an improvement. Another half sheet might be constructed merely containing the survey of a few of the principal harbours in the Bay (for the harbour of Bayonne I am much asked) which, when added to the other half would form a convenient and useful chart.

I have been tempted several times to make it up with a blank half but the thing would then look imperfect, whereas a little management, and very trifling expense as my connexion extends.

I already begin to find the tide turning in favour of Admiralty Charts and with little attention, I make no doubt they will soon establish a name, which will make them a universal request. Hoping you will take my proposal and plan into consideration.

Before Beaufort even had time to consider his response, less than a week later she had written again on 3 August:

Sir,

I have hit on an experiment to avoid the awkwardness of the Bay of Biscay Chart, which will enable me to make it more acceptable to the public, until you have more time to attend to it. I send it for your inspection and hope you will approve the plan. The man in joining it has not managed as I would have wished. The scale down the middle must be left out and likewise the black *border* on the right of the small chart. In the next I have put together, the little piece appears from the colour like an old housekeeper, but the difference of colour will not appear in the next. I am in hope this arrangement, *for the present*, will make it better liked.

I am Sir

Yours obliged
Janet Taylor

It was just as well that Beaufort was open to her ideas and was sympathetic with her frustrations in the delay in the supply of charts. She was not a lone voice in airing her concerns and the associated problems with Bate. John Norie had also been having troubles of his own. He wrote:

> Having frequently applied to your agent Mr Bate for charts ordered by correspondents, we have on several occasions been much disappointed by not being able to procure them from his house, and consequently obliged to delay executing the orders, and in some cases to omit altogether at your office.

Norie, it seemed, would now be an ally in her cause rather than an enemy. Although it had only been less than twelve months since he caused her to republish her *Principles of Navigation Simplified*, his long-standing reputation, both as a seller of blueback charts and one of the original sub-agents for the sale of Admiralty charts, made him someone of considerable standing in the nautical community. When he also complained about Bate, it added substantial weight to Janet's own concerns.

The situation at last reached a point where her patience finally ran out and she came to the view that it was really no use to ask Bate for charts at all. All the while Bate had known about her complaints and this made him even more unwilling to assist with her enquiries. He harboured a deep resentment that, while the sub-agents could still sell private charts, he could not. And so he decided to do some complaining of his own in return, writing to Beaufort that he was 'woefully disappointed in my expectations from all my agents'. Rather than attending to their frustrations, he simply turned the blame back onto them.

Janet had come to signify many threads of the frustrations of Bate's own life and he simply could not bring himself to like her. She had first come across his path when she and George undertook their 'exploratory' visit to his shop and again came to his notice in 1833 when she published her first book. And all by a woman just twenty-nine, *and* twenty-two years his junior. He relished the review in the *Nautical Magazine* that 'the Authoress had ventured rather beyond her depth', an opinion with which he heartily agreed. But now she had gone too far in *daring* to complain to the Admiralty about him. Who did she think she was, intruding upon his territory? The unfortunate Bate had been beholden to women all his life, and here again yet another one was unsettling his universe, and more particularly his sense of self. Well, he would certainly not make it easy for her, and he still had friends in high places to call upon if necessary. He was, after all, a man of standing; and she was nothing. Or so he convinced himself.

In the meantime, Beaufort had grown sympathetic and responsive to her suggestions, realising just what a thorn in her side Bate must have been. When he received her recent letters, recommending changes in the charts, he acknowledged to Becher that, in the barrage of correspondence, there were some good ideas, and enquired whether they could do as she recommended with the Biscay chart. Beaufort also directed Becher to enquire discreetly about Janet's health and if all was going well with her pregnancy, in view of the loss of the child the year before.

A few weeks later, on 16 September 1836, Janet gave birth to another son, her fourth, whom she named Deighton, her mother's maiden name. Once again, the *Nautical Magazine*, as well as *The Times* on this occasion, acknowledged the event:

> On the 16th Sept., of a son, Mrs Janet Taylor of 103 Minories, the celebrated Authoress of 'Luni- Solar and Horary Tables' and of 'Navigation Simplified' &c.

Like others in the nautical world, Bate saw the announcement and strode angrily about his office. 'Celebrated authoress, indeed!' he fumed. Tight-lipped with rage, he was determined that, one way or another, Mrs Taylor would have no celebration of him.

XII

International Recognition

And so another boy had arrived in the Taylor household and George's daughter Emily, now eighteen, just shook her head. There were her own brothers George, one year older than she, and her younger brother Charles Frank, four years her junior; then her half-brothers Herbert, almost five; Henry Frederick, a month shy of his third birthday; and now Deighton. It all seemed too much.

Elizabeth Juggens, who had been in the household since December 1831 when Herbert was born, had just turned nineteen herself and had her hands full with three little boys in the house. The years had been hard for her too, especially when Seymour died. She dearly loved the children and at that time Herbert had just turned four and Frederick was barely two. Janet had to cope not just with her own sense of loss but with a grieving Elizabeth, when all she really wanted to do was to close her study door and disappear into her work. It was a mechanism to disconnect from the realities of her domestic world altogether and to sail with the mariners she imagined every day on their journeys across the seas.

She was also very mindful of baby Deighton's health, both because she was nervous after losing Seymour, and because Deighton was also quite poorly from the outset. Withdrawing as much as possible from public life, she became immersed in the private universe of her own work and her family. Pressing on her mind was also that she remembered full well her own mother's death from complications surrounding the birth of her youngest sibling.

In trying to find a way to explain to her boys about their baby brother's death, Janet used her own key reference point and source of solace. She used the stars to show her young sons a way of imagining their baby brother. In addition to working on her books of *Tables* and *Principles*,

Janet had begun working on a map of the heavens to provide in picture form a chart of the skies. This was a real labour of love, and one that she kept for the few quiet and less hurried times in her life. It would take her many years to complete. To her boys, she pointed to her chart of the stars and said that was where their baby brother was, 'swimming and laughing with the fishes in Pisces', playing with the Big Bear, Ursa Major, his friend and her father, their grandfather Peter.

Considering the difficulties encountered in the previous twelve months, Mrs Marton was increasingly concerned that the added burdens in the household were all getting too much for Elizabeth. She had been an ideal choice, a hard worker and a caring young woman much loved by the little boys. Seizing the moment, she felt this would be an excellent opportunity to bring Elizabeth's younger sister, Caroline, having now turned fourteen (the usual age for going into service), to the growing family at No. 103 Minories. After a moment's reflection, Janet readily agreed as they could now afford the extra expense, at least for the time being, and Mrs Marton seemed to have a keen sense of things in this particular aspect of the household arrangements. It had been apparent to all how Elizabeth was much loved by her little boys and another pair of hands would certainly be welcomed.

By the time of Deighton's christening at St Katherine Coleman in November, Caroline had joined the Taylor household. The prospect of living with her sister again also lifted Elizabeth's spirits greatly. She and Caroline also found Janet's descriptions of the stars as intriguing as the boys did, managing to slip the 'Big Bear', 'Fishy Pishy' and 'Poppa Peter' into their nursery games. Down the years these would be passed on to each of the new Taylor children as a way of learning about the stars and remembering their family.

The time now came for Janet to give the boys more formal instruction in mathematics. Herbert had shown a great interest in anything mechanical from a very early age and was clearly very excited at the sight of his mother working on ideas for instruments. And it was even more fascinating whenever his father took him to the workshop where the men were undertaking the fledgling manufacturing side of the business. His eyes would open wide with eager anticipation when his mother showed him the secret stone she had stored in a very special space, the treasured chip of grey lodestone she had inherited from her own father. So, just after he turned four years old, she was delighted to feed his curiosity and show him simple things, such as basic times tables, elementary arithmetic, reading and writing. He took to these lessons earnestly, but not enthusiastically, reserving his interest and serious attentions for the machines.

By the end of the summer in 1836, when Frederick was almost three, he too seemed ready to join in the instruction. For Elizabeth Juggens it was a merciful break, as the boys were active, bright and, at times, a bit of a handful. Frederick showed much greater interest in arithmetic, even at such a young age, and increasingly revealed an aptitude with numbers. As they grew, however, both boys and their siblings to come loved the time when their mother would take them into the classrooms where the navigational pupils had their lessons and could show them the globe of the Earth and the charts that indicated to the sailors how to find their way across the vastness of the planet. They were fascinated with how it would spin on its axis and reveal such strange and magical places on the other side of the world. 'Where would you like to go today?', she would ask them. They started with countries beginning with 'A' and worked their way through the alphabet from Africa to Zanzibar. But they showed their greatest interest in the lands completely on the opposite side from England, the East Indies and Australia, the place where they 'transported' the prisoners. To them it was the most intriguing thing in the world that the people could sail there and not fall off. For young boys, it was magical.

Teaching her children for a few hours every weekday morning was a task Janet added to her busy schedule and her already full life. Education was the key, she thought. It was both her duty and her gift to her children to be able to show them a little of what she had learned from her own father, to share her love of mathematics, of music, and her knowledge of French with each child as the family grew. Despite the misgivings that naturally surrounded Deighton's birth, September 1836 had, after all, proven to be a propitious month. It had also brought another man into the Taylor sphere in the shape of Dr Peter van Galen, founder of the Rotterdam Navigation School in Holland.

In February, at the suggestion of her sister Isabella living in Rotterdam, Janet had written to the Dutch government about her books, as Isabella had seen the great interest in Holland in navigation matters. Just maybe Janet could secure further sales abroad. While there had already been interest in her books in Holland, particularly the third edition of *Lunar Tables*, it was essential to build on this wherever possible, as she had quite rightly proclaimed that the book sales were 'the bread of my family'.

By late September she had almost given up hope of a response, when out of the blue a letter arrived from van Galen, requesting a visit to speak with her about the possibility of his doing a Dutch translation of her book. Janet had heard about him previously from Isabella, as she had spoken of his navigation school in Rotterdam, established in late 1833. Janet immediately grasped the importance that such a meeting could have for her reputation, and her finances, and her curiosity was heightened by the tone and style of the correspondence. She had deduced that it was penned by a reasonably senior man and she was rather taken aback when the thirty-one-year-old Dutchman, indeed only eighteen months her junior, arrived at No. 103 Minories several weeks later. It was true that his receding hairline did make him look a little older, but, like Janet, he was already well established in the field of navigational teaching – and with his own school. She could not help but be impressed, not to mention delightfully surprised, since van Galen had been asked to be an emissary of his government and was not simply there on his own behalf.

Van Galen went straight to the point in professing his personal admiration for Janet's work, gratifying enough in itself, but then he wasted no time in handing her an official letter which, he admitted, rather overshadowed his own reason for wishing to speak with her. The document, from C. G. Wolterbeck, the Director-General of the Marine of His Majesty the King of the Netherlands, not only requested 100 copies of her latest edition of *Lunar Tables*, but also announced that the king had decided, by royal decree personally signed by him, to confer upon her a gold medal 'with a suitable inscription, in testimony of His Majesty's gracious approval of the aforesaid tables, so important in navigation'.

The words danced in her head as she read them several times over. She had of course known of these awards – the Dutch King had been conferring a silver or gold medal on those who produced a significant book or work of art of international standing since 1817 – but to win one herself was completely unexpected. A purchase of 100 copies of her book *and* the gold medal! It was almost too much to bear, such was her delight. And as a bonus, it seemed, she also found van Galen the most charming company, and there were so many things to discuss with him. Thrilled with the possibility of the translation of her *Lunar Tables* into Dutch, his visit extended into many hours of conversation on the puzzles that had intrigued and perplexed her. After the death of Seymour just a year before, the anxieties surrounding the birth and health of the new baby, Deighton, and this news from Holland, not to mention its emissary, were a breath of fresh air.

Janet was also not the only member of the household who was enchanted at the visit of the charming and eloquent Peter van Galen. Much the same could be said of the eighteen-year-old Emily, who was captivated by the intriguing stranger. He had made a memorable contact with two women that day and he had grander designs for both of them.

The gold medal was presented to Janet by King Willem's Envoy Extraordinary to Britain, the sixty-year-old Sir Salomon Dedel (1775–1846). It was inscribed in Latin:

HONESTISSIMAE
I TAYLOR
OBLATIS TABULIS
NAUTICARUM RATIONUM
CAUSSA EGREGIE
AB IPSA
CONFECTIS
REX
D
A°. MDCCCXXXVI

Translated, this reads:

THE HONOURABLE
J TAYLOR
IS BESTOWED THIS AWARD FOR
NAUTICAL METHODS
RESPONSIBLE FOR EXCEPTIONAL ACCOMPLISHMENTS
BY HERSELF
KING
ON THIS DAY
AD. 1836

By November the news had reached the ears of the *Atlas Magazine* which announced that it was 'very glad to extend the publicity of the following note, addressed to the authoress', even including the letter from Wolterbeck in full.

While the previous year had ended with much sorrow, 1836 had ended in triumph with a happier note that held much promise. As the chill of New Year's Eve settled around London, she reflected upon the fact that such recognition came not at home, but from abroad. Such irony was not lost on the reviewer of the third edition of her *Lunar Tables* as well as the third edition of *Principles of Navigation Simplified* in the *Liverpool Mail* of February 1837:

Hommage aux dames! We have had very few of what are designated 'learned ladies'. With the exception of Mrs Somerville, and the author of these works, we have scarcely any females who have published works on what may be called the more abstruse science. In mere work of imagination lady authors have fairly kept their ground in competition with writers of the manly sex, but whether it be the fault of education or their actual incapacity of intellect to grasp severe studies, they have *not* all become distinguished scientific writers.

Mrs Janet Taylor, author of the two important works before us, is one of the few exceptions to this general rule. We shall briefly state the nature of her publications and leave the public to decide whether she is not, indeed, a very extraordinary woman. It will excite their additional surprise to learn that she is very young.

The first work (now in a third and much enlarged edition) is literally what its title signifies – 'The Principles of Navigation Simplified'. It is divided into two books. In the first she takes the science of Navigation from its source (to use her own words) elucidating it in the easiest manner, by those problems in geometry, which are necessary for practice, and likewise by a careful selection of such theorems from Euclid, as are useful in demonstrating the different rules and methods introduced in the work …

The second part of 'Navigation Simplified' is dedicated, more especially, to nautical Astronomy. The introduction to this science is written with eloquence and clearness. The luni-solar and horary tables belong to this part of the science, to which their application is explained here, too, we have a simple and improved mode of finding the longitude by lunar observations and chronometers, and the latitude by meridian and double altitudes and elapsed time. The actual use of the tables is (to sum it up in a word) to allow the observer to dispense with all the tiresome calculations and allowance heretofore in practice, previous to clearing a Lunar Distance from the effects of parallax and refraction which cause the error in the angular distance.

The use of the 'Lunar Tables' (also in the third edition) is to obtain the true distance from the apparent altitudes. There is a short treatise on the construction and use of the chronometer and different plans for rating the instrument.

Having given as detailed of these works as a careful examination of them has permitted, we have but to add the opinion of a friend which should have some weight as he is one of the best seamen out of the port of Liverpool. He writes to us thus: 'I return Mrs Taylor's work on which you request my opinion. I have sailed my ship by them for the three last voyages and they have relieved me from fully two-thirds of the tedious calculations I formerly made. They are above all praise and a sailor cannot well dispense with them.'

Mrs Taylor indeed merits high praise, and may we add national gratitude. She has removed the chief difficulties which obscured the science of Navigation; she has simplified its practical part and she has thus laid the foundation for raising the ability of mariners, as well as materially increasing the security of commerce by increasing the safety of navigation. We have no hesitation in saying, as far as we can judge from a very careful examination of the work, that here is the most complete treatise on Navigation which has ever been published. That it should be a woman's work increases its value.

We learn from a notice in 'Lunar Tables' that the King of Holland ... sent her a valuable gold medal; with a suitable inscription. What acknowledgement has been made to her by our government? NONE!

While Janet had good reason to be extremely pleased with such a positive review, it also brought home, in a really public way, the sharp contrast between her recognition abroad and the lack of it at home. And the comparison with 'Mrs Somerville' irked her deeply. Mrs Mary Fairfax Somerville, indeed the well-connected Mrs Somerville, daughter of an admiral, married to a doctor who was a member of the Royal Society, and friend and associate of leading mathematicians and scientists. What had she really done to *earn* an annual civil list pension? Sir Robert Peel had granted her £200 a year in 1835, increased by Lord Melbourne to £300 a year in 1837.

The civil list pensions were formally granted in the name of the sovereign on the recommendation of the Prime Minister, then known as the 'First Lord of the Treasury', according to principles agreed in the House of Commons in 1834. They could be awarded in recognition of 'personal services to the Crown, by the performance of duties to the public, or by useful discoveries in science and attainment in literature and the arts'. Mrs Somerville was largely known, and recognised, for just two works. The first was her translation of Laplace's *Mécanique Céleste* with extensive commentary in 1831, at the age of fifty-seven, while the other was *On the Connection of the Physical Sciences* in 1834, on the interrelationship between gravitation, heat, light, electricity and magnetism. At the time they were acclaimed and popular, but even on Mrs Somerville's own account, many years later, there was no originality in her works.

Janet mused that if 'Mrs Somerville' could secure such recognition, why couldn't 'Mrs Taylor'? Had Mrs Somerville been recognised by the King of the Netherlands? What had *she* done that Janet had not? Somerville's main claim to fame was her 1831 translation of Laplace's work, with some commentary. Janet felt strongly that such pensions were supposed to be granted only to those who had made useful discoveries in science and there was certainly no *discovery* in Mrs Somerville's work, in her assessment. Janet sensed that there must have been other factors at play. It even occurred to her that she was somehow being punished for being born the daughter of a country curate and not an Admiral, or even for being married to a solid (if somewhat stolid) man like George. She just wasn't grand enough.

But this was not a time for pointless reflection and if having connections was important to securing the recognition that equated to ongoing financial stability, such as a civil list pension, then she clearly needed to use all her mastery to drive the point home in her case some other way. Meanwhile, maintaining cash flow was a constant problem. Despite having high hopes for substantial revenue from chart sales, they were providing little profit, and by this stage she had expended several thousand pounds, 'all her means', in the production of her books and the work on the Mariner's Calculator. It then crossed her mind that the Bishop of Durham could be enlisted to help her cause. If only she could win his support and that of others in high places, her claim may be advanced towards an acknowledgment that she was worthy of a pension after all. It would necessitate making the long trip to Durham again to press her case in person, but fitting it in with her hectic life would prove quite a challenge. As an additional string to her bow she felt that before setting out it might be worth her while to approach George Airy, the Astronomer Royal, as his influence had already been demonstrated in the case of Mrs Somerville, or at least Mrs Somerville's association with him had not detracted from her cause.

In the meantime, Beaufort had read of the Dutch tribute to Janet and went to some pains to ensure that the communication lines were clearly still open between them. But there was an additional motive since in April 1837 he needed to ask her a very large favour. It turned out that he had the need to translate, from French into English, a 'Pilot Book' for the Coast of Brazil. This work was originally entitled '*Pilote du Bresil, ou Description des Cotes de l'Amerique Meridionale*' and had been the outcome of a survey by the French admiral and surveyor Baron Roussin. Having charted the east coast of South America between 1818 and 1821, he published his findings in French in Paris during 1827. Beaufort was anxious that it be made available to English mariners and he turned to Janet for help. In doing so he demonstrated a considerable trust in her, along with a recognition of her abilities, but it would also prove to be a time-consuming burden which yielded no income.

Beaufort could readily have undertaken the task himself, being fluent in French, if he had the time. But Janet saw it as a peace offering of sorts, providing an opportunity to mend a few fences with him. It was also akin in her mind with Mrs Somerville's being asked to translate Laplace. And so she obligingly accepted the assignment although, as she wrote:

> My manifold occupations leave me but little time for even necessary relaxation … but I trust that with the blessing of my usual health and spirits and long days of summer to accomplish my task to your entire satisfaction.

National life that spring and summer of 1837 was counted in the rituals of mourning and celebration: 24 May – Princess Victoria's eighteenth birthday; 18 June – Waterloo Day – the twenty-second anniversary of the Battle of Waterloo and victory over the French. While Janet set aside time to embark upon this new task during this period, the nation as a whole suddenly became focused once more upon royalty. King William IV had survived to see, as he desired, 'another anniversary of the battle of Waterloo', but on Tuesday 20 June 1837 he died of cardiac failure and bronchopneumonia. This precipitated the succession of his niece, the eighteen-year-old Victoria, as queen, and on 13 July the new queen moved into Buckingham Palace (the renovations, started by George IV, just completed), gaining her independence from her overbearing and overprotective mother, the Duchess of Kent, so beginning her new life as a woman and as queen.

As the months passed, Janet continued painstakingly upon her work. Like others around her, especially those in London, she watched with interest and entertainment – and, at times, disdain – the royal goings-on, as they all had done with the queen's uncles George IV and William IV. The young Victoria was a year and a half younger than Janet's stepdaughter Emily and what responsibilities now descended upon her. At least the eternally vexed issue of the succession of the monarchy had finally been resolved, none of her uncles having been able to produce a surviving legitimate heir. Victoria was the last of the German house of Hanover and Britain had not had a queen regnant in over a century, the last being Queen Anne, who marked the end of the Stuarts in the early years of the eighteenth century.[14] For a woman to reign was very much the exception.

Janet's stepdaughter Emily paid keen attention to the fashion of the queen and, like so many young women that summer, changed her hairstyle to the sleek and smooth style of Victoria's, parted in the middle with corkscrew curls at the side of the face. It fell upon the unfortunate

Elizabeth Juggens on many an evening to spend hours tying the rags in young Emily's hair to produce the curls for the next day.

It turned out that Janet's plan to complete the translation of Roussin over summer was overly optimistic, severely underestimating the other activities that would invade her life. It was not only King William who fell ill that summer. Baby Deighton again became unwell and, as was usual in young families, the illness went from one to another in the Taylor household, and there was the continued pressure of maintaining the business. Feeling the need to provide some explanation to Beaufort for her delay in the translation, she wrote to him on 26 June:

> Sir,
> Amidst the mighty and passing events of these times, it is hardly to be supposed you remember me or the work on which I am engaged, but, nevertheless, I feel anxious to account for any apparent dilatoriness about Rouissin's Brazil Pilots. My young family have been ill for some weeks past, and during the last fortnight my Baby has not been expected to live from day to day.
>
> Unlike a lady you once named to me, who could by magnetism, or some other ism communicate maternal care and attention to her children though *separated* from them, my mind and *personal* attendance has been accorded to them night and day, and I am thankful my cares have been rewarded by the restoration to health of my darlings, and now with freshened activity I shall return to my literary duties, the trying interference with which I have been kept, rendering such exertions of the mind comparatively trivial.
>
> In a week or two I hope to shew you that I have not been idle.
> I am Sir
>
> > Your obliged
> > Janet Taylor

Like her correspondence with the anonymous reviewer she had taken on in the *Nautical Magazine* in 1835, Janet had proved herself very assertive in certain contexts, as in making plain to Beaufort her views about Robert Bate. But in relation to his request for the Roussin translation, she remained extremely deferential and respectful. For his part, Beaufort had also intended the translation to act as a bridge-building exercise of his own and found the tone of her letter somewhat disarming and unnecessarily self-deprecating. Responding immediately, he asserted that he was 'really most rejoiced to learn that the improving health of her children has enabled her to resume her industrious pursuits' and indeed was looking forward to hearing her views personally about Roussin's book. This turned out to be a considerable acknowledgment, indicating that he preferred to discuss such matters with her personally rather than in writing.

In due course the task was completed, passing with little fuss and barely any notice. This was mainly because Beaufort's attentions, by this time, were squarely focused elsewhere. While the death of his wife Alicia in 1834 had caused him profound grief, and even propelled him into the desperation of an incestuous relationship with his adoring sister Harriet, at the age of sixty-two Beaufort was now courting again. This time he had become smitten with Honora Edgeworth, eighteen years his junior and the stepdaughter of his sister Frances, who had married his friend Richard Lovell Edgeworth. Such was his infatuation, they were to marry on 8 November the following year. This meant that his correspondence with Honora, along with his travels to Ireland to see her in the year preceding, greatly overshadowed the diligent work of Mrs Taylor.

By the end of 1837, the winter hit hard in London; although always cold at this time of year, this winter exceeded itself with its harshness. With freezing temperatures came the coal burning and the resulting smog haze that draped the city every winter in a yellowing pall, sometimes rising over 200 feet above sea level. It was 'as if a sponge had wiped out London'. The foggy winter shadows of the street also proved the perfect cover for the escapades of 'Spring-Heeled Jack', or the 'terror of London' as he was called, first appearing in the chill of the autumn of 1837. With eyes that 'resembled red balls of fire', a black cloak and gloves with sharp metallic claws, he leapt from behind corners and over walls to frighten his unsuspecting prey. All women in London, and even their husbands and fathers, feared for their safety. Children shivered under their bedcovers to hide from the newest bogeyman, supposedly with springs in his feet and power to leap right over high walls. Young Caroline Juggens was particularly terrified as the anecdotal stories and the exaggerated press accounts of his escapades rippled around the streets. Intriguingly, he was never captured or even identified.

Exceeding even the most pessimistic forecasts, the temperature kept falling as the winter progressed and the River Thames finally froze over. It hadn't frozen completely since 1814, before the new London Bridge had opened. The combination of constant coal burning and the freezing of the river created their own disasters on several levels. Fires in London winters were an ever present danger (between 1833 and 1841 there were a reported 5,000 fires in the City of London) and on 10 January 1838 fire roared through the Royal Exchange, the sixteenth-century building between Threadneedle Street and Cornhill that housed the foreign exchange market of Britain. This was the place where London merchants met daily at the centre of the country's industry.

The fire engines could do little in the face of the intensity of the blaze. It is said that the chimes in the tower even began to play 'There's nae luck about the house'. With the Thames frozen, the fire engines could draw no water from the river and the building burned to the ground as the fire raged on throughout the next morning. When daylight came the streets were still thronged with onlookers. Smoke filled the air and the smell of fire stretched over the neighbourhood, well down to Minories and St Katharine Docks. The smoke from the Royal Exchange only added to that of the ubiquitous winter coal fires, making the day as night and the air unbreathable. For those forced to endure this, year after year, it took a considerable toll on their health, with chronic respiratory conditions a normal part of London life. For those with already weak lungs, like Janet, it could become unbearable.

George thought it was a good time for Janet to be out of the City. Her desire to renew her campaign for the support of the Bishop of Durham in aid of a grant of a civil list pension suddenly seemed like a good idea. There had been renewed discussion over the award of the civil list pensions in the context of the allowances by Parliament to the new monarch. The size of the awards attracted criticism in the debate in the Commons in November and December 1837 that 'the only real effect which these pensions produce is confined to a select circle under the Minister's eye' and that the pension system, confusing merit and need, only served to create injustice. Indeed, Mrs Somerville's pension was one of those singled out for criticism as 'a waste of money'.

With public attention on the awards, it seemed like a good time for Janet to continue in pursuit of her own cause. The Lord Bishop of Durham had indicated that he would support her and, with this backing, she wrote to Professor George Airy, the Astronomer Royal. She had written to him earlier in the year, trying to solicit his opinion on her tables and on that occasion he had been somewhat encouraging. Now she needed to enlist his more particular support in aid of her wider claim. Enclosing a copy of her 1834 book, *Principles of Navigation Simplified*, she wrote on 29 November 1837 that:

> The polite attention you gave a former request I made to you has again induced me to trouble you though on a different suit.
>
> The Bishop of Durham (in whose See my Father was many years distinguished, not only as exemplary in the discharge of his duties

as a clergyman but likewise as a very clever man) has kindly offered to advocate my cause, and to endeavour to obtain for me some consideration for what I have done to facilitate the working of some problems in navigation, and for the general service I have tendered to the *practical* science. Of course, experience as to the best arrangements of such works for the benefit of that class of men for whose use they are intended could only be purchased by time and *innumerable* sacrifices.

This much has now been dearly bought and, were my resources less limited, my works in a short time would be more suited for practice than any in present existence. The scientific writers on the subject can know little of the seafaring community or their confined education – my object has been to make my works universally useful and I have in part succeeded.

I would now ask you to look over the accompanying book and do me the favour to give your opinion of it and my exertions. With that and the interest I have made in influential papers, I hope to have some attention paid to my claims.

I have worked bodily and mentally for some years past to benefit a large and useful portion of my countrymen and it is to bring my plans to perfection that I now seek your assistance.

Pray pardon me for troubling you and likewise for requesting as early an attention to my requests as you conveniently can.

Janet's message was a double one, alluding both to the value of her contribution and the limited nature of her resources to continue her work. Lest what she wanted was left a little unclear, she wrote again a month later, after the Commons debates, saying that Airy's opinion would assist her 'in obtaining some consideration from government', reiterating that this would enable her 'to bring what [she had] already done to perfection', as civil list pensions could provide a breathing space for writers.

Airy was polite, but unfortunately reluctant to give any assistance. He excused himself, saying that he was 'really incompetent to give any opinion upon a work intended for a class of person whose habits and methods of proceeding are so different from mine'. He was a scientist, an astronomer, whereas Mrs Taylor's work was 'applied' and for the mariner. Hedging his response, he suggested that 'many scientific officers of the navy could speak to this matter with much more greater certainty and with more advantageous influence' than he could. It was, as Airy declared:

Almost useless for me to remark when the principal thing to be ascertained is whether the work is likely to be practically useful to mariners and on this point I am very little qualified to give an answer.

While he was not the willing ally to her cause that she had hoped for, Airy was not entirely dismissive either, commenting that her theories of trigonometry and different kinds of sailing seemed to him to be 'very clearly done and probably the astronomy also'. Twenty years later, he would need her as an ally in his own cause.

The rebuff was clear and for the time being Airy was a dead end. She didn't dare press her luck with the Admiralty again, having offended Beaufort enough already in seeking the Navy's support on more than one occasion. If she was going to have any success at all she needed to secure help from elsewhere. An added catalyst to her campaign was that she had received another gold medal, this time awarded to her by Friedrich Wilhelm III, the King of Prussia. She determined to enlist the support of Edward Maltby, Lord Bishop of Durham.

But he was many miles away – and what would he make of a request by a woman in such cause?

XIII

A Visit to the Bishop

Having firmly decided to recruit the Lord Bishop to her cause, Janet wrote
to Maltby on 15 January 1838:

> My Lord,
> I again take the liberty of addressing you, having just received another
> splendid testimonial of the utility of my works on Navigation. It was
> sent to me by the King of Prussia whose Consul here made enquiries
> respecting me at the Admiralty, the result of which was a gold medal in
> approbation.
>
> I am anxious, My Lord, to have an opportunity of showing the medal
> to you and I trust you will allow me to wait on you at your leisure,
> when I think My Lord, I could suggest a plan which would meet your
> approval and ensure my petition attention. Professor Airy professes to
> know nothing of nautical astronomy nor of navigation and refers me to
> practical men, which of course renders his reply to my request of no use.
>
> I trust, however, your Lordship will permit me to see you when I can
> better explain my motives for troubling you now.
>
> With great respect
> I am, My Lord,
>
> > Your Lordship's Humble and Obedient Servant
> > Janet Taylor

(My Lunar Tables have been reprinted in America and the most useful
methods in the Longitude Work have been introduced into their best
work on navigation.)

Beyond a letter, she knew she also needed to pay him a personal visit in Durham, at Auckland Castle. Fortunately, the timing was now also agreeable to George. Understandably worried about the women in the house with the hysteria of Spring-Heeled Jack echoing all around him, George decided it was timely for them to be out of London. The time was now ripe for the planned trip to Durham. It was agreed that Caroline Juggens should accompany Janet, and that the boys, Herbert, just turned six on 30 December, Frederick, four years three months, and even sixteen-month-old Deighton, or 'Dite' as they called him now, would go along as well, as he was now much stronger after his summer illness.

Janet was also aware that the ruthless smog of that winter could precipitate it all again, for Dite and herself, and leaving smogbound London outweighed any such risks. Moreover, it would provide an opportunity for them all to catch up with the Durham cousins and to visit grandfather Peter Ionn's grave in Wolsingham. In this way Janet could also have her meeting with the Bishop and impress him with her medals while pleading for his backing in her petition for a pension. Meanwhile, Mrs Marton would keep her usual good eye on everything and George's concerns about Spring-Heeled Jack were allayed with the family out of harm's reach.

Travelling was slower in winter, but the journey now was much smoother than it was when Janet, as the nine-year-old Jane Ann Ionn, had made the long journey south so many years ago to go to Queen Charlotte's school at Ampthill. For the boys, it was a great adventure and the older boys delighted in meeting their cousins who were living in Durham. Janet's older sister Joyce, married to the Reverend Matthew Chester, the incumbent of the parish church at St Helen Auckland, had three children: Jane, twelve, and two younger boys, Thomas, eight, and George Heber, aged five. Janet's journey also proved an opportunity in another respect. It gave her a chance to catch up with her sister Emeline.

After living with their brother Seymour at No. 44 Oxford Street, Emeline had spent several years with the Wilkinson family as governess, before marrying the chemist James Hardy in June 1833 and settling in Gateshead, near Newcastle. Emeline and James had two children, a son James, born in April 1834 and now nearly four years old, and a daughter, Jane Ann, born in August the following year and now nearly two and half years old. But sadly, Emeline's husband became ill and, after a long illness, passed away in early December 1837. Their younger brother, Frederick, had spent most of the year with them to do what he could to help with the business and their two young children as James had faded. When they learned that Janet and her boys were coming to Durham, it lifted their spirits and Joyce was only too happy to welcome the three siblings into her home.

Reverend Chester was delighted to lead the expedition to see Reverend Peter Ionn's grave in Wolsingham in the graveyard of the parish church of St Mary and St Stephen, although with all the extra children they needed to arrange two carriages. The journey along the Wear River and through the villages of the Weardale to the place of Janet's childhood brought back such a collage of memories. And the contrast with London was profound. Janet's boys were intrigued to see all the names on the tombstone in the church graveyard, not only that of their grandfather, but also those of grandma Jane and great-grandfather Matthew Ionn.

Janet was especially proud to see the splendid plaque in the back of the church erected in her father's honour. She was also overwhelmed to see her sisters and her brother again, even with the sadness of Emeline's husband's recent death in the background. Janet thought Reverend Chester an admirable but rather sombre man and was profoundly grateful that he took charge of the large family group. It was precisely this sort of outing that evoked strong memories of her childhood visits to grandfather Seymour Deighton and his family home at Wolsingham Park surrounded by the farms of Lower and Higher Doctor Pasture.

But soon enough it was time for the business at hand, and the next day Janet sought counsel with her brother William's legal firm in Bishop Auckland in preparation for the upcoming meeting with the bishop and how best to plead her case. Her initial plan was to ask Maltby to include a copy of a petition and testimonials with his own letter of commendation. After some contemplation, the legal advice was not simply to leave things in a 'please, sir' form, but rather the matter should be put much more directly and formally. In other words, minimise the effort required by the Lord Bishop by providing him with a proper document that he could submit, with his support, on her behalf.

In the last days of January, William got to work and prepared a memorial summarising her case for consideration that she took with her, along with the testimonials from the kings of the Netherlands and Prussia – a strong case indeed, they thought. Edward Maltby, now aged sixty-seven, had been appointed Bishop of Durham in March 1836, the first such bishop after the abolition of the office of Prince Bishop that year. He was of liberal leanings, a supporter of the Whigs and a member of the Society for the Diffusion of Useful Knowledge. In theory, at least, he should have been an ideal candidate to support Janet's cause.

Janet pulled her coat around her and walked determinedly from the Market Place to the castle, but the winter was very cold. The town had grown up around the castle over its 800-year history, and Market Place, and William's office, sat close by the castle walls, just over a stone's throw from the castle gate. Her arrival was announced and at last she had her audience with the Lord Bishop. Janet approached nervously. She proceeded through a series of rooms before reaching the King Charles Room. It was one of the bishop's smaller formal rooms, and easier to keep warm in winter, but it was still intimidating.

The chubby, bald-pated bishop, with white hair and sideburns, was not of overly frightening appearance, but Janet knew that he was highly respected for his scholarly attainments and spiritual publications, as well as being often controversial for his openly political actions. This was particularly evident in his support for the Reform Bills propounded by Earl Grey in 1830 and 1831. She was also apprehensive because she was again pregnant – six months at the time of their meeting – something that was difficult to conceal, although she hoped that the folds of her winter clothing provided at least a minimal disguise. It was one thing being female, but being pregnant was quite another.

Immediately challenging her as to the subject of her interest, Maltby speculated that it was a rather odd subject for a woman to pursue. Janet had no hesitation in responding to this question, informing him of her father's work as curate of the parish church at Wolsingham and schoolmaster, and how he had taught the boys, and herself, the principles of navigation. And although that may seem strange to others (including his Lordship, she thought inwardly), for her it was 'the most natural thing in the world'. To amplify her claim, Janet pointed out that her mother's family, the Deightons, also came from the county, and they had encouraged her in her inquisitiveness, even before she had gone as a child to Queen Charlotte's school.

Maltby considered all this for a moment, and recollected her family, particularly the well-respected Deightons, but he still found it somewhat peculiar. Surely she should leave such concerns to others, as weren't there many others – men – in this field? Janet felt on firm ground in her response. Although there were men, she agreed, they did not do it well enough, and, as she said, there were 'many merchant captains who are such ignorant men', and that when a ship is once insured, 'the owners do not care whether she goes to the bottom or not'! To say the least, Maltby was shocked at such outspokenness, especially in a woman. Her forthrightness, once she overcame her initial nervousness, had caught him off-guard and he found it distinctly unnerving.

And if his lordship thought it strange for a woman to pursue such subjects, Janet could not help but point to the case of Mrs Somerville. Maltby was clearly familiar with Somerville's works. He was, after all, a committee member of the Society for the Diffusion of Useful Knowledge, which had requested her to undertake the translation of Laplace's work, and a Fellow of the Royal Society, as was Somerville's husband. But Maltby was also a political man, and aware that Mrs Somerville's worthiness for her pension had come under sustained attack when the issue of civil list pensions had been scrutinised by the government and the press in the last two months of 1837. Targeting her, they attacked her on two grounds: that her work was not adding to knowledge, and the size of the amount, recently increased to £300, was the same as that awarded to eminent men of science like George Airy, the Astronomer Royal, and Michael Faraday, the discoverer of electromagnetic induction.

Janet felt some sympathy with the first prong of this attack and resorted to a well-worn formula by condemning her with faint praise. She acknowledged that her work was most commendable, but why should Janet be regarded as any less deserving than she? Janet's work, was, after all, *far* more original, she argued, as well as being practical. Mrs Somerville's works were merely *description*, with no formulas or tables. What good was this to the practical man or the mariner? Janet also argued that while Mrs Somerville had friends and helpers in high places, Janet had laboured largely on her own. Maltby shifted uncomfortably in his chair, and after a few moments reflection, rose and extended his hand, saying that he would see what he could do and would, at least, write on her behalf to the Prime Minister, Viscount Melbourne. After that, it would be up to him.

True to his word, on 5 February 1838, Maltby wrote to Melbourne, enclosing a copy of the testimonial from the Prussian government and her petition. Although giving the appearance of supporting her claim for a pension, he managed to express himself in most guarded terms:

If her works be of the value they are said to be and if her character corresponds to her talent (neither of which I have any reason to doubt, but I never vouch for what I do not myself know) she is more deserving of a pension than Mrs Somerville; because the works of Mrs Taylor are of such practical usefulness in a branch of knowledge important to this country.

The formal petition enclosed was addressed to the Home Secretary, Lord John Russell. After narrating the history of her dealings with the Admiralty and the honours bestowed upon her by the King of the Netherlands as well as the King of Prussia, it continued:

That your Petitioner relying not upon her own opinion of her own works, nor even upon the opinions of private and disinterested persons however numerous they may have been, but upon the testimonials of their worth which she has received from the Sovereigns of Foreign Countries and from the public authorities to which she has alluded, is unwilling to believe that her works are unworthy of encouragement from the Government of her own Country and feels confident that upon proper enquiry they will be found to be of great national utility, worthy of being adopted by her Majesty's Navy and of being recommended by those in authority to the mercantile community.

And that if your Petitioner shall be granted such enquiry she will undertake to prove the practical utility of her works by personal demonstration and the testimony of several officers of her Majesty's Navy and commercial navigators with whom they have been in use for several years.

May it therefore please your Lordships to presume consideration of your Petitioner's ... application and to remit the same to the Lords of the Admiralty for their Report with instructions to submit your Petitioner's works to competent officers for special enquiry into their merits and thereafter to do in the said application as to your Lordships shall seem just to your Petitioner and most advisable for the interests of her Majesty and her subjects.

And your Petitioner shall ever Pray etc.

Janet Taylor

Melbourne was somewhat baffled by the tone of the petition, and Maltby's peculiar 'reference', and transferred the matter to the first Lord of the Admiralty, Lord Gilbert Elliot-Murray-Kynynmound Minto. Minto's response, just over three weeks later, was not at all encouraging. While acknowledging that Mrs Taylor had published 'some useful tables', for which she had received a 'gratuity' of £100, and that she was, he understood, 'a very respectable person', the bottom line in his assessment was that 'her works are not of such value nor of such a character as to give her a claim to a pension'. So, for now, she was not included in the civil list.

Janet received the news of the rejection with a mixture of anger, frustration and disappointment. She loathed having to petition in this way and her sense of the unfairness of it all irked her deeply. Not surprisingly, it also made her more resolute to show them just how wrong they were, continuing to revise and improve her *Lunar Tables* for a further sixteen years, running into seven editions. Moreover, her *Epitome of Navigation* had an even longer lifespan. She had not the slightest doubt that her best work was still ahead of her, despite what Minto might think.

While Janet was preoccupied with gaining the recognition in England that she felt unfairly eluded her, George had to deal with some trouble of his own. Alcohol is an easy accelerant of tension and so, too, it was for George. During their joint business enterprise, George had continued his involvement in the brewing business, and particularly in a managerial capacity with Meux's. This meant, at times, that he was conveyor of hard news: a contract lost, business rejected, and so on. On 20 April 1838, one such recipient was Edward Hall, victualler. He didn't take the news well at all, and he touched a raw nerve with George when he called him 'Mr Janet Taylor'. George, enraged, threw a punch. Hall enlisted the police and George was charged with assault. Meux was able to settle things down, but had a quiet word to George that perhaps, with a glass or two less on board, he may not have reacted with such a short fuse.

Meanwhile, with optimism and expectation, all Britain and beyond watched the succession of Alexandrina Victoria. The coronation, set for the coming summer, was sure to draw the eyes of the world to Britain and to Westminster Abbey once again.

XIV

The Victorian Age Begins

On 28 June 1838, all London stopped for the coronation and the 'Victorian Age' began. Never had the city been more crowded. The summer brought with it the highpoint of 'the season' for the upper classes with the social round of parties, galas, balls and entertainments, and with it the brokering of aristocratic marriages. But this particular summer saw the coronation bringing an estimated 500,000 extra people to the overcrowded streets of the nation's capital. The hordes besieged the city from every direction that fine day and on every form of transport possible, including the new railroad lines from Greenwich, Southampton and Birmingham. How magnificent the spectacle, they cried, and how short the queen! She was barely five feet tall – a full head shorter than Janet. From their home in Minories, the Taylor family could hear the guns thundering in salute of the new queen at the Tower and, further afield, in Hyde Park.

Like many others, Janet and George devoured the newspaper reports of the coronation and found a degree of amused satisfaction that the Bishop of Durham, who was less than enthusiastic in supporting Janet, had performed so poorly during such an important event. Maltby had presented the orb to the queen far too early and it was so heavy, she nearly dropped it! 'What am I supposed to do with it?' Victoria was reported as saying.

And, like the rest of the City, the Taylors took part in the festivities of the times, including a visit to the magnificent fair in Hyde Park, held after the coronation. While the heavens had opened to drench the crowds who gathered for the ceremony, the summer rains managed to clear for the fair. The tents, tumblers and balloons filled the air, creating a wave of excitement, energy and optimism in the carnival atmosphere. The Taylor children took special delight in the pastries, shaped like kings and queens, and, of course, the fireworks. The fireworks! What fireworks they turned out to be, enough to make the boys whoop and holler for weeks to come. Meanwhile their parents took the opportunity to enjoy, for a moment, the anonymity that large crowds engender, to dance, crowding almost to suffocation with thousands of other Londoners in the booths especially erected in Hyde Park.

Setting aside her disappointment with respect to securing a civil list pension, for now, Janet shared the optimism and excitement of the occasion. At the back of her mind, however, there were the ongoing frustrations and problems to contend with – especially concerning Admiralty charts. Being a sub-agent was a vital aspect of the business, providing a particular indicator of standing, but it was all falling apart with the charts regularly not available in time. To add to her troubles, even when they did arrive, there were never enough of them and their quality was often poor. As her customers were now making more frequent trips to the southern hemisphere, their need for immediate, accurate and readable maps was insatiable: Port Jackson in Sydney; Table Bay and False Bay in Cape Town, South Africa; Demerara in Guyana; Rio de la Plata in Uruguay to Valparaiso in Chile (now Santiago); and the coast of Brazil.

As merchants travelled further and further, their need of charts expanded, the sailing trade and empire relying upon good and accurate information. Whenever she couldn't get them through Bate, Janet would go around him, sending long lists to Becher of any charts she needed. And if she considered the charts were too light or too faint – 'scarcely visible' – she personally outlined the coasts in Indian ink. Although this was an act of defiance, she considered it essential, despite knowing full well the fury that would come from Bate's direction once he learned what she was doing.

Not only did 1838 see the coronation of the queen, it also quite literally brought the 'Railway Age' to Janet's doorstep when demolition began for the London and Blackwall Commercial Railway. The first London railway had opened on 14 December 1836. It ran from London Bridge to Deptford, near Greenwich, and extended to Greenwich two years later. The first brick was laid on 4 April 1834 and, within a year, 400 arches had been built. By the end of the first week of opening, such was its popular appeal, it had been used by 20,000 people. Each year, new lines and new kinds of rail transport developed, with train tracks being built in every direction between the major cities. These arteries fanned out from London to traverse the nation, carrying its lifeblood in trade and people. It was the great democratisation of transport, not just for London, but the entire country and, indeed, the whole industrialised world.

Demolition in its cause came to Minories in 1838 when No. 105 and upwards were razed to the ground. The promoters naturally painted a favourable picture:

> The intended railway will be constructed like that to Greenwich on a succession of Arches, thereby reducing the whole line to almost a perfect level which will be travelled with the advantage of light and air, free from dust and dirt and without having recourse to ditch and tunnel, stationary engines or dangerous curves from any part of the line. The Arches will be of a sufficient height to admit of an easy junction with the Northern, Eastern Counties and other projected railways without interfering with the traffic on Commercial Road.

A three-and-a-half-mile line was built from Minories, running eastwards to Blackwall via Stepney, the first section to West India Docks sitting on a viaduct above the road. Not everybody rejoiced, however, with this development. In particular, the owners of St Katharine Docks were alarmed that by linking the East and West India Docks with the City, their income would be cut considerably, given that the principal purpose of the rail line was to transport goods. And, as many suspected, it would also change the face of Minories forever.

This 'progress' was greeted with very mixed emotions by the Taylor household at No. 103, situated only two doors from the worksite at No. 105. All through the latter months of 1838 and into the New Year, the demolition and the building continued, creating month after month of noise, dust and disruption. Janet had to endure all of this while trying to close off the outside world so that she could continue her writing. But young Herbert found it all fascinating and was eager to learn more about the engines that would run on the line. To provide some diversion, as well as some practical instruction for the boys, George had one of the workmen construct a very simple steam model that provided them endless hours of amusement. Janet was especially grateful for this during the worst of the noise and chaos in the spring of 1839 as, once again, she was heavily pregnant.

On 16 April, amidst all the disruption and turmoil, another son, Jon Justinian, joined the Taylor family. Awarding him the honorary title of 'coronation baby', on 13 May, Janet's thirty-fifth birthday, he was christened at St Katherine Coleman. Where her other children were dark-haired and brown-eyed, like she and George, Jon looked utterly different. He was unusually fair, with the palest of skin, blonde hair and reddish eyes. She gave him a special middle name, after Justinian the Great, the Byzantine Emperor of Rome.

Three weeks later, on 6 July, the railway finally opened with Minories as a temporary terminus, the main one at Fenchurch Street being completed the following year.[15] At first, there was only a single track, with a second being added later in 1840. The viaduct that straddled Minories was first enclosed, as it was feared that horses at street level might take fright from the noise and smoke of the engines as they darted overhead. These fears proved groundless, the horses having to manage countless other distractions in their daily rounds, and the coverings were subsequently removed.

While the Railway Age may have been widely welcomed as an expression of industrial maturity and development, the Taylors' perspective on noise and disruption, with a household brimming with young children, students and servants, was an intensely personal one. The years of construction had been deafening, and the operation of the train itself was not much better. Until 1849, to eliminate the risk of fire, cable haulage was employed and, notwithstanding the initial spruiking of the promoters, stationary engines were installed both at Minories and Blackwall, driving the thunderous cable drums, twenty-three feet in diameter.

Where the railways opened up the country, shipping opened up the world, and industrialisation had a huge impact on the sea as well as on land. Steam power took to the sea with the introduction of steam-driven paddle vessels using wood burning furnaces, the ships becoming bigger and bigger and the journeys faster and faster. Perhaps the prime example took place on 19 July 1837 with the launching of the SS *Great Western*, 236 feet long and almost sixty feet wide across the paddle boxes. Designed by the great railway engineer Isambard Kingdom Brunel, and named for the Great Western Railway Co., it was purpose-built for the long and arduous Atlantic crossing. On her maiden voyage in April 1838, as an expression of ability, power and sheer bravura, the *Great Western* raced another steam-driven British ship, SS *Sirius*, chartered by the rival company British and American Steam Navigation Co., in a dash across the Atlantic to New York. (The ship the company was building, the *British Queen*, was still in the shipyard, hence the Irish Sea steam packet *Sirius* was chartered for the task).

While the *Sirius* narrowly beat the *Great Western* to arrive, it was the *Great Western* that took the honours. Although she left several days after the *Sirius*, the crossing only took fifteen days. The *Great Western* also arrived with 200 tons of coal still on board, while the *Sirius* only completed her journey by burning the cabin furniture, spare yards (the spars on masts from which sails are set) and anything else combustible on board. (This was said to be the inspiration for the fictional journey of the character Fogg in Jules Verne's *Around the World in Eighty Days* (1872), where all the wood on board was used as fuel for the journey.) These ships carried sails both as an extra form of propulsion (and only means of it, if the coal supply had been exhausted) but also to stabilise the ships in rough seas, to maintain an even keel and the paddles in the water. But, as they quickly learned, it was impossible to use steam engines and sails at the same time because the cinders from the smokestacks could set the sails on fire. Rescuing her own claim to a place in history, however, the *Sirius* later became the first steamship to cross the ocean without using a sail.

Not only were the new ships using steam, but their method of construction was changing significantly – and using more and more iron. First, similar to the *Great Western* and the *Sirius*, they had iron straps around their wooden hulls. Then, by the 1860s, propelled by war, first plates of iron encased the wooden hulls – the 'ironclads' as they were known – and then, eventually, ships were constructed completely with iron hulls. This now provided the next great challenge for navigators, as the iron wrought havoc with compasses. A compass that was not accurate meant death to mariners and for those involved in navigation with the aid of navigational instruments this was to be the greatest challenge of the coming years.

The compass was based upon the fact that a magnetised needle had a propensity to point north. A card was mounted upon the needle and it was enclosed in a wooden box to protect it from the wind. As time passed, the card was marked with the thirty-two points of the compass. By the Middle Ages the compasses of the Christian world signified the north point with a *fleur de lis* and the east point with a cross. The *fleur de lis* was the successor to the top-most indicator on the Italian 'wind roses' of the thirteenth century. The circular wind rose showed the eight prevailing winds of the Mediterranean. The north wind was the 'Tramontana', abbreviated on a wind rose as 'T'. The cross of the east represented the location of the Holy Land, brought under European rule as a result of the Crusades from the eleventh century.

While the magnetic compass was a seemingly magical aid to the mariner, it was also one whose magic could deceive, unless its true properties were known, respected and adjusted for. The first significant thing to be recognised was that the *magnetic* north pole is not the same as the *geographic* north pole. This difference, or 'magnetic variation', agitated scientists and seamen alike. The information that eventually filtered back from the great voyages of Portuguese and Spanish discovery from the fifteenth century (Spain's Christopher Columbus who crossed the Atlantic on his way to America in 1492, and the Portuguese navigator

Vasco da Gama, who rounded the Cape of Good Hope in 1497 and pioneered the sea route to India) and the circumnavigation of the globe by Sir Francis Drake at the end of the sixteenth century, revealed that magnetic variation was also not fixed or constant. It varied across the globe and also over time.

In 1701, for example, Edmond Halley drew attention to the fact that the magnetic variation in the English Channel had changed from east to west in 1657 and the dangers of navigating the Channel if the latest changes in compass variation were neglected. 'If they miss an Observation for two or three Days, and do not allow for this Variation, they fail not to fall to the Northward of their Expectations.' The challenges of the magnetic compass were not just those of variation. The greatest challenge of all was posed by magnetic deviation since any iron near the compass would cause it to deviate. Iron nails in the compass box, iron cannons, iron anchors, indeed any iron at all, could cause the compass needle to deviate.

But before the introduction of iron vessels catapulted Janet into another major chapter of her life, events on a more immediately personal level were the order of the day. During 1839, Peter van Galen had been busily occupied in completing his translation into Dutch of the third edition of Janet's *Luni-Solar and Horary Tables* as well as putting the finishing touches to his own book, *Introduction to the Theory of Navigation*, written in Dutch and English, side by side – a clever and useful innovation. He was keen to finish these undertakings as quickly as possible as he had set his sights on a partnership of another kind, in marriage to Janet's stepdaughter Emily. The letters between Peter and Emily had started shortly after his meeting them both in late 1836 and the affection between them each had continued to blossom. He was smitten with the enchanting young girl and in September 1839 paid another visit to No. 103 Minories, bringing with him the newly published books as a pretext. It would have been a believable and sufficient reason on its own and sufficiently masked another personal mission that was his principal task. Soon after his arrival he suggested a family outing to Greenwich to see the time ball at the Royal Observatory as a ruse to hide his still private plan.

The three boys – Herbert, Frederick and Dite, now eight, seven and three years old respectively – were all naturally very excited. While baby Jon had to stay at home with Caroline Juggens, even George set aside his busy work to join them all for the day out. The first stop was to be ferried across the river by wherry to Pepper Alley Stairs, just past the new London Bridge and close to the station at London Bridge on Tooley Street, where they were to take the train to Greenwich. The line was the first steam railway built for London passenger service and proved hugely popular, carrying over a million passengers a year. Herbert especially was fascinated by railways and everything about them. Janet, meanwhile, and for once, sat quietly, letting the whole scene wash over her and fill her with the sheer warmth of being a family, together, and thoroughly diverted.

Their destination was imminent when they finally reached the bridge that crossed the point where the River Ravensbourne met Deptford Creek. The station at Greenwich was in Church Row, close to St Alfege Church.[16] As they had been in a musical mood, albeit prompted by Herbert's youthful exuberance, they paid their respects to the famous English composer Thomas Tallis, buried in the churchyard. George also pointed out the new church spire, built only a few years earlier when the old spire was struck by lightning.

While the excursion was Peter's idea, George took the lead for the moment, pointing out the elegant buildings of the Royal Naval Hospital by the Thames for sailors wounded in Britain's wars, built on the instructions of Mary II. In the spirit of the moment, he asked his ever-curious boys if they knew why was the building divided in two? For Herbert, the answer was obvious: so they could put another railway line in the middle! The answer, as their mother explained, was because the queen didn't want to lose her view of the winding Thames.

At this point, Peter turned their attention towards the park and their planned destination of the Royal Observatory on the top of the hill. From King William Walk to the Avenue and then, for the benefit of the boys, a run up the hill to the Observatory and the time ball. Janet had told them all about this during her morning lessons: the Greenwich Meridian from which the counting of the lines of longitude began, zero degrees from the North Pole to the South Pole and running through Greenwich, along with the time ball, the signal for captains to see when their chronometers would all be set true to Greenwich time.

Such a simple thing, the time ball. From 1833, at 1 p.m. each day, the red ball would drop from the windvane on top of the main building, selected because it was easily visible by telescope by captains in port. What a lovely adventure, with another train journey home; it was to be a full, tiring and delightful day. But there would be another surprise in store – as Peter had planned. Amid all the hubbub and mayhem of the family outing, while the boys were pelting helter-skelter up the hill, he seized the moment for a quiet, very personal word, with Emily. Indeed he had planned the excursion with precisely this mission in mind. Emily had secretly hoped for this moment too and was inwardly pleased at the scheme Peter had quite clearly devised to declare his intentions.

They couldn't wait a second longer to tell Janet and George, particularly to seek George's approval of the match, and so, over their fish and chips and a glass of cider in a Greenwich pub, they announced their news. There was no need for any words, as Janet threw her arms around her beloved stepdaughter and, between laughter and tears, realised that she would be the learned Dr Galen's mother-in-law.

1840 was to be a year of weddings. On 10 February, amid torrential rain, Queen Victoria married her handsome cousin Prince Albert, the son of Ernst I of Saxe-Coburg-Gotha, in Westminster Abbey (although, as a reigning monarch it was Victoria who had to propose to him).[17] Only a few months later, on 4 July, in contrasting bright summer sunshine, Emily married Peter, son of Henrik van Galen, a physician, in the Taylor family church of St Katherine Coleman. By now, George was feeling quite comfortable in the business, notwithstanding its difficult times. So much so that pride on this special day for his daughter led to his describing himself on the wedding certificate simply as 'gentleman'. The celebration was a relatively modest affair, with a simple wedding cake that contrasted starkly with the 300-pound monster cake for Victoria and her prince, adorned with cupids and satin love knots, and topped with a large figure of Britannia blessing the bride and groom. But the joy of the occasion was in no way diminished for the Taylor clan.

It was a period of widespread optimism for the nation, although tinged with undercurrents of tension, both domestically and internationally. Movement along economic and political fault lines, opened up by the French and industrial revolutions, had the potential to rip through the very fabric of society, with chaos, disruption, dislocation, disease, death and mass emigration following in their wake.

Britain soon found herself embroiled in international conflict again, the day after Emily's wedding declaring war on China. It concerned the profitable opium trade; British merchants wanted to get the opium grown in British India into China, so from the end of the eighteenth century, British merchants had been shipping it illegally into Canton (now Guangzhou). In 1839, the imperial Chinese government sought to block the trade, seizing and burning all opium stocks in the city. The British community was kept under virtual house arrest in their warehouses until allowed to withdraw to Hong Kong. The 'Opium Wars', as they became known, revealed the strength of the East India Company gunboats, with their 32-pounder guns. The Treaty of Nanking, signed on board the British warship HMS *Cornwallis* in 1842, ended the war and led to Britain's acquisition of Hong Kong, access to several ports and significant trade concessions.

Back home, meanwhile, Janet faced a continuing war of her own on the subject of chartselling and, in particular, with Robert Bate. It had reached Bate's ears that both she and John Norie had been complaining about him to the Admiralty – and behind his back. He was greatly aggrieved, the more so because they could still sell private charts, where he could not. Bent on revenge, he hit upon the idea that the *Nautical Magazine* would provide the principal vehicle of his attack. It took the form of an anonymous letter from 'a skipper' who roundly condemned the private charts and, by implication, their sellers, claiming that they were simply Admiralty Charts with a few embellishments:

> The ground work of the whole, namely the Admiralty Chart, can be had in its simple and correct form, for next to nothing.

It was true that the private charts were more expensive, costing even four times as much as Admiralty charts. But despite this vast difference they were nevertheless still sought after because they were viewed as far more accurate and up to date. No price was too much to pay for that. Bate had also heard whispers that Janet had not only wanted to obtain charts directly, but had the effrontery to demand precisely the same discount allowed to him.

Considering Norie too powerful to irritate, Bate decided to target Janet, firstly by publishing a major book directly in competition with hers, *The Practice of Navigation and Nautical Astronomy*, by Henry Raper, a naval Lieutenant. To make matters worse, it was an excellent work, for which Raper was awarded the gold medal of the Royal Geographical Society the following year. Bate was delighted at its impact and its potential in consequence for making her life difficult. But he sought to undermine her further at the Admiralty by telling Lieutenant Becher in September 1840 that the Taylors' shop had no real interest in promoting Admiralty charts and promoted the bluebacks in preference whenever they could, as they yielded a higher profit.

Greatly alarmed, Becher contacted George on 8 December, expressing grave concern at the publicity they may have been giving to the private charts over the Admiralty charts, and requiring their accounts of sales. Janet replied immediately, livid that 'some unfavourable impressions may be afloat at the Admiralty on the subject' (and knowing only too well who was their likely source); and protesting that *only* Admiralty charts were ever displayed in the shop window. In an effort to put paid to the blatant untruths, she gave particulars of the sales that amounted to £165 18s 9d for the prior three months alone. Although such sales figures spoke for themselves, she was 'never happy' until she or her conduct was 'placed on a fair footing'. In her view, she had always given her best and was a strong believer in the cause of Admiralty charts. In one instance, on 12 February 1839, she had earnestly assured Beaufort of her 'exertions to extend the circulation of [his] Charts as a public benefit', and although she had hoped for 'a better allowance' on them, as there had proved to be little profit in their sales, she 'did not wish to ruffle the temper of Mr Bate or interfere with his arrangements'. That she had even *asked* for such a discount, once he learned of it, did indeed ruffle the temper of Mr Bate.

By the end of 1840, Janet and George had realised that, in relation to the Admiralty chart sales, as she had written to Beaufort in February 1839, 'business done without *any* profit, *must* be attended with loss', so it became imperative to build upon all the other aspects of their enterprise. In any case, they had already been looking to other activities to bolster their income. There was of course the Nautical Academy, along with the manufacturing of nautical instruments of their own. They had even been successful in obtaining key agencies to sell those of others, such as the sole agency they had obtained in 1835 for Dent's and Arnold's Chronometers, one of the leading clock-making firms. (In 1852 it was Edward Dent's firm that won the commission to make the great clock for the Houses of Parliament at Westminster – familiarly known as 'Big Ben', which he completed in 1854.)

But all the skirmishes with Bate paled into insignificance when it came to meeting the challenge of iron. And it was to the universal problem of magnetic deviation to which Janet now turned.

XV

Iron Ships

The problems of distortion of the compass due to variation and deviation were reasonably well understood by the beginning of the nineteenth century. But the challenge of seafaring was about to be transformed when, in 1822, the first iron-hulled vessel, the paddle-wheeled steamer the *Aaron Manby*, crossed the English Channel and steamed up the Seine River to Paris.[18] From that moment on, iron-built ships would entirely change the face – and hazards – of shipping, as the iron severely affected the compass. Its unreliability provoked serious discussion and heated debate as to how the situation could be remedied. As if the loss in shipping due to the problems in ascertaining longitude and poor charts were not enough, the effect of iron on compasses now posed another, and perhaps even more serious, crisis for navigation.

Although the issues surrounding iron and compasses were apparent, the problems were only exacerbated with iron ships, as their very construction set up permanent magnetic fields. The ship itself acquired its own magnetic portrait or signature, depending on its direction, or heading, as its iron plates were hammered and riveted into place, each hammer blow adding to the complexity of the ship's magnetic character: the 'hard iron' or permanent magnetic property of the ship. The compass is also affected by the magnetic state of things around it – components of the ship's structure, like its beams. This is known as the 'soft iron' property of the ship, caused by transient induced magnetism in vertical and horizontal structures. And a global solution to the dilemma seemed unlikely because the problems were individual to each ship. It was clearly going to take the work of dedicated, meticulous scientists and navigators to solve the challenges of iron.

One of the pioneers in finding answers was the masterly hydrographic surveyor Matthew Flinders, who had investigated the problem of distortion of the compass while undertaking his surveys of the coast of Australia. In March 1805 he presented his findings to the Royal Society based on his observations of the changes in the compass on board the *Investigator* arising from an alteration in the ship's heading. 'Whilst surveying along the south coast of New Holland, in 1801 and 1802,' he began:

> I observed a considerable difference in the direction of the magnetic needle, when there was no other apparent cause for it than that of the ship's head being in a different direction. This occasioned much perplexity in laying down the bearings, and in allowing a proper variation upon them, and put me under the necessity of endeavouring to find out some method of correcting or allowing for those differences; for unless this could be done, many errors must unavoidably get admission into the chart.

This landmark paper represented 'a systematic effort to investigate the laws of ship magnetism with the object of discovering a method of correcting a disturbed compass'. In 1812 Flinders then pressed the case to the Admiralty for regular testing of their compasses by 'swinging the ship' (or 'swinging the compass'), comparing the compass bearings through 360 degrees against known fixed positions on shore.

Swinging the ship involves moving the ship into positions according to the markings on a compass card which usually remains pointing north, the process ideally taking place in a suitable location in open water with plenty of room for manoeuvring the vessel. While the ship remains steady on each of the eight primary compass points, existing compass headings or bearings are compared with what is known the actual magnetic headings or bearings should be, the difference being the 'deviation'. During this procedure, any magnetic fields created by the ship's structure or equipment which might cause the compass to deviate are reduced or eliminated. This may be achieved by creating equal but opposite magnetic fields using compensating correctors that are placed inside the compass binnacle or near the compass.

A man of forthright opinions, Flinders' recommendations also contained stinging criticisms of the Admiralty itself outlining their general negligence in relation to the treatment of compasses on board. This of course had the effect of ensuring that his report would only be circulated in an abridged form. Flinders' research was very much the work of the *applied* scientist:

> Constant employment upon practice has not allowed me to become much acquainted with theories, but the little information I have upon

the subject of magnetism has led me to form some notion concerning the cause of these differences, and although most probably vague and unscientific, I trust for the candour of the learned in submitting it, as well as the inferences above drawn, to their judgment.

He said, however, that he would 'leave it to the learned on the subject of magnetism' – the *theoretical* scientists – to form a hypothesis from observations, such as his, 'that may embrace the whole of the phenomena'. One theoretical scientist, the French mathematician Siméon Denis Poisson, devised a theory in the 1820s to explain the variation of the compass due to terrestrial magnetism. But this was only part of the problem. Flinders also noticed the deviation effect of two guns that had been standing near the compasses and devised a novel solution by placing a vertical bar of soft iron on the binnacle, the housing for the compass, as a corrector. (This later became known as the 'Flinders bar'.)

Another who was keen to enter the debate was the famous Arctic whaler, and keen observer, William, later Reverend, Scoresby, who contributed his own suggestions for solving the iron problem. On his many voyages into the Arctic, Scoresby had noticed how the many iron items in a wooden ship, lying or hanging vertically, became magnetised by the magnetic field of the earth. Like Flinders, he also observed the phenomenon of latitude, which caused magnetic variation, which occurred least when sailing north or south, and greatest when sailing east or west. There were multiple varying effects.

But the suggestions of Flinders and Scoresby, and others at the time, were focused upon wooden ships and not the far more problematic iron ships. With ships made of iron, the issues, including the challenge of permanent magnetism, seemed overwhelming. Francis Beaufort was one who was only too aware that something had to be done, and quickly. His proposed committee, the Admiralty Compass Committee, met for the first time in July 1837, the month following Victoria's ascension to the throne, to consider the 'compass problem'. Any lingering question about the need for such a body evaporated when the iron paddle steamer and Channel mail packet SS *Rainbow*, the largest iron-hulled steamship yet then built, came close to being shipwrecked on her maiden voyage from the Mersey to the Thames in 1837. Beset by heavy fog, the *Rainbow* was reliant on her compasses, but they became wildly distorted by magnetic deviation. Hearing of the near disaster, Beaufort decided to enlist the Astronomer Royal towards finding a solution.

George Airy was a man of some considerable accomplishment. Lucasian Professor of Mathematics at Cambridge University (a position later occupied by the renowned Stephen Hawking for thirty years between 1979 and 2009) in 1826 at the precocious age of twenty-eight, prestigious Plumian Professor of Astronomy two years later, Astronomer Royal in 1835 and Head of Greenwich Observatory in 1838, Airy was the epitome of the theoretical scientist. Although a principal concern of the position of Astronomer Royal was lunar and planetary observations, Airy quickly recognised the importance of magnetic observation to assist in maintaining the lunar-distance method of longitude determination, and established a Magnetic Observatory at Greenwich.

In an effort to find a solution to the magnetism 'problem', Beaufort asked him to make a close examination of the *Rainbow*. From late in August 1838, Airy used the large basin of the Royal Dockyards at Deptford to swing the ship through a full circle to measure the deviation and find the compass error on each heading – the method Flinders had recommended.

Even one as well qualified as Airy 'struggled with the numbers', as he wrote in his autobiography, and he only succeeded by examining 'horizontal magnetic intensities', by which 'the explanation of the whole was suggested at once'. The disciplined and meticulous Airy conducted his task precisely, and he was shocked by the findings that, on some headings, the deviation was up to a staggering fifty degrees. Working over many days in July and August, on the ship, on a raft, and in experiments in the Magnetic Observatory, he devised his solution, and he was ready to try it:

> On Aug 20th I carried my magnets and iron correctors to Deptford, mounted them in the proper place, tried the ship, and the compass, which had been disturbed 50 degrees to the right and 50 degrees to the left, was not sensibly correct.

Through his experiments and calculations, Airy concluded that it was necessary to tackle both the problem of the permanent magnetism of the ship itself, as well as the problem of induced magnetism in soft iron on board. For the former, he used a permanent magnet; while for the latter, compensating soft iron in the form of, for example, chains placed on either side of the compass, either inside or around the binnacle. To test this theory, the *Rainbow* was taken on a test run to Antwerp. The captain reported that he was 'perfectly satisfied with the correctness of the compass', a verdict that Airy's method was indeed sound. Airy documented all his work with customary thoroughness – 'the ruling feature of his character was undoubtedly Order'. For corroboration, he was asked to do the same thing for another new ship, the aptly named

Ironside, the world's first iron-hulled sailing ship. Much to his delight and satisfaction, the ship sailed to Brazil with the compass remaining steadfastly correct throughout the voyage.

At the same time, Airy took the opportunity to improve the method, with fixed magnets to compensate for permanent magnetism and iron chain links in two boxes for the induced magnetism. Airy documented all his work with the utmost thoroughness and published it for others to follow, presenting his findings to the Royal Society on 9 April 1839. While the Admiralty remained unpersuaded by the outcome of Airy's experiments, 'the general success of the undertaking soon became notorious' amongst the maritime community.

Although the issue was of unmistakable importance to the seafaring world, for Airy it was but a distraction from his main work. So much so that, once he considered he had successfully devised an effective method for compass correction using the appropriate theory, he left it to others to implement: that 'every sea-going ship should be examined by a competent person', as he put it. The problem was, however, that it was exacting, and if instructions were not followed to the letter, the compasses would still be out. When the gunboat *Nemesis*, supposedly corrected according to Airy's method, ran aground in the winter of 1839/40, there were those who were quick to lay the blame squarely at Airy's feet. And when the *United Service Journal* in May 1840 claimed that his method was 'a sealed book to all but men of high science', he responded immediately in a lengthy, defensive letter to the editor, dated 15 May and published in June, arguing that the compass must have been moved and naturally he couldn't be responsible for that. As to the suggestion that his method was difficult for the practical navigator, Airy responded that if the writer *had* perused *all* of his 1839 paper on the subject:

> He will find a description of the very process used by the captain of a merchant ship (with no more instructions, I believe, that are there detailed), by which, in my absence, he completed the correction of the compass *before breakfast*. And I fully believe that your correspondent, after ten minutes' attention to that paragraph, will find himself perfectly competent to carry out the correction of the compass in any iron ship.

Airy was confident that his method was correct; his experiments on the *Rainbow* were manifest proof of this. But the problem was still far from solved in both the eyes of the public and the Admiralty Compass Committee. This six-member group, comprising Captain Francis Beaufort, Commander Edward Johnson, Captain James Clark Ross, Major Edward

Sabine, Professor Samuel Hunter Christie and Captain Thomas Best Jarvis, had already spent three years agonising over the compass dilemma, their work leading to a report in June 1840. As a result, the committee decided upon recommending a standard compass design for all naval compasses and the adoption of deviation tables. The compasses were to be checked regularly for deviation by swinging, but they were *not* to be corrected, a deviation table being kept to ensure that the deviation for each particular compass was tracked. This 'tabular' approach was in contrast to the 'mechanical' approach of Airy, relying on compensating magnets.

While the Navy was now locked in to the tabular method, merchant seamen, meanwhile, clamoured to have their compasses corrected according to Airy's system. As to which was right, or better, it would take years of repeated testing at sea. Continued shipwrecks and loss of life proved that the issue was far from resolved and led to the questioning both of Airy's method and the competence of the examiners his method had spawned. For those with an entrepreneurial bent, however, there was now an opportunity in the field of compass adjusting for the Merchant Navy. And so, a new profession was born.

Janet had been caught up in the challenge of iron from her childhood, her kitchen games of pots and pans representing naive musings on the effects of magnetic deviation. But this was no longer a game. Peter van Galen was similarly fascinated by the challenge and undertook his own experiments, all the while corresponding actively and intently with his new mother-in-law and writing a book on the subject. Janet followed the exchange in the *United Service Journal* with a degree of fascination, and felt considerable sympathy for Airy, having been the subject of unfair criticism herself. She wondered whether she should write in support of him, but thought, no, the moment wasn't right. She had, after all, sought his support in 1837 when she was seeking a civil list pension, and he had been dismissive. While her own observations and experiments suggested that Airy was, indeed, correct, there would be a better moment to broach the subject, when she felt that she was on firmer ground.

In the meantime, domestic events were overtaking the royal household, along with that of the Taylors. On 21 November 1840 the sound of bells filled the streets of London, pealing in greeting for the birth of a royal baby, the Princess Victoria Adelaide Mary Louise. For a moment, even the winter chill and the London fog seemed to clear away, although this winter it was so dense that ships twice collided in the Thames. The next spring, at No. 103 Minories on 2 May 1841, Janet gave birth to her sixth child, and first daughter, whom she named Janet. This was her 'wedding baby' as she called her privately to George, as she had been conceived in the giddy excitement of the celebrations for Emily's wedding. Two days later, Janet turned thirty-seven. Once again she had to face the tribulations of infancy, as her tiny namesake was gravely ill from the outset and her survival measured in days. Janet remained resolutely at home through this difficult period, recovering from the birth and anxiously caring for the baby.

Shortly afterwards, on an early summer's Sunday evening, 6 June 1841, it was census night – the first great census since Domesday (the eleventh-century survey conducted by order of William I 'the Conqueror'). Although there had been a census held in each of the years 1801, 1811 and 1821, these were mainly of local concern, being the responsibility of the 'Overseers of the Poor' and the clergy, mainly focusing on matters like the numbers engaged in certain occupations and the condition of housing stock. The records of these censuses are now lost to history, many of these early returns having been destroyed. In sharp contrast, the 1841 census was centralised under the control of the Registrar General and the Superintendent Registrars who had been responsible for the registration of births, deaths and marriages since the General Registration Act of 1836.

The types of questions were also different from the earlier censuses, requiring a much more detailed analysis of individuals and family households and the communities in which they lived. And despite the apparent good intentions of the government, there was suspicion from the general public as to precisely how these statistics would be used (even though the census forms would not be accessible to the public for another 100 years). There was also considerable inaccuracy as ages could be rounded down and the census recorder often muddled the information received.

In the Taylor household that night, it was George who took charge of the form. The evening had been a pleasant one, with baby Janet seemingly on the mend, and the family felt they could relax for a moment. The prospect of the census form caused some amusement, both as to what occupations to list as well as to their ages. As his occupation, George curiously chose 'clerk', while Janet assertively listed 'chartseller'. And with respect to their ages, they both rounded their ages down liberally, and more than the nearest multiple of five as directed: George as forty, not his real forty-eight; and Janet as thirty, not her thirty-seven. The servants in turn followed this example and took liberty with their ages, rounding them down: Mrs Marton, forty; Richard Tyley, thirty; Elizabeth and Caroline Juggens, twenty and fifteen. The children were listed correctly: Frederick (seven), Dite (five), Jon (two) and baby Janet (still to be christened). Of the other family members, Herbert (nine) was away at school and George's sons, George Jr (twenty-one) and Charles (nineteen) were launched on ventures of their own. Emily was also settled back in Rotterdam.

Their neighbours, the Richardson family at No. 102 Minories, undertook their task more diligently. The rather dour household head David, who was meticulous in his counting of his grocery stock, insisted on precision: for him, thirty-eight; his wife Mary, thirty-four; Henry Pugh, the shopman, twenty-eight; Betty Strange and Mary Benton, servants, twenty-one and sixteen respectively; and the children, George, ten, David, two, Maria, three, Jennett, one; each as exact as apples on a shelf. There would be no rounding down on the Richardsons' form. The Browns, meanwhile, at No. 104, 'rounded down' strictly as directed on the form, but not with the licence or fun of the Taylor household. The report of the inhabitants recorded: William Brown, linen draper, fifty; his wife Jane, forty; their three children, Mary, twenty, Ann and Jane, both entered as fifteen years old; a relative Thomas Brown and James Hall, both 'journeyman drapers', thirty and twenty respectively; a servant, Mary Waterman, twenty; Elizabeth Dale, twenty-five, a woman of independent means; and a five-year-old child called Mary Webster.

In Rotterdam, Peter van Galen was busy working on his second textbook, *Praktische Zeevaartkunde* (*Practical Navigation*), and he and Emily were eagerly anticipating the birth of their first child, named Georgeanne Emily, born in September 1841. Peter acknowledged his great admiration of his mother-in-law, in dedicating his book to her:

Dear Friend

I am extremely pleased that you have allowed me to dedicate this small work to you. Indeed, there is nobody better qualified than you to whom a work which attempts to further the interests of navigation, could be offered. You have achieved lasting fame with the publication of your works on navigation and anybody studying this branch of science is much obliged to you. Thus placed under your protection, I trust that this small work will be received more favourably and will serve its intended purpose more readily.

I hope, dear Friend, that you will continue to find satisfaction in the difficult task you have set yourself and in the well-earned tributes universally paid to you, and that you will enjoy the happiness surrounding you in your home-life for many years to come. Please allow me to express the wish that the ties linking us become closer still.

Yours very sincerely
Peter van Galen

Back in England, as the autumn cool overtook the summer in the evening of 30 October 1841, it seemed from Minories as if the world had caught alight, as a great fire engulfed the Tower of London. By the next morning, local residents and thousands of other spectators had lined Tower Hill or crammed onto watermen's wherries on the river, watching in amazement and horror as flames consumed Bowyer Tower; and the precious Crown Jewels were passed from hand to hand by policemen to get them out of harm's way. The onlookers stared with great consternation as, in confusion and enormous haste, the collection of ancient weapons and a large supply of gunpowder were dragged out of the Grand Storehouse. The docks adjacent to the Tower, with their storehouses and thousands of ships, were in immediate peril, as was Janet's shop, full of charts, nautical instruments and books, and the businesses of her neighbours, like the Browns' linen drapery. The sparks and embers threatened everything and it took several days before the fire eventually burned itself out.

Even when the immediate crisis had passed, the smoke lingered in the air for weeks, causing great concern especially for families with small children, and those like Janet who were prone to chronic bronchitis. The winter months were already difficult to endure, when the smog of coal fires clung to London like an olive-green blanket, but the Tower fire so close to home aggravated her condition badly. At the same time Janet had to watch her baby daughter carefully as she struggled through the winter, sick one moment and seemingly better the next. And then, by April 1842, Janet also realised that she was pregnant again.

Emily and Peter came to visit No. 103 during the following summer, but the joy and excitement of the visit, as well as the success of Peter's book in Holland, was overwhelmed by sadness when their precious Georgeanne Emily passed away. She was only ten months old when she was buried at St Katherine Coleman on 21 July. Overcome with grief, her distraught parents immediately returned to their home in Rotterdam.

Janet, too, was devastated at the loss of her grandchild, but she didn't have time to dwell. Baby Janet's health was also now sinking deeper and deeper and, as if the heavens mirrored her own feelings, fierce storms battered the coast and the Thames overflowed its banks. And while the nation greeted the birth of a son to the queen, Prince Albert, on 9 November – the first legitimate royal prince since George IV was born in 1762 – the Taylor household filled with mourning yet again when baby Janet died on 24 November, aged just nineteen months. This was the second child that Janet had lost. First it had been Seymour, who died on 25 October 1835, and now she had lost her daughter, some eight years later. What made it worse was that two treasured baby girls had gone within months of each other, casting a heavy shadow over the Taylor household and making it a sombre Christmas period for the family. It was with great trepidation that on 29 January 1843, at the age of thirty-nine, Janet gave birth to another daughter, Ada Marian, christening her on 20 March at St Katherine Coleman. Ada, mercifully, seemed to be thriving and Janet was able to get back into the regular rhythm of her work and now focused on the problem of iron ships.

As the 1840s progressed, iron-built ships were becoming more and more commonplace. The Admiralty, having decided upon the tabular approach to compass deviation, appointed Captain Edward Johnson RN, a member of the Admiralty Compass Committee, as superintendent of the Compass Department in 1842. It was an important part of his duty to swing every naval ship to determine the extent of deviation for its compasses, ensure that this was duly recorded in its Table of Deviations, and establish that each was ready to travel. Meanwhile, merchant seamen clamoured to have their compasses 'corrected' using Airy's mechanical method of correction. This provided a catalyst for a significant expansion of the Taylors' business in the compass-adjusting department; and they quickly established their reputation in this new and growing field.

In late 1843 Janet was faced with a considerable challenge – to adjust the compass of a ship that was not only made of iron, but also loaded with an iron cargo. Now, she thought, was the right time to contact Airy, writing on 8 November:

Sir,
Before troubling you I have made every enquiry possible, that I might avoid the necessity of applying to you as you have, no doubt, but little time for answering enquiries of the kind. I am applied to for the best Treatise on correcting the deviation of the compass on board Iron steam vessels, and for the requisite instruments for making experiments. The first attempt is to be made on board an Iron vessel 120 ft long, 30 ft broad, draught 4 ft and with a cargo of Iron. I shall be greatly obliged if you will inform me where I can get the required information and what apparatus is necessary to perform the experiments, which you have recommended.
    With apologies for troubling you,
    I am Sir,

Yours obediently
Janet Taylor

Airy was in a much more receptive frame of mind when he read her letter. While he found the correspondence from her curious, coming from a woman, after all, she was writing as an admirer of his principles and, besides, he needed all the allies he could muster. He immediately obliged by sending her two copies of his own exposition on the subject, including specific instructions for compass adjustment using his method and details of the relevant instruments to do the work. (His official full volume on the subject, *A Treatise on Magnetism*, didn't appear for another twenty-eight years.) But her letter had another important consequence: he was now on notice that the Taylors' navigation warehouse included compass-adjusting services – and according to his method.

Looking back on the kind of task involved in the adjustment of compasses, one can only but wonder how Janet would, or could, have carried out the actual work of compass adjusting, especially on top of all her other activities. Compass adjusting was also very much a man's business and it would have been considered unseemly for a woman to undertake it. While Janet understood Airy's principles thoroughly, she was well aware that it would be very difficult for her to perform the task of swinging ships herself. It was outdoor, physical work and had to be undertaken in all weathers to ensure the compasses would be ready when needed. Her lungs were delicate and very susceptible to the cold. As a woman, even her clothing would have conspired against her.

To add to her burden she also had a household full of children, with the approaching Christmas of 1843 heralding colder and colder weather. Ada was not yet a year old and Janet also realised she was pregnant yet again, expecting her eighth child. It was painfully apparent that she needed an apprentice. The twenty-two-year-old Frederick Wiggins was the right man in the right place at the right time. And by the end of 1845, she had assembled a team of men to undertake the fixing of magnets according to Airy's system.

Living up to her expectations, Wiggins was a keen and willing pupil and under her watchful eye made rapid progress. Armed with his tools of trade, including a brace of assorted magnets of varying shapes and sizes, she showed him how to put Airy's principles into practice. When Wiggins had completed his apprenticeship to her complete satisfaction, he became the first person in Britain to take up compass adjusting as a profession. Her fee to hire him out was thirty guineas and he could swing up to three ships in a single day. It also provided a timely boost to her finances. Whenever possible Janet would supervise his work on site, and when she could not, she made it her business to review his findings back at Minories, meticulously going over his report sheets on his work with each ship.

1. Jane Ionn (*née* Deighton).
(Authors' collection; photographic
copy of original painting held
privately)

2. Peter Ionn portrait. (Authors'
collection; photographic copy of
original painting held privately)

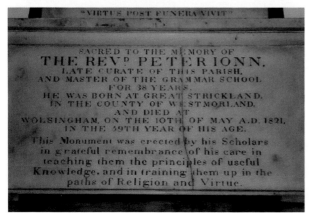

3. Forged extract regarding Peter Ionn's baptism. (Durham University Library, Durham Diocesan Records, Ref. DDR/EA/ CLO/3/1784/11)

4. Dedication to Peter Ionn – plaque in parish church of St Mary and St Stephen, Wolsingham. (Authors' collection)

5. Stone plaque at Wolsingham Grammar School. (Photo by Geoffrey Wearmouth, provided by Anita Atkinson)

6. Pastel portrait of Janet Taylor (Jane Ann Ionn). (Authors' collection; photo by Bec Lorrimer)

Left: 7. Spine for *Mrs Taylor's Epitome of Navigation*. (Authors' collection; photo by Bec Lorrimer)

Below: 8. *Epitome of Navigation* flyleaf, 1845. (Authors' collection; photo by Bec Lorrimer)

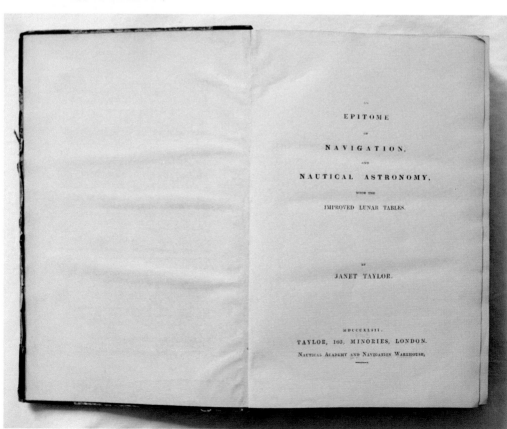

AN

EPITOME

OF

NAVIGATION,

AND

NAUTICAL ASTRONOMY,

WITH THE

IMPROVED LUNAR TABLES.

BY

JANET TAYLOR.

MDCCCXLIII.

TAYLOR, 103, MINORIES, LONDON.

NAUTICAL ACADEMY AND NAVIGATION WAREHOUSE,

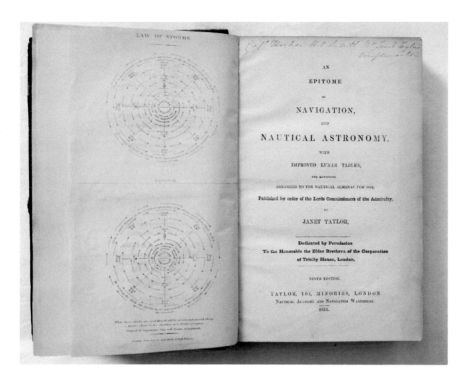

9. *Epitome of Navigation* flyleaf, 1851. (Authors' collection; photo by Bec Lorrimer)

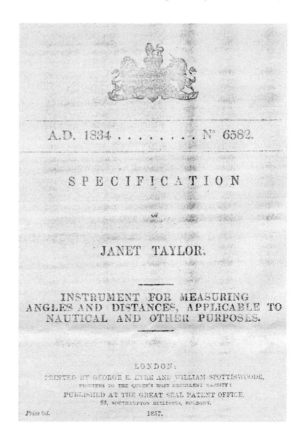

Right: 10. Mariner's Calculator specs (original). (Patent Office London. Patent No. 6582, A.D., 1834)

11. Mariner's Calculator replica. (Authors' collection)

Left: 12. Janet Taylor binnacle. (Authors' collection; photo by Bec Lorrimer)

Right: 13. Janet Taylor binnacle, with detail showing 'Mrs Janet Taylor'. (Authors' collection; photo by Bec Lorrimer)

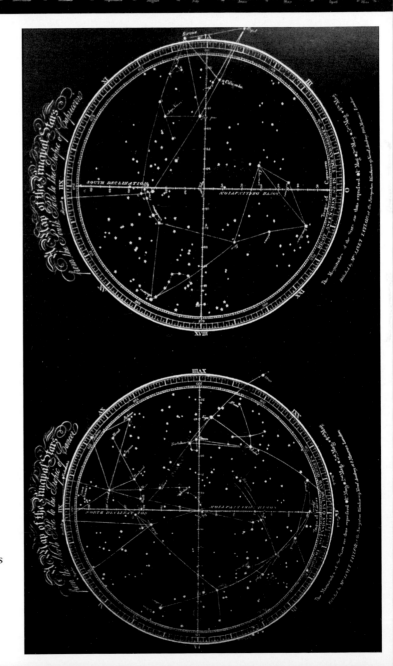

14. & 15. Two images of the Planisphere of the Stars. (Authors' collection)

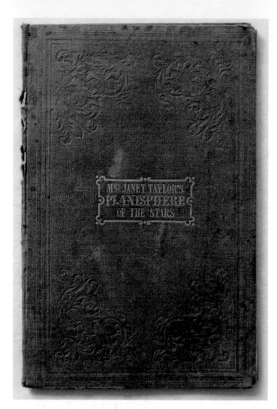

Left: 16. *Planisphere of the Stars* cover. (Authors' collection; photo by Bec Lorrimer)

Below: 17. *Planisphere of the Stars* flyleaf. (Authors' collection; photo by Bec Lorrimer)

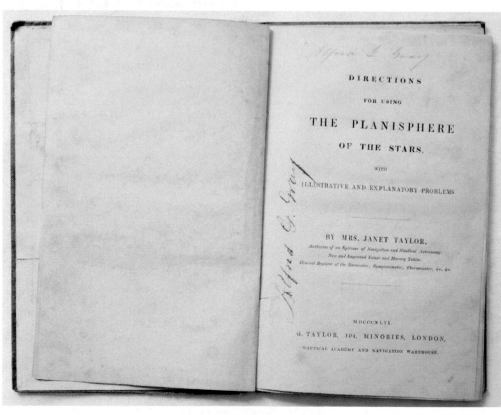

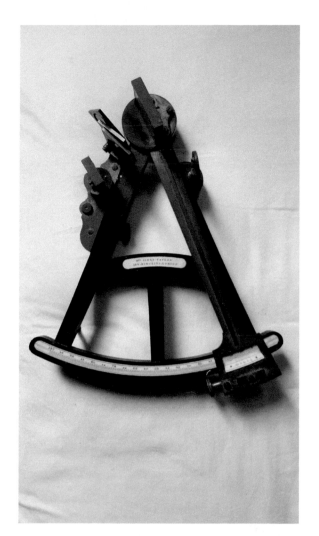

Right: 18. Janet Taylor
Octant. (Authors' collection;
photo by Bec Lorrimer)

Below: 19. Janet Taylor
Octant detail inscribed 'Mrs
Janet Taylor & Co' – detail of
image shown in 18. (Authors'
collection; photo by Bec
Lorrimer)

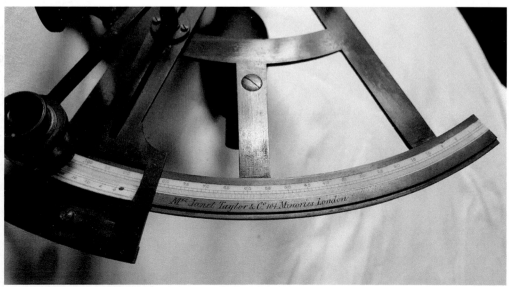

Above left: 20. Janet Taylor Octant – reverse of octant in 18. (Authors' collection; photo by Bec Lorrimer)

Above right: 21. Janet Taylor aneroid barometer. (Photo by John Croucher; item held by the Alger family)

Below: 22. Royal Exchange. Nineteenth-century engraving. (Authors' collection; photo by Bec Lorrimer)

Above: 23. Trinity House. Nineteenth-century engraving. (Authors' collection; photo by Bec Lorrimer)

Above: 24. Admiralty. Engraving from *c*. 1820. (Photo by Bec Lorrimer)

25. Janet Taylor compass. (Authors' collection; photo by Bec Lorrimer)

26. Janet Taylor compass (2). (Authors' collection; photo by Bec Lorrimer)

Right: 27. Janet Taylor telescope. (Authors' collection; photo by Bec Lorrimer)

Below: 28. Janet telescope showing detail, 'Mrs Janet Taylor & Co'. Nineteenth-century engraving. (Authors' collection; photo by Bec Lorrimer)

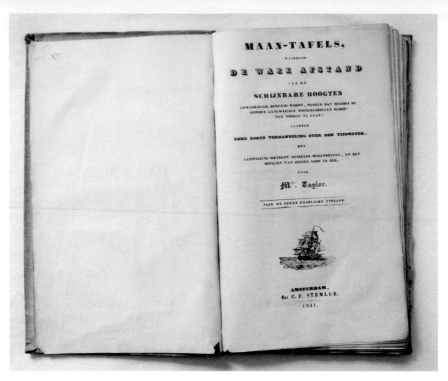

29. Dutch translation of Lunar Tables. Flyleaf of 1841 book. (Authors' collection; photo by Bec Lorrimer)

30. Peter van Galen. (Photo by John Croucher; item held by the Alger family)

31. Janet Taylor's grave in 2016. (Photo by Geoffrey Wearmouth, provided by Anita Atkinson)

32. Frederick Peter Ionn authorship block from his Ionn family chart. See p. 252. (Authors' photograph; in private hands)

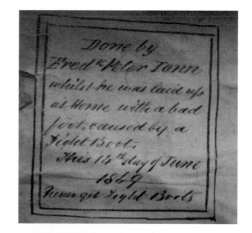

33. Jane Ann Ionn shield. Ionn family chart. See p. 252–53. (Authors' photograph; in private hands)

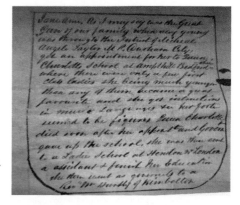

34. Entrance to London Docks. Nineteenth-century engraving. (Authors' collection; photo by Bec Lorrimer)

35. Paddle steamship. Nineteenth-century engraving. (Authors' collection; photo by Bec Lorrimer)

The winter of 1843 merged into a busy spring, with compass-adjustment papers and more books spilling over her desk and table. In May the following year, the publication 'New Navy List containing the names of all the Commissioned Officers in Her Majesty's Fleet' revealed the annual remuneration to three persons of interest in Janet's life. These were Captain Beaufort £800, his principal assistant Commander Alexander Becher £400 and secondary assistant Lieutenant Alfred Miles £156 10s. Three months later on 4 May Janet celebrated her fortieth birthday; and on 9 August she gave birth to her eighth and last child, her fifth surviving son, Alfred Robert. While pregnant with Alfred, Janet's mind had turned again to the possibility of a civil list pension. The catalyst was her third award from an international source – this time, the Pope.

It had caused quite a stir in the Taylor household when the letter from Pope Gregory XVI arrived at the door, complete with yet another medal to honour her achievements. But it only served to remind her again that Mrs Somerville had received recognition from her own Government while she had been dismissed. It was the Pope's medal that provided the impetus to write again.

In March 1844 she wrote to the Prime Minister, Robert Peel. She reminded him that two years earlier, in December 1842, the Reverend Hodgson had sent Peel a copy of the first edition of her *Epitome of Navigation and Nautical Astronomy*. Hodgson, renowned for his study of antiquities, came from the Durham area, was well acquainted with her family and advanced her claim for consideration in Peel's eyes. Janet's petition was not so much about money, it was about recognition:

> During the last 16 years my life has been devoted entirely to the advancement of education amongst British Seamen, and though I have been incumbered by innumerable difficulties, I have done much towards the improvements of that large and diffuse portion of Her Majesty's subjects and would still do more, could I meet with support that such an undertaking requires, and merits – and you, Sir, I now appeal whether I have such true claims on the consideration of my country.

That 'consideration' was based on her scientific contribution, acknowledging what she had done for the welfare of mariners. Distancing herself from 'fashionable readers', she argued that her works were 'unknown in such circles'. Her claim rested on much higher ground:

> I can say with the honest pride of an Englishman that there is not a Port in which the British flag is unfurled where my name is not mentioned with feeling of gratitude by the British mariners.

But if the Prime Minister were mindful of personal matters, she had a bundle of those to throw in to strengthen her argument:

> Having a large family (principally boys) to educate, and my own health impaired by great sacrifices I have been compelled to make, I am urgent to be heard and I think at your leisure you will give me that attention, you will find on enquiry, I deserve.

Her boys Herbert, twelve, Frederick, eight and Dite, now seven, were all at school, and good schools at that, receiving a classical education to fit them well for all possibilities of advancement in life. Jon, only five, needed special attention as a result of his poor eyesight. Juggling the demands of her growing family; George's issues in the liquor trade, which were not always smooth sailing; the vagaries of the chartselling arm of the business; her book sales sometimes hostage to the fate of the reviewer into whose hands they fell; all her money from her father gone in the pursuit of the business; and the fact that her own health always subject to the trials of the winter, the cold and smog often triggering chronic bronchial troubles that she bore stoically from year to year; all of this could rightly be called 'innumerable difficulties' without needing to spell it out. And still her name was spoken of abroad. It was the British mariner who was her truest ally.

That Janet's plea intertwined issues of merit and need spoke of a wider conflict, or confusion, about the proper basis for the award of civil list pensions, which had been a subject of some political contention in the 1830s. The pensions had first come under scrutiny in 1834, with allegations of political favouritism and cronyism being made, leading to the following guide being prescribed by the Commons in February of that year:

> That it is the bounden duty of the responsible advisers of the Crown to recommend to his Majesty for grants of pensions on the Civil-list such persons only as have just claims on the Royal beneficence, or who, by their personal services to the Crown, by the performance of duties to the public, or by their useful discoveries in science, and attainments in literature and the arts, have merited the gracious consideration of their Sovereign and the gratitude of their country.

With the death of William IV and the ascension to the throne of Victoria, discussion over the award of the civil list pensions was renewed in the context of the allowances by Parliament to the new monarch.

There was a fundamental confusion as to the nature and purpose of the awards. Was the claim to 'Royal beneficence' based on need; or was it for merit – for 'useful discoveries in science' and 'attainments in literature and the arts', or both? In November 1837 such ambiguities fuelled a lively discussion in the Commons again when the removal of the civil list pensions altogether was proposed. This inherent tension was also reflected in comments about the awards: in particular, how much should be given, to whom and for what?

With respect to contributions of a scientific kind, Airy and Mrs Somerville were the only beneficiaries recognised in the civil list in 1835. The size of the awards attracted criticism in the debate in the Commons in November and December 1837, that 'the only real effect which these pensions produce is confined to a select circle under the Minister's eye' and that the pension system, confusing merit and need, only served to create injustice:

You pay a compliment to one man of science, or to one public man, but you create a feeling of dissatisfaction and wounded pride in the bosoms of a dozen others ... Why, Sir, the only good which the pension does is the gratification which it imparts to the favoured individual, and it surely, therefore, is not improper to take some account of the contrary feelings experienced by others. But then we are told, that the pensions on the civil list are not to be distributed according to public services alone, or to scientific merit alone, but partly to charitable purposes also ... Your pension list is then to be an asylum for public servants or for persons of literary eminence when they happen to be in a state of comparative distress ... Now this seems to introduce entire confusion and perplexity into the distribution of pensions.

This was the occasion when Mrs Somerville's pension was one of those singled out for criticism.

Janet's correspondence with Peel sought to cover all possibilities, addressing both merit and need. But the response was devastating when Peel simply scrawled across the top, 'no costs can be appropriated to her'. And that was that. From the Pope a medal, but from her own Prime Minister, nothing. Perhaps it had not been such a good idea to mention the Pope. After all, the Prime Minister had been nicknamed 'Orange Peel' when, as Chief Secretary for Ireland (1812–18), he opposed claims for Catholic emancipation. When word arrived at No. 103 Minories, George knew it was time to withdraw for a while. He had witnessed Janet's stormy pacings before. He exchanged a knowing look with Mrs Marton before he hastily retreated to the warehouse, to the brewery, or anywhere out of earshot of Janet's angry outpourings. Her anger, especially when pregnant, was something definitely to escape from.

Her fury gradually dissipated over the ensuing weeks and George, along with Mrs Marton, breathed a shared sigh of relief when Alfred was born on 9 August. It was also apparent that setbacks actually energised Janet, propelling her to prove herself yet again in whatever venture she set upon. On this occasion George encouraged her to continue her work on the *Planisphere* in addition to the annual editions of *Lunar Tables*. The former was a book very close to her heart: to map the heavens in a simple, yet beautiful way. She worked on this quietly over several years, saving it for special moments. It was a labour of love on so many levels. In her Introduction she wrote:

> The science of Astronomy offers to the reflective mind, a wide field for study and contemplation, and tends much to raise the heart and feelings beyond the scenes of this life, to that Almighty Being, who has spangled the heavens with innumerable orbs, each rolling in infinite space, and yet all maintaining the same beautiful order, and harmony in motion, as when first they issued forth from the hand of the Creator.

But the winter months brought sadness once more to the Taylor household as on 20 November 1844, after four months of suffering, her brother Seymour died of 'consumption' (the old name for tuberculosis). Janet had seen little of him since their days at No. 44 Oxford Street. After the failure of his business there he had taken up work in Hastings late in 1829 and married Emma Ross two years later. The death of his wife saw Seymour return to London where he then married a widow, Mary Barnes, who had some property of her own, settling in Oxford. They subsequently had six children and he took up a new business as a stationer. He was only forty-two when he died: the same age as his and Janet's mother. His death of consumption placed him among the 15,000 Londoners killed by it each year, against which the so-called 'remedies', from creosote even to boa constrictor excreta, made no impact in its unrelenting swathe.

XVI

The Business Grows

The new year of 1845 began with mixed emotions at the sadness of Seymour's passing and the disappointment again at the lack of recognition of Janet by the government. But there was no doubting the optimism at the exciting new possibilities for the business with the compass adjusting side of things starting to grow and other aspects revealing their potential. It was a time of rapid expansion that required extra room for both an instrument warehouse and instrument manufacturing. There was also a significant opportunity on the horizon as the Government was now discussing the introduction of examinations of competency for mariners. Though not implemented at first, it would only be a matter of time before such requirements were introduced and the Taylors wanted to be well and truly ready. And in preparation, early in 1845, the family made the decision to move.

The business was relocated into No. 104, only next door, but with much more scope and potential for growth. The family, however, moved around the corner to No. 1 Hammet St where they set up their domestic establishment. As Hammet Street ran into a crescent at right angles to Minories, with No. 102 Minories on the corner of both streets, the rear of their home provided easy access to their business, not only yielding the extra space but also allowing some separation of the business and domestic aspects of their lives. Their previous neighbours, the linen draper William Brown and his family, had moved out three years earlier, and it had remained empty ever since. Although the construction of the Blackwall Railway had proved too much for the Browns, No. 104 was larger than No. 103 and suited the needs of Janet admirably. George had been astute in his early assessment of the location of Minories for the establishment of a nautical enterprise, and the fortuitous opportunity of renting both No. 104 and No. 1 Hammet St for their plans of expansion was now abundantly clear. It also provided a practical way of distancing themselves from the sadness and disappointments of the previous year.

The first six months of 1845 were spent consolidating the enterprise at No. 104, particularly the nautical instrument manufacturing arm as well as the teaching facilities. The business stationery now included the official logo of her school, the traditional anchor with intertwined rope for nautical establishments, with the words 'Mrs Janet Taylor's Nautical Academy, 104 Minories' written around the border. It was also a time for settling the family into their new surroundings, in particular ensuring that Alfred was closely watched and tended through the precarious early months of childhood. His 'big' sister Ada had turned two on 29 January and with her three eldest brothers away at school, and Jon requiring special attention, Janet had been somewhat relieved when baby Alfred was born. Ada would have had a bigger sister, had baby Janet, eighteen months her senior, only survived. They would have been lovely companions as little girls together, reflected Janet sadly at times. But little Janet was buried just two months before Ada was born and she would just have to make do with a baby brother. And, at the age of forty, Janet felt sure that Alfred would be her last child.

The move to Hammet Street also proved an opportune time for some restructuring of the household. Mrs Marton, now in her mid-fifties, decided that it was time to take less of a role in the family. Suffering as silently as she could for several years, she had found all the stairs increasingly hard on her hips. Hammet Street was simply too daunting. Dealing with her mistress when Mrs Marton was hale and hearty was one thing, but with her own health now dragging her down, her patience with Janet's 'strangeness' was getting harder to maintain. Sensing her chance had at last arrived, she suggested to Janet that Elizabeth Juggens step into the role of housekeeper. Elizabeth had proven herself indispensable to the household over the years since her introduction into the family in 1832 to look after the first child, Herbert. And now at age twenty-eight she had shown herself to be responsible and, more importantly perhaps, the children loved her. As Janet's concern was primarily for continuity and reliability, she readily adopted the suggestion.

Although George considered it his duty to find Mrs Marton a place where she could be more at ease in her remaining years, she had already arranged this for herself. She had family in Essex, and her cousin, also a widow, had a small cottage they could share. George also encouraged her to take along Caroline Juggens, making sure that she had a small allowance to provide for her modest needs in 'retirement'.

The important thing now was to find someone to help with the youngest members of the Taylor family, Ada and Alfred, as well as to assist in the general duties of the house. In no time two young women, Sarah Dobson and Hannah Butt, nineteen and twenty respectively, were found to join the household. This would suffice to start with. Janet was very grateful to Mrs Marton when, after settling in Essex, she also enlisted for her two very able young people for the household. William Bates would act as a secretary and Caroline Harding would assist in the household or with the boys in the school.

Janet and George could now deal with the immediate task of developing their nautical instrument manufacturing facility, a bold enterprise that complemented the chartselling, book writing, compass adjusting, teaching and other activities. The factory was designed for the manufacture of sextants, quadrants, compasses, barometers and other types of meteorological and nautical instruments and, whenever the boys were home from school, they loved to visit it. To oversee this new phase of the business, the talented William Reynolds, formerly apprenticed to the well-known Liverpool instrument maker John Gray, was engaged as foreman. Reynolds was widely regarded as brilliant in his craft and with Janet's guidance they would produce some of the highest quality devices of the time.

One notable example of the Taylor–Reynolds combination was a dry card compass, constructed using the design of Sir William Snow Harris, an English scientist who contributed a number of papers to *Nautical Magazine* and other journals on the study of electricity and in particular the damage that lightning caused to ships. A particular feature of this compass was the thick copper ring (about 1.5 inches deep by 0.5 inches thick) for damping or calming vibrations of the card while the pivot was mounted on a spring contained in a socket. The card was made of mica and graduated to half points, and a pin fitted to the verge glass to prevent the card coming off its pivot. Janet's name was clearly outlined around the centre.[19] She also developed a new instrument, called the 'Mariner's Compass', an artificial representation of the horizon.

Over the next few years the trail to No. 104 Minories became increasingly well-worn as the reputation of all aspects of the business grew. Merchant seamen and captains beat a steady path to her door seeking charts and for their compasses to be adjusted. The standing of her firm in the domain of compass adjusting strengthened daily, with the numbers of ships they had 'swung' now numbering in the hundreds. Frederick Wiggins was still applying himself conscientiously to the role and his expertise and stature grew with each compass he adjusted. Both he and Janet trained other assistants using Airy's method, while she continued a lively correspondence with her son-in-law Peter van Galen about its various twists and turns, as he continued his own experiments in Holland. By the end of 1845 she felt sufficiently confident to approach Airy again, seeking his approval and referrals of business in the area, writing on 20 December:

> Sir,
>
> From the number of Iron Vessels now building I understand you are frequently applied to for competent persons to adjust the compasses on board. I have therefore taken the liberty of asking you, should you have an opportunity of referring parties to me, if you will have the kindness to do so.
>
> I have instructed some of my best men to fix the magnets by your pamphlets and likewise from various experiments made by my Son in Law, Doctor van Galen, whose little work I sent you some time ago, on this subject. He is employed by the Dutch government to fix the magnets on board their Iron vessels.
>
> I feel a confidence in preferring this request to you knowing our efficiency and that you will not have any cause to regret your recommendation.
>
> Trusting you will excuse my troubling you,
>
> I am Sir,
>
> Yours obediently
Janet Taylor

As it happened, word of her firm's compass adjusting had already reached the ears of the Astronomer Royal and he was quietly pleased to hear from her, especially as her compass adjusters were demonstrable advocates of his methods. She was delighted in turn to learn that he had already been sending business her way:

> Mr Airy presents his compliments to Mrs Taylor and will not fail to mention Mrs Taylor's name to any persons who may apply to him respecting the correction of the compass in Iron Ships.
>
> A few weeks since Mr Airy recommended the Captain of an Iron Ship in which some change had been made, to apply to Mrs Taylor, but does not know whether application was accordingly made.

Before long, her firm had begun to lay claim to being the establishment of choice for compass adjusting. One notable instance was that the captain of the Portuguese warship *Duke of Oporto* had specifically asked her to adjust his compasses, after the rival adjusting firm Lilley, with whom her instrument maker William Reynolds had worked the previous year, had made a mess of the job. When the ship was swung her assistants found gross errors in the compass readings and in the readjustment she also tried out some small variations in Airy's method that she found worked most effectively.

Sensing that she now had his attention, her next letter to Airy outlined the exercise along with some 'improvements'. In particular she wanted to know if it was in order to utilise, contrary to his recommendations, smaller magnets placed outside the boxes, or 'binnacles', which contained the compass. Binnacles were becoming standard fare on iron ships, usually made from a special stand of non-magnetic material including a brass hood, and built into the hull of the ship for housing the compass. They were also fitted with a light, usually a lamp with a wick, by which the compass could be read by a mariner at night. Airy's correction method involved placing magnets either inside or around the binnacle to counteract the effects of any metal that could affect the direction shown by the compass.

The timing of her letter was not particularly opportune. During the previous summer Airy had had enough of quarrelling and quibbling after a public brawl with the astronomer Sir James South who attacked almost everything Airy did in the Observatory. Janet's 'improvements' may have worked well, but he wasn't a man who took kindly to the proposal that his method needed any improvement at all. And of course he bristled at the suggestion 'in reverse to those you recommend'. He replied the very next day:

Madam,

I really do not perceive what has been your difficulty in regard to the compasses on the 'Duke of Oporto'. If you will refer to my printed notes for correction, you will see that there is nothing said about the use of the magnets or about their being equal – and in fact much more power is usually mounted in one direction than the other.

Also, there is nothing said which prevents you from placing the magnets out of the centre, or high or low, so as to suit your convenience at the same time as to correct the compass. The directions are explicit – that if you draw a chalk + on the deck, the centre of either magnet may be anywhere on either line, or above it or below it, but not in the angles between the lines.

If the person who does this much for you still finds any difficulty in understanding this, he had better come to me some morning before

2 o'clock with my printed notes in his hand and perhaps I can help him. I cannot give him much time.

In regard to the strength of the magnets, it is a very desirable object to put them out of the reach of water. A position *below* the deck (in the ceiling of the cabin) is better than above. But it may be raised above the deck if you think fit. A place upon the deck is the worst of all.

In regard to the strength of the magnets, it is sometimes desirable to place two or more magnets side by side two or three inches apart instead of one. This is better than using one large magnet as the large magnets are seldom made so well.

I am Madam

Your obedient servant

G. B. Airy

His tone said it all. Although supporting her firm as an exponent of his method, he was certainly not about to brook any 'improvement' of it. While she appreciated that he was speaking to her directly and he was willing to show her men personally and to assist them, *his* method was *his* method, and that was that. After her earlier experiences with Beaufort and overstepping the various unwritten lines of decorum and dealings among men, Janet decided simply to keep her mouth shut on this point. She would keep going with her experiments and just not tell him about it. In the meantime, replying graciously on 12 February:

Sir,

I am exceedingly obliged by your attention to my queries regarding the magnets and we now so thoroughly understand the matter, that I shall not have occasion to avail myself of your kind offer respecting my assistants.

I am Sir

Your obliged and obedient servant

Janet Taylor

Besides which, rather than trying to press points with Airy when he wasn't interested in hearing suggestions, she still had her hands full with other matters. In 1846, No. 104 Minories became a 'Post Office Receiving House' on a five-year contract. Letters were given in to receiving houses, usually located in shops and much like the post offices of today, then collected and taken to the Chief Office in London and dispatched with amazing efficiency. Adding the role of 'official receiver' to her repertoire, the logistics of the operation first entailed sorting the letters on flat tables.

Young Jon, who turned seven in May, liked to help in this work, supervised by William Bates or one of the others that George employed to oversee the task. Once sorted, the letters were then marked with the cost of delivery and passed on to the letter carriers for London delivery or bagged for distribution by mail coaches to other towns. New business, such as this, was welcome and diversified the enterprise. It helped to distract from some continuing irritations of the other aspects of the business, particularly the persistent problem of securing charts in a timely fashion.

Bate never delivered enough charts, nor on time. His apparent indifference to the fate of mariners fuelled her indignation. So when one of her regular customers, Captain Robson, lost all his charts when shipwrecked on the coast of China and needed to replace them urgently, Janet wrote directly to Beaufort. Convicts were still being transported to the Australian shores and merchant vessels were travelling with increasing frequency into the waters of the southern hemisphere. The need for charts of the dangerous waters of the Torres and Bass straits lying at the fringes of the Australian Continent, north and south, was pressing. And when captains were sailing they needed their charts, and they needed them *now*. Her messages were overlain with urgency and her frustration with Bate:

> My messenger will call *early* tomorrow morning for your reply. The Captain of the vessel wished me to obtain them if *possible*, which must plead in extente for my troubling you –knowing very well it is no use applying elsewhere.

Beaufort was torn. He felt the same urgency and empathy when it concerned men of the sea, but he still had some attachment to Bate. Old habits of deference died hard, even for one who had earned his laurels many times over, as had Beaufort. Bate was still a man whose family had their own 'bearings'. He had connections. So when Janet implied yet again that it was Bate himself who was the problem, it distressed him greatly. But her plea, scrawled in a note at the bottom of her letter, struck home. You can hear her voice in that simple, potent message: a plea to the heart and to the soul of the Admiralty:

> Would it not be better to let us have a few copies of these Charts by which so many vessels *have* sailed in safety, than to let us be entirely without?

Beaufort complied with such requests, notwithstanding the difficulty, indeed irregularity, of his doing so.

The problem was not just in delays in getting Admiralty charts. They contained many errors; and corrections and amendments took a long time to be incorporated into revised versions. Merchant seamen often preferred private charts, the blueback charts, even though they cost much more than the Admiralty charts. But improving the chances of sailing safely by having the latest charts was priceless. Janet's shop stocked both the Admiralty and the blueback charts as she felt that mariners should have not only what they needed, but what they wanted. Norie charts in particular continued to be popular, although Noric himself had died in 1843. And it was one such Norie chart, of the English Channel, that was purchased by one Captain Rawlinson of the *Tribune* on 7 November 1846 at the cost of 13s, instead of the Admiralty chart for 3s.

At the end of his travels over the next year he used his Norie chart as he wended his way home. As fate would have it, he managed to come to grief, hitting an unmarked reef, and the *Tribune* was lost. Rawlinson survived. Now he sought to blame Janet for selling him the private chart.

XVII

A Fierce Defence and Education of Mariners

When Captain Rawlinson's letter arrived at the Admiralty, concern rippled through its Whitehall chambers. What was an 'Agent for the sale of the Admiralty Charts' doing selling bluebacks in preference? A justification was requested by Beaufort's second assistant, Captain Alfred Miles. Alarmed when she received his 'please explain' letter, Janet immediately put pen to paper:

> 1 Hammet Street
> 16th February 1848

Sir,
I think it best to give the 'explanation' required in Capt. Miles letter to you direct which I will do briefly.

In the first place I regret that Captain Rawlinson was not asked why he selected Norie's Charts at 13/– in preference to that published by the Admiralty at 3/– because you would then have heard the painful truth which the gentlemen in my establishment receive in 99 cases out of 100 from Captains who have the advantage *here* of selecting their charts from the best and most recent publications viz: 'that the Admiralty Channel Chart is on so small a scale and consequently so confused with soundings that it is of no use'.

I have been an agent for Admiralty charts ever since I came to reside in the City, and I think a reference to Mr Bate's books prior to and since that period, will shew that the publicity I gave to them in the Merchant Service where they were not known or scarcely so, will prove that I have been a more efficient Agent than the Admiralty ever had, and it is with regret I so frequently see their charts returned to our shelves, and charts of less merit selected.

It is not the low price of a chart that will induce a man to take that which he considers of no use in preference to one of double its price – neither, I beg you to believe, is it the paltry extra profit I might derive that would induce me to supply one I knew to be incorrect. I have had the Admiralty Channel Chart coloured, framed and mounted in my windows ever since it was published, besides copies of it in my portfolios which are exhibited on all necessary occasions.

I have regularly supplied all the Captains trading between here and the Irish Coast with Admiralty Charts of that Coast, and, since they were published, with the Irish Channel, but there is not one of them that *will* take the Admiralty Channel Chart. I cannot see how I am accountable for Captain Rawlinson's acts, neither can I see in what way his having made the selection he did nearly 18 months ago can have had anything to do with the loss of the 'Tribune'.

I remain Sir

Yours respectfully
Janet Taylor

Beaufort found the logic of Janet's explanation compelling. Perhaps if merchant sea captains were better taught they might not seek to put their own failings onto others. Compulsory examinations surely would be of benefit. Here they were both of one mind. But, for now, the matter of the charts could be settled by a well-placed notice in Janet's shop and in any advertising, so that the Admiralty concerns could be allayed. This was readily done:

Mrs. JANET TAYLOR,
Chart and Nautical Bookseller and Publisher,
Agent for the Sale of Admiralty Charts

———————

Mrs. TAYLOR begs particularly to call the attention of Purchasers of Charts to her Establishment, where no restriction is made in selling the Publications of certain authorities only, to the exclusion of many others of better repute. The best known and most authentic Charts and Sailing Directions are selected from those published by the Admiralty, East India Company, Horsburgh, Laurie, Norie, Hobbs, Wilson, Imray etc. and every care is taken to exclude from her Stock any that may be considered incorrect.

And no more was heard from Captain Rawlinson.

In the meantime, Beaufort was grateful for continued reports of information of errors or amendments needed to the Admiralty Charts and welcomed her regular correspondence on such matters. Business was indeed booming and it came as no surprise that she received a great deal of intelligence of alleged errors in charts, passing them on to Beaufort if she felt they had any credibility.

'A gentleman just returned from ....', or 'One of my Captains', she would write, with news pertaining to charts. One lost his vessel:

> On a sandy point running out to the Eastward of Cape Farewell, the north point of the South Island of New Zealand. He positively asserts that the Longitude of the Cape is laid down on your Chart as well as on several others, nearly 30 miles in error.

(Cape Farewell, situated at the northern most point of the South Island of New Zealand, is a treacherous place. Nowadays there are two lighthouses, the Farewell Spit Lighthouse and the Pillar Point Lighthouse, but in Janet's day there were none.)

Another, Captain McKnight of the merchant ship *Admiral Morrison*, reported that:

> The Chart lately published by the Admiralty is very erroneous, particularly at the entrance and that if a vessel were to attempt to enter by that Chart, she would get on the sand bank that out on rounding the point before getting into Bahrens Bay. He was there at the time HMS *Modeste* got aground. He copied for his own use a chart made by Mr Allen Scarborough, who is sailing out there for the Hudson Bay Company, and if you would like to see it I shall have much pleasure in forwarding it to the Admiralty.

Beaufort leapt at such information, along with the opportunity to meet the men who conveyed it. Immediately he, or Captain Miles, would write in thanks, and welcome a meeting with a captain, such as McKnight, to see the charts and news of reefs, points, sandbanks and anything that should be added to charts.

Janet bundled up McKnight's charts and despatched them to Beaufort and advised that he would be pleased to see him at his convenience. The information provided by McKnight had been confirmed by other sources as well, only serving to underscore Beaufort's appreciation of Janet's continued interventions:

> Madam – I return the charts which you were so kind as to lend me – as I find that Captains Gordon and Killett had sent me plans of the same places – but that does not lessen in the smallest degree the sense I have of your very obliging effort to be of use.

And upon receiving the information about the Cape Farewell chart, Beaufort scribbled the instruction 'Communicate this to Capt. Stokes'. The commander of the steam paddle ship *Acheron*, Captain John L. Stokes was about to undertake a detailed survey of the coast of New Zealand on behalf of the Royal Navy to determine if economic development could be encouraged there. Janet's source was correct. The longitude in the Admiralty chart had been adapted from a survey undertaken by the explorer Jules-Sebastien-Cesar Dumont d'Urville who charted and discovered several Pacific islands, along with mapping the New Zealand coastline during his three-year voyage from France on the *Astrolabe* and *Zelee* between 1837 and 1840. Beaufort was very appreciative:

> Madam – I am much obliged to you for the information about the longitude of New Zealand, in our charts. It was adapted from the survey of Durville – and his logs. In other parts of the group do not differ very widely from Captain FitzRoy's. I should be thankful for any other particulars that he can give on the subject – or if he be in town, if he will be so good as to call on me.

At other times captains would bring her copies of other charts and surveys that she conveyed to Beaufort. One captain 'just returned from the China Seas' left with her a copy of a Dutch survey of the Straits of Rio showing a passage 'both desirable and safe' that was neither in the blueback nor the Admiralty chart. Another 'very clever man in the Merchant Service' brought her surveys of New Caledonia and 'the Carolines' (the Caroline Islands north of New Guinea), where he had been navigating for some time. Due to the 'very imperfect knowledge of the position of most of these islands', she felt sure they would be of use. On each such occasion Beaufort or Miles sent the message that he would be 'most happy' first 'to see the gentleman with the chart of Rio in his hand', secondly to see the author of the Caroline charts 'at leisure'. Always he was 'most obliged' to Janet for giving him such opportunities.

On another front, she maintained an abiding concern about the education of mariners, saying that she was 'devoted entirely to the advancement of education amongst British seamen'. But she was not alone in this aspiration. The decade before, in 1836, James Silk Buckingham had introduced a bill recommending improvements of the British Merchant Service arising out of the deliberations of the committee he had chaired, prompted by complaints about officers in the service. It led to a report on shipwrecks and a bill that included recommendations for the introduction of formal examinations for captains and mates. Janet was a strong supporter of such moves, and, in writing to Beaufort about it, she urged:

> Could the Committee now sitting in the House of Commons have one tenth the experience I have had ... they would without much debate, decide on the momentous importance of there being an examination of Captains and Mates. Much of the existing ignorance may be attributed to the shameful manner in navigation has *been* and *is* generally taught. We know of numberless instances where men are teaching it without knowing anything but the application of rules, for which they cannot account nor properly explain.

Janet also anticipated that the bill would be passed and put herself forward in the role of examiner:

> Events which are at present agitating the minds of the Seafaring World, and which have raised some speculations in my own mind now induce me to request you will, in the suit I prefer, make my cause your own and plead for me as you did on a former occasion. From the Report published by the Committee on Shipwrecks, it appears that an examiner of the Masters and Mates in the Merchant Service will be appointed ...
>
> Test us to the extreme and ascertain whether we are or are not equal to the office of Examiner or, should that post go into higher hands, as *Preparers* for the Examination. Then if you find us worthy, aid me in obtaining (for my husband *nominally*) the situation.

Even at this time, when her enterprise was really in its infancy, she aspired to such endorsement. And of course George was only 'nominal' in this part of the business. Unfortunately, on that occasion, the bill failed in the face of considerable hostility from shipowners and some Merchant Service officers.

But in 1845 the matter came before parliament again. This time Robert FitzRoy, who had commanded the *Beagle* on its epic voyage in 1831, attempted to introduce a bill aimed at improving the British Merchant Service. Once again there was resistance to the introduction of competency certificates as, after all, many men had commanded ships for many years. Although the bill was again unsuccessful, it was only abandoned when the government promised to introduce *voluntary* examinations leading to 'First, Second and Third Class Certificates of Competency for Masters in Merchant Ships'. This was based on assurances from the Board of Trade and, true to its word, the board introduced the anticipated regulations. Much to Janet's irritation, no private examiner was appointed and Trinity House itself conducted the examinations.

Despite the promises being kept, the scheme was far from successful. Right from the outset there was a great reluctance on the part of Merchant Service officers to submit themselves as candidates for the voluntary examinations. Why should they have to be subjected to further tests? Hadn't they been tested where it really counted – at sea? Who were the members of a 'Board of Examiners' assigned to test them? To make matters worse, although the government insisted on the requisite qualifications being held by all officers on merchant ships under government charter, these were but a small percentage of the 30,000 ships in the British Merchant Service at that time. It was also apparent that there were many influential shipowners who considered it prejudicial to their own interests if their patronage, and appointed officers of their ships, were required to include possession of a certificate of competency.

The concept of examinations provided only a limited incentive to men to acquire one of the new qualifications and, in March 1846, the *Nautical Magazine* reported that, in the first five months of the operation of the Board of Trade regulations, only twenty-six serving masters and eight mates had gained certificates. And in the period 1 November 1845 to 1 July 1846 a total of only ninety-seven certificates had been awarded. The *Nautical Magazine* scornfully added that it wasn't known if any of the officers thus qualified had as yet 'received the benefit of any new appointment as the reward for their boldly submitting to the ordeal of this new state of things'. It was not satisfactory at all. But for Janet Taylor's Nautical Academy it presented an opportunity and classes were now offered between the hours of ten and four, and also in the evening from 6 to 8 p.m.

The specific requirements were that for a Third Class Master, the candidate was obliged to be able to find only latitude by meridian altitude, whereas a Second Class Master required, in addition, an ability to find longitude using a chronometer. Only for the rank of First Class Master was the candidate required to have additionally 'a general knowledge of nautical astronomy, including the determination of the latitude by reduction to the meridian, and of the longitude by lunar observations'. Janet adjusted the advertising of her Nautical Academy's programs to reflect the new regulations:

> Mrs Taylor's Academy is under the superintendence of Masters highly qualified for the important situation and she has made arrangements in her Establishment which will be found highly advantageous to Captains wishing to read and prepare for passing as FIRST, SECOND and THIRD CLASS MASTERS; likewise to Officers, Midshipmen, and young men desirous of obtaining such a thorough knowledge of Navigation, as will fit them for the highest grade in their profession. Mrs Janet Taylor's School under the patronage of the Admiralty, Trinity House, and East India Company, offers every facility for acquiring that knowledge, instruction being aided by lectures on Astronomy, the Use of the Globes, and other illustrations tending to simplify and explain the subjects. Separate rooms are appropriated for the different classes and Private Apartments for those who wish to study alone.

The upper school rooms, under the direction of 'a highly qualified master', were used for the preparation of masters and mates in the Navy and Merchant Service. The lower school rooms, under the supervision of 'a mathematical master', were used for other classes. As George had promised, her Nautical Academy was finally living up to its title.

But she no longer had her 'promising genius', James Griffin. While Janet had taken him under her wing and given him all the encouragement she could, he never quite fulfilled her expectations. For his part, Griffin felt under-valued and under-appreciated. He had ambition and a greater sense of himself than had Janet, coming to believe in the publicity in which she had suggested that she had a 'brilliant teacher' at the helm. Not contented with simply quitting, he joined the opposition at the firm Blanchford and Imray, only a few doors up the road at No. 116 Minories. He also emulated his former mistress by publishing, under the Blanchford and Imray banner, his new book, *An Epitome of Practical Navigation and Nautical Astronomy*, curiously an almost identical title to Janet's own book, *An Epitome of Navigation and Nautical Astronomy*.

Upon sighting his latest effort Janet was not so much angry as disdainful. 'How presumptuous!' she scoffed. "*Sanctioned by G. B. Airy, Esq., Astronomer Royal*", indeed!' Her assessment proved accurate and the *Nautical Magazine* agreed on this occasion in the biting sarcasm of the review of Griffin's book:

> Now we are far from saying that a good book cannot find its way into the world from a house in Minories, but we do mean to say that to call this work 'A Complete Epitome of Practical Navigation and Nautical Astronomy' is a downright, deliberate misnomer! It is a treatise on nautical astronomy with some explanations of the method of keeping a journal at sea.

As for the so-called 'testimonials' of Airy, the review was scathing: 'Why this letter should be called a testimonial is beyond our solution.' And to aid the reader, a table of translations of Griffin's comments was given, pricking the bubble of his puffery:

Recommendations	Explanation
'This volume comes before the public with at least four strong recommendations'	This volume comes before seamen with at least four strong recommendations!
1. 'Its author is evidently a practical man.'	1. Of the author's practice we have given proof above!
2. 'It is printed and, technically speaking, it has been read with extraordinary care and accuracy.'	2. A very 'extraordinary' recommendation indeed, technically considered!
3. 'It is honoured by the high sanction of G. B. Airy, Esq., the Astronomer Royal.'	3. See the references to the Astronomer Royal's letters above-mentioned
4. 'And it is dedicated, by permission, to the Right Honourable the Lords Commissioners of the Admiralty. Thus it may be regarded almost as an official publication. At all events, we can unhesitatingly pronounce it to be the best work of its class extant.'	4. Several works have been dedicated to their Lordships merits remaining unimproved and their official character unestablished thereby. Therefore, this cannot be regarded as an official publication. At all events we cannot unhesitatingly pronounce it so.

Where Janet had risen to the stinging attack of a savage review, Griffin crumpled. He was not given the opportunity or he didn't try, but whatever the truth of the matter, he was certainly not in Janet's league. Being associated with her name assisted him initially, even to get a hearing of sorts from Airy, but after that he was on his own. And, on his own, his talents and abilities were shown to be wanting. While Griffin's star went no further, the name of Imray never disappeared from the publishing scene, with the firm of 'Imray, Laurie, Norie and Wilson Ltd.' still publishing charts today in St Ives, Cambridgeshire, England, describing themselves as the 'oldest nautical publishing house in Europe'.

Griffin's departure allowed Janet to recruit others to fill the growing need for skilled teachers, or at least those who could become so under her watchful eye. While they got on with the teaching, Janet continued her publishing ventures. In 1846 she produced an intriguing volume entitled *Diurnal Register for Barometer, Sympiesometer, Thermometer and Hygrometer* that she dedicated to Colonel William Reid, the Governor of the Bermudas (1839–46), Governor of the British Windward Islands (1846–48) and Governor of Malta (1851–58). He was knighted in 1851:

> This little work enables mariners and others to register at any hour, the different readings of the various Meteorological Instruments generally used at sea, by a most simple method; space is also given in the form for recording the direction and force of the wind, the state of the weather &c. on the plan ordered by the Lords of the Admiralty to be adopted for the use of Her Majesty's Navy; it contains also a brief description of the Mercurial and Aneroid Barometers, the Sympiesometer, Hygrometer and Thermometer and the principles on which they are constructed. By Mrs Janet Taylor.

The *Athenaeum* considered it 'a useful work, with excellent directions'. As if responding to her particular interest in weather evident in this publication the heavens responded with a fierce hailstorm that summer, breaking panes of glass all over London, including considerable damage to Buckingham Palace.

Janet also at last completed her *Planisphere of the Stars Accompanied by a Book of Directions*. The *Planisphere* volume contained no text but consisted of several beautifully printed large foldout maps of the heavens (each about one foot by one foot) which were coloured dark blue and, as well as mapping the stars and planets, linked them up with astrological symbols. The *Book of Directions* contained instructions on how to read these maps while also presenting a short exposition on astronomy. (The copy now held by the British Library has a handwritten note on the flyleaf: 'Given to Captain Becher with Mrs Taylor's compliments.')

Both publications proved enduring contributions. The *Diurnal Register* was such a popular and handy book that it remained in print for nearly twenty years, although later with a slightly different title, *Barometers, Air & Water Thermometers, Aerometers, Hygrometers and all kinds of Meteorological Instruments.* The *Planisphere* and *Book of Directions* were still in print seventeen years later, running through seven editions. As the art of 'taking lunars' remained for so many years the crucial test of the good navigator, using stars and planets to find a position at sea, her *Planisphere* achieved the reputation of being the best of its kind anywhere in the world. At the same time Janet kept up regular editions of *Lunar Tables*, publishing the fifth edition in January 1847. The preface revealed a woman confident in her abilities, embracing in her interests, sincere in her faith and passionate in promoting the health and safety of mariners:

Although much is already known by man, and indefatigable as he may be in promoting his energies and extending his knowledge, yet there can be little doubt from what is already known we have still but a very imperfect knowledge of the space around us; which seems filled, as far as the eye can penetrate, with stars in countless myriads. What for centuries appeared but as white clouds in the firmament are now resolvable, by the help of good telescopes, into clusters of stars, some no doubt regular systems like our own and, could the eye be carried still deeper into the regions of space, yet might it rest on worlds still farther remote; and while the contemplation of such vastness strikes insignificant home to our hearts, it makes us unconsciously acknowledge the Omniscience of the Supreme Being 'who telleth the number of stars and collecteth them all by their names' and raises the mind of contemplation of Him in the grandest and most sublime works of nature.

Few men have had more frequent and glorious opportunities or more leisure for such a thing than seamen, whose career is on the bosom of the mighty deep, which is itself an object for meditation; and to them I would recommend a careful search after that knowledge which will not only assist them in their perilous path across the ocean, but lead them to a dependence on Him who can alone guide and protect them in the midst of those dangers which daily and hourly encompass them.

To the untutored mind the heavens may present a confusion of bright objects only distinguished from each other by different degrees of splendour, but the ingenuity and talent of man has so divided, arranged and even numbered them, that the relative positions of the most minute have been determined.

It is to Astronomy we are indebted for the means of measuring *time* for *time*, being deduced from *motion*, it is necessary that *motion* should be uniform, and nowhere can we find that regularity, but in the heavenly bodies; from them likewise, we derive our seasons – thus both the husbandman in the cultivation of his field and historian in recording the rise and fall of mighty nations are alike indebted to the Science of Astronomy.

To the Navigator it is, if possible, of still greater importance, as from the positions and revolutions of the celestial bodies, he is enabled to calculate his exact position on the trackless ocean and to determine the latitudes and longitudes of all places on the globe; inspired with confidence from these circumstances, he fearlessly commits himself to the mercy of the mighty waters, transverses unknown seas and wafts back to his native shores the riches and treasures of other countries which, but for the confidence imputed by the sciences of Astronomy, might have remained as unknown lands.

It would be impossible in the pages of this Work to pursue the subject to any satisfactory result, I would therefore recommend the seaman, anxious to store his mind with the knowledge which will render him a useful and intelligent member of his profession, for several weeks now before the public, and confine my remarks in the following pages, to subjects more immediately committed to *practical* Astronomy, so far as it relates to Navigation.

At the end of 1847 one important chapter in Janet's life closed. On 27 December, at the age of sixty-five, Robert Bate passed away at his Hampstead house in north-west London after several years of ill health. He was but one casualty of the thousands who died in the influenza epidemic that swept the country that winter, targeting especially the young and the old. Apart from the sympathy she had for Bate's widow, Betty, who had helped him in the practice, Janet was acutely aware that it also created an immediate vacancy for the position of Principal Chartseller. She and George discussed it at length and considered presenting a case for them to assume the role.

Although at first keen, she really was very occupied with other things, and, after all, the chartselling really didn't contribute much to their overall financial position. Besides, the Principal Chartseller could not deal with the blueback charts – and they were still very much the preferred chart on many occasions. Janet thought it simply wasn't worth it, as the real interest lay with the bluebacks and there were too many constraints in being the Principal. But George remained unconvinced, and such a chance would not come up again for some time. And so he personally wrote to Beaufort on 3 January 1848:

> Sir,
> Presuming that some alteration may now take place in the Agency for the Sale Of Admiralty Charts, I beg to offer my services as Admiralty Agent. In doing so I wish to recall to your remembrance, that for some years past every exertion has been made in my establishment to promote the sale or the Governments Charts and to give publicity to their publications in the Merchant Service.
> Trusting to your favourable consideration and recommendation of my application.
> I have the honour to be, Sir,
>
> Yours obediently
> Geo. Taylor

The Hydrogapher was bemused. There were conventions in such things, certainly with an established business. Where the widow was willing to continue, and the business of good repute, this was one arena where gender did not seem to get in the way. Married women, as widows, at least had a chance, and many ran businesses – public houses, shops and the like. But in deference to his respect for Janet, Beaufort instructed his assistant to write George a brief note. Quickly he penned six words on the bottom of his letter: 'Tell him to state his terms.'

His application wasn't exactly met with wild cheering at the Admiralty, but rather they put the matter back upon him. What could he do for them? And what did he want them to do for him? Captain Miles wrote:

> Sir – I am desired by R. A. Beaufort to ask (in reply to your letter of this day for the Agency of the Admiralty Charts) the terms upon which you would take it – what connexions you have at the outports and whether you propose to have an auxiliary shop near the Royal Exchange.

George was taken aback at this reply. The Admiralty was quite specific in asking if he planned to open a shop near the Royal Exchange in Threadneedle Street, about four blocks from Janet's business. This area was a marketplace, originally set up by Sir Thomas Gresham in 1566, where London merchants met each day and it had soon become the centre of the country's industry. George had expected that, if granted the role of Principal Chartseller, he would have been able to conduct operations from No. 104 Minories – well, rather, in reality Janet could do so while he continued his other work. She was right. It was too much bother and things were better left just as they were. So, he let it go and Betty Bate stepped into the role.

While the day-to-day business at No. 104 Minories continued its familiar pattern of comings and goings of mariners and the hectic activity of the warehouse, the school, and the domestic life at No. 1 Hammet Street, for many others it seemed as if the world were falling apart again. The French Revolution of 1789, the Terror and the Napoleonic wars that followed were thought to have been long put in the past, but the cracks in the social and political fabric opened wide again when in February 1848 shocking news came from France of a coup that had overthrown the seventy-four-year-old king Louis Philippe.

The restoration of the monarchy in France in 1814 had led to an uneasy stability, but the resurfacing of trouble in Paris again brought back bad memories to those who had suffered in times past. It was said that 'when the throne of the Bourbon collapsed, every throne in Europe trembled'. If it could happen in France, to a much-liked king with a large army in a fortified city, could it happen in England too? Rumours, gossip and alarm rippled across London. Queen Victoria, nearing the end of another pregnancy, this time with the Princess Louise, her fourth daughter, shared the City's alarm. The fall of Paris was echoed in a wave of revolutionary activities across Europe as popular rebellions toppled incumbent rulers once more. Many fled to London as refugees. In her diary Victoria wrote of 'these awful, sad, heart-breaking times' and that 'I feel grown old and serious, and the future is very dark'.

The year was grim not only politically, but also economically. These were the 'Hungry Forties', as they have gone down in history. The Irish potato famine still echoes down the centuries as a time of major national catastrophe. The humble potato, the staple food of Irish farmers, was struck with blight and the crop rotted in the ground. And it was not just one failed year, but another and then another from 1846. The stark choice was to flee or to starve.

It wiped out as many as 1.5 million of the population and generated the great Irish Diaspora, as over a million fled to England, to America and beyond. In England things were also bleak, as Britain struggled with economic depression. Firms were failing. The slums of London, many so close to Minories, were bursting at the seams and the stench and chaos of so many poor souls crammed together made the public health risks of the summers of the late 1840s extreme. The starving immigrants brought typhus with them, the 'Irish fever' as it was dubbed, and over a thousand Londoners perished of the illness in the last months of 1848.

Unrest was fuelled by high bread prices. The Prime Minister, Sir Robert Peel, thought that perhaps the bread crisis could be alleviated by allowing easier importation of grain from the Continent. So on 31 January 1849 he led the removal of the protections of British grain prices through the so-called 'Corn Laws' that had been in force for some forty-five years. This move divided his own Tory party, dominated by landowners who had profited from the barrier to the importation of grain that led to high local grain costs. High wheat prices meant higher bread prices, and these hit hardest in Britain's fast-growing towns and especially its slums. They also stoked the fires of unrest and food riots broke out all over Britain. And as bread prices went up, so did the workers' pressure for improved wages.

On 10 April the radical working class group, the Chartists, a movement that took its name from the People's Charter of 1838, called a large public meeting on Kennington Common clamouring for government action. The queen, her advisers and senior political leaders were very much on edge. How many would respond to the call and attend the meeting? It was just such a gathering that led the rebellious Parisians to overthrow the king and forced him to flee. As the bands of men, banners unfurled, marched through the streets in the days preceding the meeting, they even adapted the tune of the *Marseillaise* to their cause.

The City was on high alert. After several anxious days the queen was sent out of the capital two days before the meeting. Like so many Londoners, the Taylors were anxious as to what might happen. Kennington Common seemed well away from Minories, across the Thames and upriver some way, but the feeling, and fear, of unrest was on everyone's doorstep. Businesses were told to close and the streets were all but deserted except for the processions of workers marching towards the Common and the rows of unarmed police constables that lined the streets. While the mood was agitated, the masses were not, and where hundreds of thousands were anticipated, those that gathered were far fewer than this. The weather also conspired against the mood of the moment and drenched the hardy protesters who, by the middle of the day, began to disperse. Calm returned to London, and to England.

Disaster, in the form of the Continental overthrow of monarchies, had not ensued. And business at No. 104 Minories returned to normal. By the end of the decade Britain could number 200,000 seafarers amongst her population. They all needed teaching, charts, navigational instruments and their compasses adjusted on their many voyages – all the stuff of daily fare for Janet's enterprises.

The Taylor boys found their place in the varied activities of the business as well as finding distraction in the sights of the river so close to them – like the bright red 'blood worms' that appeared in mudbanks at low tide, the freezing of the river in the winter of 1846, the Chinese junk that arrived in 1848 and the demonstration that same year by 3,000 British seamen who processed in a stately line of boats with colours flying to Westminster, supported by guns firing from shore and ships. They were protesting against a proposed amendment to the navigation laws that would allow foreign sailors to work on British ships.

When they were home from school the boys loved to visit the factory. Herbert, ever mechanically minded, was fascinated by the machines that were needed to craft the precision elements of the instruments. Frederick, more mathematically inclined, enjoyed watching the activities of the school and the navigational problems the boys and young men were untangling.

Dite was a different one. Having a love of music, he had shown a talent for the violin. Janet encouraged him in this, so long as it did not detract from his other studies, and enjoyed his contributions to the musical evenings the family shared. But Frederick Wiggins took a shine to him, taking him under his wing and revealing the magical art of compass adjusting. Feeling somewhat overshadowed by his older, and bigger, brothers – he being much slighter in build than they, even accounting for their age differences – Dite was delighted to be singled out in this way. It was such an adventure for him to be taken down to the Channel and to participate in the swinging of ships on the great 'swinging buoys' at Greenhithe before their great voyages on the seas. When he returned to Hammet Street on such occasions he loved to tell his younger brother Jon all about it. Jon's eyes filled with wonder. Such excursions were out of reach for him and he hero-worshipped his brother Dite, who was kindly disposed towards him.

After the unrest of 1848 faded and the economic climate turned demonstratively for the better, Janet's business continued to grow. George took on more men to meet the demands of their clients and by the end of the decade there were over fifty employees, making it five times larger than any similar operation in the United Kingdom today – and nearly three times the size of Bate's workforce in 1820. Business was indeed booming. And on the home front, as the year 1849 drew to a close, their oldest child, Herbert, turned eighteen. Of the other children, Frederick was sixteen; Dite, thirteen; Jon, ten; Ada, almost seven; and Alfred, five. Janet, now forty-five, and George, nearly fifty-seven, surveyed their domain with considerable satisfaction.

The optimism was shared in the royal household as well. The monarchy was secure, there were royal heirs in abundance – two sons, four daughters and the queen was pregnant again – and, in January 1850, Prince Albert was appointed to head a Great Exhibition, to celebrate prosperity, progress and the marvels of the age – and the ascendancy of Great Britain itself.

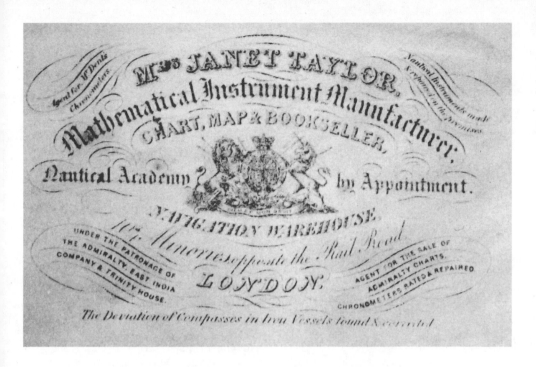

Above: 36. Mrs Janet Taylor Trade Card. (British Science Museum Library Trade Cards Collection)

Right: 37. Logo for Mrs Janet Taylor's Nautical Academy.

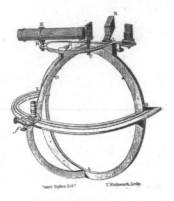

Left: 38. Advert for the Mariner's Calculator. *Flyleaf, Lunar and Horary Tables*, 2nd edition (1834), inside cover.

Below left: 39. Janet Taylor's Mariner's Compass. From Janet Taylor's *Epitome of Navigation and Nautical Astronomy* (1842), p. 6.

Below: 40. Janet Taylor advertisement for compasses for iron ships. From Fitzroy's *The Weather Book* (1863), p. 48.

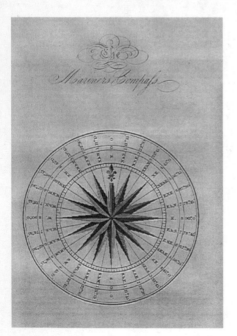

41. A view of Minories area in London in the 1830s. Adjacent properties here had consecutive numbers. For example, Nos 102, 103 and 104 Minories are adjoining and on the same side of the street. From a watercolour by an unknown artist. The original is believed to be in Canada, with a copy held at Guildhall Library, London (No. 1532).

42. 102 Minories, *c.* 1850. Taken from the title page of James Imray's 1851 catalogue. Published in *Mercator's World*.

43. Minories station on the London and Blackwall railway, *c.* 1840. (Public domain)

TABLE XLII.

LATITUDES and LONGITUDES

Of the principal Ports, Harbours, Capes, &c. in the World, from the latest Observations, Surveys, and Charts.

NOTE.—As I considered *all authentic* positions of Places were published for the benefit of the public, I unfortunately copied the Table of Latitudes and Longitudes in Mr. Norie's Epitome, which he obliged me to suppress. For this however I thank him,—for on comparing his Table with those Works on the subject, which are recognized and used by Government, and which ~~Capt. Beaufort and~~ Lieut. Becher of the Admiralty, and Capt. Maconochie of the Royal Geographical Society subsequently lent me, (to whom I take this opportunity of returning my warmest thanks,) I find it to differ from them most materially. For instance, the entire Coast of Africa, according to Capt. Owen's Survey, is wrong; several Islands on the Eastern Coast which must be passed (if not touched) daily, by vessels to India, &c. are laid down from 1 to 5 *degrees* in error; some important points on the South and East Coasts of Italy are many miles from their true positions; and it is with surprise I look at the East Coast of Greenland aslaid down in " the Epitome," where there are errors of from 2 to 10, and even 13 degrees. Indeed discrepances of this nature are too numerous to particularize in the brief space of a note: however, this may be a sufficient hint to the mariner. Mr. Norie insisted that his Tables were constructed according to *private authorities* on which he founded great originality, but I find that, since the suppression of my Copies, he has edited his Tables with some alterations in his boasted original positions; but I think there yet remains numerous instances in which *originality* prevails at the expence of accuracy.

To Mr. John Arrowsmith I am indebted for much useful information on this subject, as well as for the reference he has allowed me to make to his valuable Works.

From the Meridian of Greenwich.

Places.	Lat.	Lon.	times	rise	Places.	Lat.	Lon.	times	rise
	° ′	° ′	h. m.	ft.		° ′	° ′	h. m.	ft.
ENGLAND.					Eddystone Light .	50 11N	4 15W	5 15	18
South Coast.					Ram Head.......	50 19	4·12	5 45	
LONDON, St. P..	51 31N	0 6W	2 7	19	Plymouth Dock .	50 22	4 10	5 30	18
Greenwich, obs. .	51 29	0 0			Drake's Island ...	50 21	4 8		
SheernessFlagStaff	51 27	0 44E	12 0	15	Fowey...........	50 20	4 38	5 30	16
N. Foreland, Light	51 23	1 27	11 15	16	Deadman's Point .	50 13	4 47	5 30	
Deal Castle......	51 13	1 24	11 15	19	Falmouth........	50 9	5 2	5 30	18
S. Foreland	51 8	1 22	11 6	15	Black Head......	50 1	5 4		
Dover Castle.....	51 8	1 19	11 16	20	Lizard Point	49 58	5 11	4 55	18
Dungeness Light .	50 55	0 58	10 50	24	—Penzance	50 8	5 31	4 30	19
Hastings.........	50 52	0 38	10 36		Runnelstone,Beac.	50 2	5 39		
Beachy Head	50 44	0 13	9 45	20	Land's End	50 4	5 42	4 30	
Brighton	50 50	0 8W	10 6	16					
Shoreham	50 50	0 16	9 21	16	*West Coast.*				
Arundel	50 51	0 36	9 20	16	Scilly Islands,				
Owers Light	50 40	0 40	11 0	15	—St. Agne's Light	49 54	6 19	4 40	18
Portsmouth Ch. ..	50 47	1 6	11 40	18	—St. Mary's	49 55	6 17	4 40	18
					The Seven Stones.	50 3	6 6		
Isle of Wight.					Cape Cornwall ...	50 8	5 41	4 25	22
Cowes...........	50 46	1 16	11 0	15	St. Ives..........	50 13	5 28	4 30	22
Bembridge Point .	50 41	1 5	11 40		St. Agnes, Beacon	50 18	5 12		
Dunnose.........	50 37	1 12	8 56		Trevose Head	50 33	5 1		
St. Catherine's Pt.	50 36	1 18	8 30		Padstow	50 35	4 55	5 0	24
Needles Lights ...	50 40	1 34	8 56	9	Tintagel Head	50 40	4 45		
					Hartland Point...	51 1	4 30	6 0	
S. Coast of Eng.					Mort Point	51 11	4 13		
Hurst Lights	50 42	1 33	10 0		Lundy Isle	51 10	4 39	5 15	30
Poole	50 43	1 59	9 0	7	Flatholm Light...	51 23	3 6	6 28	36
St. Alban's Head .	50 33	2 5	7 30		Bristol	51 27	2 35	6 45	12
Weymouth.......	50 36	2 27	6 30	7	Nash Point	51 24	3 33		
Portland Lights ..	50 31	2 27			Mumbles Point ..	51 34	3 57		
Exmouth Bar	50 37	3 22	6 25	14	Worms Head.....	51 34	4 19		
Torbay, Berry hd.	50 24	3 28	6 0	20	Caldy Island	51 38	4 40	6 0	34
Dartmouth	50 20	3 35	6 5	20	St. Gowan's Point	51 36	4 56	5 30	36
Start Point	50 13	3 38	5 55	20	St. Ann's Lights..	51 41	5 9		
Praule Point	50 13	3 43	5 55		Small's Lighthouse	51 43	5 39	5 50	
Bolt Head	50 13	3 48	5 55	20	St. David's Head .	51 55	5 18	6 0	

44. Copy of the page torn by Beaufort from Janet's book with the acknowledgment to him struck through. (UKHO archives)

45. St Katherine Coleman Church *c.*
1811. From *The Churches of London*
by George Godwin (1839). The author
died in 1874.

A Statement of the Deviations of the Compasses on Board the Screw Steamer 'Australian' adjusted at Greenhithe on the 9th day of Augt 1854

True Course	Standard Compass	Compass	Steering Compass	Compass	True Course
North.					N. 0 0 E.
N. by E.					11 15
N. N. E.					22 30
N. E. by N.					33 45
N. E.					45 0
N. E. by E.					56 15
E. N. E.					67 30
E. by N.					78 45
East					S. 90 0 E.
E. by S.					78 45
E. S. E.					67 30
S. E. by E.					56 15
S. E.					45 0
S. E. by S.					33 45
S. S. E.					22 30
S. by E.					11 15
South.					S. 0 0 W.
S. by W.					11 15
S. S. W.					22 30
S. W. by S.					33 45
S. W.					45 0
S. W. by W.					56 15
W. S. W.					67 30
W. by S.					78 45
West					N. 90 0 W.
W. by N.					78 45
W. N. W.					67 30
N. W. by W.					56 15
N. W.					45 0
N. W. by N.					33 45
N. N. W.					22 30
N. by W.					11 15

Adjusted by Mrs JANET TAYLOR, 104, Minories, London.

46. Janet Taylor compass
adjusting report. (UKHO
archives)

MRS. JANET TAYLOR'S
NEW SEA ARTIFICIAL HORIZON.
(TO BE FIXED TO A QUADRANT OR SEXTANT.)

SEVERAL attempts have been made of late years to supply an artificial horizon of such a character as to be adapted for use on board ship. It is probable that nothing will be found so effectual for the purpose as the simple contrivance to which we here draw attention, and which has been brought out by Mrs. Janet Taylor, 104, Minories, London.

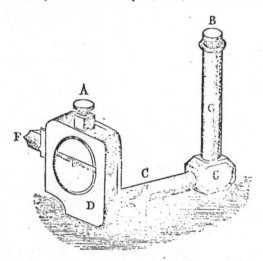

" This Artificial Horizon is fitted to the back of the horizon-glass of the instrument, by means of a clamp-screw in the arm F,—the fittings keeping it in its proper position; for accuracy in observation, put in the telescope and look towards the horizon, then turn the regulating screws A and B, *(if the screws, A and B, are not turned, the mercury does not flow sufficiently freely into chamber D)*, and give the tap C a half-turn, when the mercury will flow into the chamber D, raising a small steel bar E,—the upper surface of which represents the horizon; the altitude of a heavenly body may then be taken by bringing it down to the edge of the steel bar. When the observation is finished, run back the mercury into the cistern G, turn back the tap C, and tighten the screws A and B, to prevent the escape of the mercury; the instrument may then be laid down with safety, without taking off the horizon."

47. Artificial sea horizon. Appeared in *Mercantile Marine Magazine and Nautical Record*, Feb. 1856, p. 71.

48. Janet Taylor letter to son Deighton (Dite) 21 January 1868. See transcription on pp. 239–40. (Authors' collection; photo by Bec Lorrimer)

information dear Rachel about the
Creeks & gullies. I shall try to recollect. Have
you gone out of your way to see the Duke of
Edinburgh — I hope he will behave properly
with you & leave a favourable impression —
he has very much depreciated in public
opinion here, and I can only hope he will
see his errors & retrieve — for he was a great
favorite formerly — and promised to be a
good sensible man — the prince & he
have carried on sad games together. but it is to
be hoped as they grow older, they will grow wiser.
There is constant talk of war, and the continent
looks in a very troubled state — but I trust
shall escape. The Americans seem inclined
to be troublesome — the Fenian movement has
been very alarming, but I hope now we are
fairly roused to look the matter fairly in
the face, things will settle down again. I think
it would all have been stamped out long ago
but for the Americans — You will be well up
in all European affairs, having so many
papers & periodicals, so it is no use saying
much about such things — happily you are
far away out of such troubles — & may quietly
look on at a distance — Have you any snakes
in your part of the country. I find some of the
Australian species are very venomous, so
pray take care — Mr Somerville does, we are
told, & look bright of you, it is pleasant to

49. Janet letter to Dite page 2. (Authors' collection; photo by Bec Lorrimer)

from such friendships – I hope you will like your clergyman – remember to tell me what sort of man he turns out, & whether he truly does his duty energetically & judiciously – what class of people are the inhabitants of Strood – any educated, genteel folks among them? for it would be pleasant to find you could have a few friends at such a distance too far off to bother as morning callers, but near enough to side over to take tea & to off again – such changes are agreeable without being laborious or troublesome – I cannot dear Dite tell you anything about Fred for we have very little communication & but I can he is not doing so well as he might be & am looking forward with much delight going South in the Spring [D.V.] but I shall not stay with them – Poor Emily & her family have all been laid up with scarlet fever but by their last letters all were doing well and she desired Lucas & give her love to both of you & say she would write next mail & send her your new address – Now my very dear Children adieu – this will reach you just after you have passed your second Anniversary of your marriage – God bless you both, & grant you to be blessings to each other for many years to come – I shall think of you on the day & congratulate you in my heart – dear Dite you will remember many such happy days at home – Accept best love & wishes from your affectionate Mother
Janet Taylor

50. Janet letter to Dite page 3. (Authors' collection; photo by Bec Lorrimer)

51. Janet letter to Dite 17 August 1868, from Rotterdam. See transcription on pp. 243–44. (Authors' collection; photo by Bec Lorrimer)

her children. She tells me Frank is very well he has a situation in the Chemical Department in Woolwich Dockyard — & the Aunts has gone to live near there & take care of him. You are better off dear Rachel than I am to be within range of a circulating library — for you will scarcely believe it, there is not a thing of the sort in Bp: Auckland the nearest town to me & here at St. Helens, and I am quite dependent on my friends lending me books for I could not get on without reading in my sister's house. Mr Chester has a very fine collection of books, but they are generally of too sombre & heavy a character for me, altho' there is much I delight in and am glad to meet with, but when one wants the spirits raised, we require lighter reading — by the time you receive this your garden will be in progress and that will be a great charm & delight to you both, for I find you dear Dite are becoming quite a lover of country life & all its belongings. I was shewing your sketch of Exmoor to some friends here last night & they were delighted with it — thought it so artistically done & so interesting as representing a country one hears so much about just now. I am sorry you are having a bad season just as you begin your new life, but as it will only affect you in the shape of dear food, it will not matter much — Thanks for your

52. Janet letter to Dite page 2. (Authors' collection; photo by Bec Lorrimer)

XVIII

The Great Exhibition

God bless my dearest Albert! God bless my dearest country, which has shown itself so great today! One felt grateful to the great God, who seemed to pervade all and to bless all! The only event it in the slightest degree reminded me of was the Coronation, but this day's festival was a thousand times superior. In fact, it is unique, and can bear no comparison, from its peculiar beauty and combination of such striking and different objects.

So wrote Her Majesty Queen Victoria about the opening of the Great Exhibition on 1 May 1851, the culmination and expression of a renewed optimism to replace the political and social disturbances of the late 1840s. It was as if the confidence and pride of the nation and assuredness of Britain's place in the world were concentrated in this magical, exuberant place in Hyde Park – the 'Crystal Palace' as it was dubbed by the *Illustrated London News*. Designed by the gardener-architect Joseph Paxton, it was like an enormous conservatory, 1,851 feet long in honour of the year, and involving 900,000 panes of Birmingham glass and thousands of girders, and high enough to accommodate an existing line of elm trees.

The man above all who steered the project to its magnificent opening was Prince Albert, the queen's husband, who presided over the Royal Commission that organised the Great Exhibition. It was a bold vision, to be a 'Great Exhibition of the Works of All Nations', and it was also essentially a democratic one. It was not just for princes. The appeal for exhibits was aimed to include 'artists of the greatest genius', 'the most scientific agriculturalist' and 'skilful manufacturer', as well as 'the cottager who cultivates any seed of remarkable excellence, the cottager's son who invents any implement of increased usefulness ... the cottager's daughter who works more elegant pillow-lace than the common or plaits straw in a new and more beautiful way'.

The result was ambitious, eclectic and exuberant, with more than 100,000 exhibits in the categories of raw materials, machinery, fine arts and 'miscellaneous', all arranged over nineteen acres. The catalogue itself comprised three volumes. On the opening day, the building, bedecked with multi-coloured flags, sparkled in the spring sunshine and the crowds thronged to catch a glimpse of the queen, Prince Albert and this extraordinary building. Just before midday, nine state carriages arrived and trumpets blared to greet Her Majesty and her two oldest children, a choir of 600 voices broke into the 'Hallelujah' chorus from *The Messiah*, with a full orchestra and organ accompanying. And yet this could hardly be heard over the roaring cheers of the crowd.

The *Illustrated London News* captured the impression of entering the building at its opening:

> The first coup d'oeil of the Building on entering the nave was grand and gorgeous in the extreme. The vast dimensions of the Building, the breadth of light, partially subdued and agreeably mellowed in the nave by the calico coverings placed over the roof, whilst the arched transept soared broadly into the clear arch of heaven, courting, admitting and distributing the full effulgence of the noonday sun the bright and striking colours and forms of the several articles in rich manufactured goods, works in sculpture and other objects displayed by the exhibitors ... were blent into an harmonious ... picture of immense grandeur.

The imagination of London was captured and intrigued from the outset, even by the very process of construction of the world's first prefabricated building, which had begun in Hyde Park in late September 1850. Tickets were even sold to watch and the press kept a keen vigil on progress. The Taylor household, too, was caught up in the excitement – not just about the building, but the competition that enticed artisans and manufacturers to enter their creations. Juries set up by the Council of the Royal Society had power to make awards in respect of the quality of entries, the highest being a Council Medal, the next a Prize Medal and, below this, an Honourable Mention. Now a new obsession gripped Janet. She would contribute 'the sextant of all sextants', to display both the fineness of the quality of the instruments produced by her craftsmen, but also to be a work of beauty in itself, reflecting the aspiration of the Great Exhibition, combining manufactures and fine arts in the one breath.

The months leading up to May were witness to much focused and frenetic activity across Britain to participate in the great spectacle that was to come: to be part of the 'works of all nations'. But it also saw the second of the great censuses of the century. By 1851 the British population had climbed to 21 million and London had become the world's largest city with 2.4 million people crammed into the metropolis. It was time again for the ten-yearly census on the night of Sunday 30 March. The Taylors were still living at No. 1 Hammet Street and there were seven family members present that night. This time their ages were recorded correctly, unlike the census ten years earlier: George as fifty-eight and Janet as forty-six. But where George was described as a shipwright, employing from thirty to sixty men, Janet was relegated to 'wife'. Whether this was a perverse sense of humour on her part, or an inattentive or patronising census recorder, one cannot tell, but history's record is that on the night of 30 March 1851, Janet Taylor's status was 'wife': the universal designation of many women of her time. Together with their parents that Sunday night were five of the children: Frederick (seventeen), Deighton (fourteen), Jon (twelve), Ada (eight) and Alfred (six). There were also six others in the house. Their servants were Elizabeth Ann Juggens, or 'Ann' as she now preferred to call herself, now thirty-five; Sarah Dobson, twenty-five; Hannah Butt, twenty-six; and Caroline Harding, twenty-three. There was also Janet's 'secretary', William Bates, twenty-five, along with Mrs Elizabeth Collett, a visitor.

Such a group of servants, according to the renowned 'authority' of Victorian living, Mrs (Isabella) Beeton, placed the Taylors firmly in the respectable end of the middle-class bracket with an income of about £1,000 per annum. Meanwhile, the building at No. 104 Minories was noted as 'uninhabited' as the business was locked up after classes were finished for the day. Other members of the Taylor family elsewhere that night were their eldest child Herbert, now aged nineteen, along with all three of George Taylor's children, all now making their own way in life.

Just around the corner at No. 103 Minories, the Taylors' old address, the young Levy family also duly filled in their census forms. They were part of the Sephardic Jewish population of London, descendants of refugees who had been fleeing across the Channel since the eleventh century, and with the Ashkenazi Jews from the seventeenth century, like 'Fagin', classically immortalised in Charles Dickens' *Oliver Twist*, they formed a small, but important minority of 20,000 in mid-nineteenth-century London. Carefully listed at No. 103 that night were the head of the house, Alexander Levy, aged twenty-seven, a merchant shipper born in Middlesex; his wife, Julia, aged twenty-four, born in Houndsditch, and their young daughter, Ester, seven months. With them were also listed their two servants: Rebecca Abraham, aged twenty, born in Hackney, and Eliza Allen, aged eighteen, born in Bishopsgate.

Right on the corner of Hammet Street and Minories was No. 102, into which James Imray's 'Nautical Warehouse and Naval Academy' had recently moved. This business had been further up the road, at No. 116 but, as George had rightly predicted, being closer to the docks made a much better location. Once Minories was bisected by the Blackwall Railway viaduct, Imray took the first opportunity he could to move the business to the Thames side of it and, like No. 104, it was also uninhabited on census night, having shut up shop for the day. For their home, Imray and his family lived in Park Terrace, Brixton Road, a neighbourhood that attracted the prospering merchant middle class of the time. Meanwhile in the 'hole in the wall' nook under the viaduct, the young widow Eliza Mills, twenty-two, had set up shop as a tobacconist, with her sister Mary Ann Rugen, twenty-five, and her baby son, John, aged two.

George's designation 'shipwright' was a rather loose one. He was not a member of the livery company of shipwrights, so it was a general description of his involvement in the manufacturing side of things and recognised the increased role that he was playing in recent years. As many men who had seen service at sea, George liked a drink, but his drinking had become heavier over the years of involvement as a publican. It had taken a toll on his health and his liver had taken a beating. He had moved increasingly out of the frontline business and into other roles. Building the manufacturing business with Janet, and managing the men, provided him with a useful and constructive focus.

But George also wondered if there might be a chance at the Admiralty Chart Agency again. Betty Bate was now in her sixties, and he had heard gossip that she was about to retire. This prompted him again to try his luck again with Beaufort:

Sir,
Understanding that the agency for the sale of Admiralty Charts and other Government publications is again likely to be unsettled, I beg to offer myself as a Candidate for the appointments, feeling assured from my own references and extensive connections, that I have great opportunities of promoting the sale of all Admiralty publications, particularly of the Charts, being uninfluenced by private interests.
   I remain Sir

Your obedient servant
George Taylor

Beaufort was rather surprised by George's request and hastily scribbled a note on the back to his offsider, Becher, with instructions to check whether a vacancy was really imminent. It simply said: 'Is Bate going to give up?' Sadly for George the answer was no, as Becher advised him:

> Sir – I am desired by Sir F. Beaufort to inform you in reply to your letter of this morning on the Agency of the Admiralty Charts that he is not aware of any thing being unsettled about it as alluded to by you.
>
> A. B. B.

As it turned out, this was less than honest as Betty Bate was indeed about to retire and moves were already underway in the Admiralty to replace her – but not with George. Without advertising for expressions of interest, the Principal Agency was awarded to her foreman and shop manager, John Dennett Potter. With side whiskers, always in a frock coat and top hat, the necessary black silk plush adornment of the sartorially dressed in the 1850s, Potter became the epitome of the Victorian businessman. In fact, he proved an inspired appointment and it was the making of him, going on to operate twenty-four sub-agencies in England and a further thirty-two internationally during his forty-five years in office.

And then, on 1 May 1851, the Great Exhibition opened. All of London went to this show of shows and railways ran crowded excursion trains from all over the country. Visitors included two notable octogenarians, one being Rear Admiral Sir Francis Beaufort, who obtained that rank on his retirement from the Navy in October 1846 and was knighted in April 1848, now aged eighty. The other was Arthur Wellesley, 1st Duke of Wellington and the hero of the Battle of Waterloo, now aged eighty-three, who went several times, strolling from his house at Hyde Park Corner, and on each occasion being mobbed by his admirers. By the time the exhibition closed on 15 October, over 6 million people had paid their shilling to visit it, many more than once. It touched the whole of Britain, something Prince Albert recognised when in the opening of the exhibition he had said that 'we have to acknowledge the great readiness with which persons of all classes have come forward as Exhibitors'.

The Great Exhibition was the first international display of manufactured products and set the precedent for the many international expositions that followed during the next hundred years. In speaking at the opening of the exhibition, Prince Albert stated that 'the number of Exhibitors whose production it has been found possible to accommodate is about 15,000 of whom nearly one-half are British'. The remainder, he continued, represented 'the productions of more than forty foreign countries, comprising almost the whole of the civilized nations of the globe'. The physical presentation of exhibits reinforced this dichotomy. In the western part of the building were grouped 'the productions of [Her] Majesty's dominions'; in the eastern were placed those 'of foreign countries': thirty-four of them, in fact.

But given that this was an exhibition in Britain, with such a preponderance of British invention and imagination on display, it is not surprising that it was the British goods that attracted the most attention – Britain *versus* the rest of the world – ranging from the huge and ostentatious to the quaintly bizarre. The British half of the Crystal Palace was dominated by machinery and inventions; the half for the 'rest of the world', largely by art. The industrial and mechanical exhibits included steam engines and rolling stock, 'freezing machines' and a complex 'pen-knife'. A simple but potent expression of the steam age was the gigantic block of black coal weighing twenty-four tons on prominent display. A similarly potent expression, this time of Britain's imperial sway, was the Koh-i-noor diamond, acquired in 1850 after the Sikh wars and the annexation of the Punjab, which had taken place between 1845 and 1849. Intermingled with such exhibits were things as intriguing as the fountain that bubbled eau-de-cologne; the rabbits carved from fruit pits, contributed by Prince Albert's brother Ernest; and the items of clothing including corsets embroidered with the royal arms, 'unpickable' pockets and the exhibit of bonnets made by Australian convicts from palm leaves. The statuary attracted great attention, most especially the nudes, which the Earl of Shaftesbury demanded should be decently covered.

William Makepeace Thackeray, the great nineteenth-century novelist and satirist, captured the universal and popular appeal of the building and its myriad exhibits through the persona of 'Mr Molony':

> Amazed I pass
> From glass to glass,
> Deloighted I survey 'em;
> Fresh wondthers grows
> Before me nose
> In this sublime Musayum!
>
> ...
>
> So let us raise
> Victoria's praise,
> And Albert's proud condition,
> That takes his ayse
> As he surveys
> This Cristial Exhibition.

Another group of exhibits comprised the nautical ones, such as a scale model of Liverpool docks, with 1,600 fully rigged ships, as well as a wide range of instruments – including Janet's contribution. Recorded in Section X of Volume One of the official illustrated catalogue, covering 'Sextants, Quadrants etc.', was her magnificent and flamboyantly ornate sextant, entry No. 350 in Class VIII: 'by Taylor, Janet, 104 Minories, manufacturer – sextant for measuring angular distances between heavenly bodies'. But it was much more than a sextant, as she had sought to combine the principal aspirations of the exhibition in one, arts and manufacturing, reflected in the Royal Society that had championed the Great Exhibition, the Royal Society 'for the encouragement of Arts, Manufactures and Science'.

Her sextant was to be a metaphor for each of these elements and was designed and constructed especially for the Great Exhibition. The radius was six inches and at the centre of the instrument was the Prince of Wales crest, in the German of the Hanovers, '*Ich Dien*', 'I serve', which was also on the box. Just as the prince's crest committed him to serve his country, the sextant was an instrument that served the mariner. It was an elegant, artistic combination of metaphor, allegory and practicality. The prince himself was only eleven years old, but Janet felt sure that the royal family, particularly Prince Albert, would appreciate the nature of her endeavour.

Unfortunately, the elegance of her creation was lost on the jury. In the section relating to 'Instruments made in the United Kingdom', it was simply reported that Janet Taylor had exhibited a sextant 'intended for show rather than use' and there was no mention of any award. The instrument itself was described as being used for calculating longitude by lunar distances rather than the rapidly fashionable chronometer. The award in the sextants section went, instead, to a 'Mr Simms', while an honourable mention went to a 'Mr Barrett' for his several sextants. A 'Mr Crichton' also received a mention and a medal; but Janet's work was not appreciated for what it was. 'Intended for show rather than use' – that simple, but patronising judgment – utterly missed the point of her endeavour. It was dismissed as pretty, rather than being given a fair assessment as a scientific instrument; one was seen as incompatible with the other. Her disappointment was somewhat offset, however, by joy in the Taylor household when, on 31 August 1851, in the middle of the Great Exhibition, Janet's stepson George Taylor Jane, a merchant seaman, married Esther Elizabeth Slater at the Parish Church of St George in Middlesex. Esther, a tailor by profession, was illiterate and signed her name with an 'X'.

When the doors of the Great Exhibition finally closed it had found an enduring place in the imagination of the nation – and left a challenge as to what to do with the much-loved building. It was conceived as a temporary structure, but it had found a place in the hearts of Londoners and it could not simply be dismantled. Funds were secured by Paxton for its purchase and, in 1854, it was reconstructed on the wooded parkland summit of Sydenham Hill. Sadly, the Crystal Palace burned down in a spectacular blaze in November 1936. Despite there being eighty-eight fire engines, 438 men from four fire brigades and 749 police officers on duty that fateful night, none of the structure could be saved. As for Janet's sextant, it was indeed presented to the young Prince of Wales, later King Edward VII, and gratefully accepted notwithstanding the disinterest of the examiners – a reflection of the connection established with the royal family since the days of her childhood and her scholarship at Queen Charlotte's school. The sextant ultimately passed to Queen Mary, the wife of King George V, and on the king's death in 1936 it was presented to the National Maritime Museum in Greenwich where it remains today, occasionally brought out for display.

With the closure of the Great Exhibition it was time for Janet to focus more on the day-to-day business at No. 104 Minories. There were new products to promote: like Peacock & Buchan's Composition for preventing the fouling of iron ships, for which she was an agent, promoted in *The Times* on 29 January 1852. And, of course, there was the education of mariners, and her children, still at the top of the list.

XIX

Educating Mariners
and Their Sons

By 1850 it had become increasingly obvious that the scheme of voluntary examinations for merchant seamen established in the mid-1840s was a complete failure and by December that year the government decided to take decisive action. This time merchant seamen would have no choice when the Board of Trade at last introduced compulsory examinations.

Initially for those in foreign-going ships, Local Marine Boards conducted the examinations and successful candidates were awarded certificates of competency at five different grades:

Second Mate (17 years of age with four years at sea)
Only Mate (18 years of age with four years at sea)
First Mate (19 years of age with five years at sea)
Ordinary Master (21 years of age with six years at sea)
Extra Master (one year as an Ordinary Master)

A second mate was required to find latitude by meridian altitude; the first mate was additionally required to find longitude by chronometer; and the ordinary master was required additionally to find latitude by a star. The extra master's certificate was declared as being 'intended for persons as were desirous of obtaining command of ships and steamers of the First Class'. Only at this stage did the navigation syllabus state, 'As such vessels frequently make long voyages to the East Indies and Pacific etc, the candidates will be required to work a lunar observation by both sun and star ...'

Assuming that these syllabuses were going to reflect the methods of finding longitude in use in the Merchant Service in the coming years, it was apparent that the calculation of longitude by chronometer would soon supersede calculations using lunar distance. As a result, Janet knew that the usefulness of works like her popular *Lunar Tables* was coming to an end, and that a change in the subjects taught in her Nautical Academy was required. She quickly amended her advertising:

> The Upper School Rooms, under the direction of a highly qualified Master, are devoted to the preparation of Masters and Mates in the NAVY and MERCHANT SERVICE; and the recent alterations in the Navigation Laws, rendering it necessary that the science of Navigation should be taught, with more attention to its fundamental principles, the Lower School Rooms are superintended by a Mathematical Master, and every care taken that the junior pupils may be progressively fitted for the highest grade of examination, as they become qualified for it by age.

In addition to the terms for her courses on specific subjects, such as Navigation, Algebra, Geometry, Astronomy, Physics and Mechanics, there appeared the following list of fees for the new courses:

> For preparing Masters and Mates for Examination, under the New Regulations of the Board of Trade:

Extra Master	£3	3	0
Ordinary Master	£2	2	0
Only and First Mate	£2	2	0
Second Mate	£1	1	0

The hours of attendance continued to be 10 a.m. to 4 p.m. during the day and 6 p.m. to 8 p.m. in the evening.

As Imray was also operating a nautical academy only two doors away, Janet's advertising sought to distinguish her operation as superior, 'By Special Appointment', with the royal seal of approval for her academy, as well as the patronage of the Admiralty, Trinity House, East India Company *and* the awards from the kings of Holland and Prussia. (She did not, however, mention the Pope – having learned her lesson from her plea for recognition to the Prime Minister, it was better not to refer to His Holiness.) In addition to instruction, Janet was also able to offer something more personal – 'Private apartments for those wishing to study alone' and a particular pastoral care:

> Mrs Taylor's Establishment offers superior advantages, as she is able to place those pupils who have no relatives in town, under the care and superintendence of families, where they will receive domestic comfort and attention when not engaged at the Academy.

In 1851 her pupils and mariners in general were able to use the ninth edition of her *Epitome of Navigation*. This expanded and updated volume was massive, containing forty-eight pages of introduction, seventy-five pages on navigation and 169 pages on astronomy. These 292 pages in total comprised her original work, while the remaining 329 pages were simply nautical tables. Perhaps goaded a little by the presence of Imray's business, in the preface to this edition Janet also sought to assert the significance of her contribution to the nautical world:

> In launching this enlarged edition of my Epitome of Navigation before the Public, it will be unnecessary to enter into a detailed account of its contents. The slumbering spirit of research on this subject, which I awakened into activity, now nearly 20 years ago, has gone on adding improvement to improvement, and book to book, until the tide of information has swollen nearly to overwhelming my own little bark, which then was nearly alone on the wide ocean of mental darkness, which at that time overspread the Nautical World.

Janet was not one to be daunted by the claim of others in her domain – it *was* she who had 'awakened' the slumbering, even dormant, 'spirit of research' in this field – particularly those who were surprised, if not aghast, to find a woman venturing into such territory, and catapulted into action by her, yes, impertinence!

The ninth edition also explained the mathematical concept of logarithms, Janet's preferred technique for the multiplication and division of numbers. Although she properly credited the Scottish mathematician Baron Napier with their discovery, she went to great pains to provide her own examples of how they should be used. Seizing the opportunity, she imparted an eloquent account of her view of 'the science of astronomy', which she imagined as 'so beautiful in itself as a study, leading the mind of man into close contemplation of the mightiest works of his Creator, and which, in its practical application, is of such vital importance to the navigator', a view that she had expressed earlier in her introduction to the *Planisphere*.

While the education of other people's sons occupied a large part of the daily business at No. 104 Minories, Janet also had to focus upon the careers of her own children. While her eldest son, Herbert, had embarked on an apprenticeship as an engineer, her second son, Frederick, now expressed an interest in being made a Master's Assistant in the Royal Navy. He had often spoken with his older half-brother George about his career in the Merchant Navy and he watched attentively as the young men streamed into his mother's classes at the academy. It was now, finally, that he decided that he wanted to follow this path as well, and if he qualified directly as a Master's Assistant, he would not require actual service at sea.

All he would need was a knowledge of mathematics and a practical acquaintance with a sextant and making observations for determining latitude and longitude – and these he had already gained from his mother. But he had left his run too late, if only by a slight margin. He had turned nineteen years old only four weeks earlier on 4 October, and the rules stated that the applicant must *not* be over the age of eighteen. If there were any leeway in this rule, he would need friends in high places to press his case. And that's where his mother came in.

Janet wasted no time in enlisting the support of both Beaufort and Sir John Frederick William Herschel, son of the famous Sir William Herschel, arguably the greatest astronomer of the nineteenth century, having fixed the positions of over 380 stars between 1821 and 1823. In ordinary circumstances she wouldn't have bothered such extremely powerful and eminent men, but Janet had run up against bureaucratic intransigence in face of the age stipulation and she needed to use whatever allies she could find. Her judgment was well placed, as both men were more than happy to oblige, giving an indication of the respect she commanded. Perhaps she had, indeed, earned the description of those whom Beaufort admired when he wrote to Herschel, nearly twenty years earlier, that

> there are so few opportunities for serving those whom we admire and esteem that when they offer I seize them with avidity.

Beaufort had already demonstrated this on many occasions where Janet was concerned. And, at Herschel's suggestion, he provided a testimonial in support of Frederick's case, writing on 12 November 1852:

> The long services of the Grandfather and the brilliant talents of the father are all within my own personal knowledge and now to those claims the widow and the son may be added the wish their Lordships will no doubt feel anxious to comply if possible with the wishes of a man as high in the estimation of the whole world as Sir John Herschel.

While this was enthusiastic and positive, it was a little precipitant in describing her as a widow. Poor George was certainly failing, but his obituary would be ten months away. What is particularly notable in Beaufort's letter, however, is the recognition of George as a man of 'brilliant talents', acknowledging both his service at sea and in civilian life, and also the contribution of his father as a naval man.

While waiting to hear the outcome of her petition on behalf of Frederick, Londoners close to the river, like the Taylors, watched anxiously as its waters rose. Just two years earlier, during the winter of 1850, the waters had risen so high that the furnaces at the gasworks in Wandsworth had been extinguished and the neighbourhood had been consigned to total darkness. And once again, this time for two whole months, it had rained and there were floods in the upper reaches of the Thames. Then, on 17 November, the cry went out, 'Water's over!', that signalled that the great river had overtopped her banks. It became known as 'the Duke's flood', because it upset the funeral hearse of the Duke of Wellington as it was making its way towards London for a state funeral the next day. The duke had died on 14 September and, after lying in state at his home in Kent, he was being brought to London.

The muddy streets hampered the progress of the enormous funeral carriage, which needed twelve horses, borrowed from a brewery, to drag its eighteen tons through the mud of Pall Mall towards St Paul's cathedral. It was then only through the intervention of sixty strong men, buoyed by the goodwill and sentiment of the crowd, lamenting the passing of their much-loved military champion, that the 'Iron Duke' was finally borne into the Cathedral. Behind him came his horse, with boots set backward in the saddle's stirrups, in honour of the fallen hero. Minories was sufficiently high above the river to be clear of the flood water, but as the waters receded the stench of the debris, a mixture of mud and sewage, hung in the air for weeks.

By the end of November 1852 Janet learned the fate of Frederick's application. The support of Beaufort and Herschel might have secured his admission to qualification as a Master's Assistant were it not for the zealous Rear Admiral Sir Geoffrey Thomas Phipps Hornby, currently serving a term as the Second Naval Lord of the Admiralty. His quick reply to Beaufort had been short and to the point:

> I am sorry the Regulations do not permit her son into the Service as M. Asst. after 18 years.

But Beaufort was not to be deterred so easily and suggested, as an alternative, that Frederick could be appointed a Second Master. This opened up a new pathway and Beaufort sent the requisite qualifications to Herschel to explore with Frederick:

> To qualify an officer to receive a commission as Second-Master, he must have served at least six years at sea, three of which in her Majesty's Navy

as Midshipman or Master's Assistant; or having served six years at sea, shall actually been one year or more Master; or two years chief Mate, or three years inferior .... He shall pass such examination as the Admiralty may from time to time direct; but no candidate shall be examined before he shall have attained the age of 19 years nor after the age of 35.

Although the age issue was overcome, in this new role he would be required to spend at least six years' service as a seaman or apprentice. Disinclined to take up this option, Frederick decided to abandon the whole idea and six years later he married and went to live with his wife Elizabeth in Egypt. As it turned out, the three warrant ranks in the Royal Navy of Master, Assistant Master and Second Master were all later abolished in 1868.

But Janet had no time to dwell on Frederick's fortunes as during the year after the Great Exhibition George's condition had become increasingly worse. His bouts of hepatitis were followed by his body becoming bloated with fluid retention, or 'dropsy' as it was called (from the Greek *hydor*, meaning water), symptoms of cirrhosis of the liver. Through summer he was deteriorating rapidly, his heart now starting to fail, as well as his liver. It pained her greatly to see this once strong, physical man almost melt before her eyes. By evening his legs and feet were swollen and he could hardly manage the stairs, while in the mornings his whole face had blown up like a balloon.

By now he had given up all his interests as a publican, retaining only a nominal managerial role at Meux's brewery located on the corner of Tottenham Court Road and Oxford Street. Fulfilling this role had become too much of a struggle. A bedroom was set up for him on a lower floor at No. 1 Hammet Street. Janet had to face the fact that her husband was now dying and she couldn't be sure how long he would survive. When the Duke of Wellington died in September and the whole nation grieved, it only reminded her how soon it would be time for her to mourn again.

With the world inside No. 1 Hammet Street now focusing upon the declining health of George, at the beginning of 1853 it was a great struggle for her to publish the fourth edition of her *Directions to the Planisphere of the Stars*. They barely noticed when the bells again rang from the Tower in recognition of another addition to the royal household when the queen gave birth to her eighth child, another son, Leopold, in April. This time Victoria had asked for chloroform, applied to a handkerchief held over her nose, joining a small but growing number of women who had claimed the space of childbirth as a woman's space. And with the birth of Leopold, the queen blessed her doctor, chloroform and Providence. Sadly, though, this child had the genetic illness that was to curse the royal bloodline, haemophilia, although it would take a little time for this to become clear.

As the months passed, George's condition became worse and worse, and the strain was beginning to take its toll on Janet. By the end of June it was obvious that he was not going to recover. For nearly two years he had suffered chronic hepatitis and, combined with dropsy and jaundice, he was now in his last days. Whatever the ups and downs of their relationship, George was the father of their eight children and they had been together twenty-four years. He had tolerated, accepted and encouraged her business activities, no matter how at odds they may have seemed with the ideals of Victorian womanhood and marriage. His last will and testament reflects, ultimately, the respect he had for her.

On 1 July, knowing his days on this earth were numbered, he made arrangements for his will to be drawn up. Preferring her to all other claimants on his bounty, he left her everything:

> I give devise and bequeath to my dear wife Janet all my real and Personal Estate and Effects whatsoever and wheresoever to hold to her and her heirs executors administrators and assigns absolutely And I appoint my said wife Executrix of this my will.

Having made peace with his God and with his conscience, it was now just a matter of time, and, on 12 September 1853 at the age of sixty-one, George Taylor passed away in the family home. Janet was exhausted and overwhelmed at this moment, so much so that she could not face having to arrange the death certificate. It was their son Frederick, now aged nineteen, who undertook this sad task. A brief announcement appeared the next day in the deaths column of the *Times* newspaper:

> On the 12th instant, George Taylor, Esquire, of No. 1 Hammet Street, America Square.

A true gentleman in life, he was accorded gentlemanly status in death: 'esquire'. Nothing else needed to be said.

And now, at the age of forty-nine, Mrs Janet Taylor was a widow.

XX

Wars

Two years of watching George's suffering had left Janet feeling empty and, although in a household full of people with a large business to oversee in adjacent premises, she felt utterly alone. And right at the moment when she felt she could sink no further, William Reynolds, the foreman of the instrument side of her operation, decided to leave her. For some time now, he had been restless. Reynolds was a fine craftsman with a reputation for high quality work and had been thinking about branching out on his own. In deference to Janet's plight, he waited until George had finally passed away, but the death was so lingering that frustration had set in.

Within weeks of the funeral, Reynolds tendered his resignation and immediately opened his own business a stone's throw away, knowing full well she would be furious at his chosen location, at No. 82 Minories, almost directly across the road – a prime location for the nautical community. His advertisements in the *Mercantile Marine Magazine and Nautical Record* soon proclaimed that he was 'Formerly Apprentice to Mr JOHN GRAY of Liverpool and late Manufacturing Foreman to Mrs JANET TAYLOR, London'. Reynolds did not want George to know of his plans and so he waited until after his death to make his announcement, forcing Janet to find a new foreman to oversee her instrument-making operations.

She only managed to cope by allowing her secretary William to manage all the day-to-day matters – ensuring that their clients' compasses were adjusted when required, and making sure that Wiggins knew where he had to be and when. The adjusting business had been growing steadily and there was no room or time for grieving in her business world. All manner of merchant ships now sought out the compass adjusting of her firm. Some of them included the screw steamship ('SSS') *Australian*, swung on 22 September (just ten days after George's death) and the

2,552 ton steamer *Croesus* that left on its first voyage from Southampton to Sydney on 11 January 1854; the steamships *Sydney* and *Australian* (for the Australian Company); *Haddington* and *Himalaya* (for the Peninsular and Oriental Company, or 'P & O') – the enormous 3,438 ton steamer, then the biggest in the world and twice the size of any other ship in the P & O fleet, swung on her maiden voyage;[20] the *Empress* and the *Iron Age*; the sailing ship *Typhoon*; the mail steamer *Guanabara*.

As autumn turned into winter, the familiarity of the detail gave her reassurance in the months following George's death. She now focused on the reports of Wiggins, checking them, discussing with him the deviations through all the points of the compass, including the relative differences in the azimuth and steering compasses, the placement of the binnacle, along with, at times, the negligence of the crew. Poor Wiggins. He was used to her intense interest in his work, but it had become relentless. He didn't complain, appreciating that her husband's passing had really taken its toll on her, but he wished that Janet would give him more freedom, and trust him more.

Janet also pored over the reports from her captains as they returned to port, providing a distraction and drawing her attention back to the thing she held so dear: the safety of mariners on the seas. Without a reliable compass, their lives were constantly in jeopardy. Merchant ships were now criss-crossing the world in trade and bearing the great exodus of peoples seeking their fortunes and new lives in the colonies of the British Empire. Adjusting for deviation on short voyages was one thing, but adjusting over longer distances, especially over the change in hemispheres, was quite another, as Matthew Flinders had shown. Those endeavouring to keep ahead of the scientific challenges of magnetic interferences of all sorts relied on the first-hand observations of mariners. As each of the ships returned to port, Janet anxiously awaited the reports of her captains on the performance of the compasses and their deviation over distance. There was still so much to be learned.

At around noon on Thursday 19 January 1854, the 230-foot three-decked White Star Line Royal Mail ship, the *Tayleur*, was sailing from Liverpool to Melbourne on her maiden voyage. There were over 650 passengers and crew on board, many of them seeking their fortunes in the goldfields of the colony of Victoria in Australia, where gold had been discovered in 1851, and new lives in a new country. But during the first night of sailing the wind began to blow, and all Friday the *Tayleur* struggled against it. A howling gale set upon them and, within forty-eight hours of sailing, they ran into a heavy fog. The twenty-nine-year-old Captain Noble and his crew had no choice but to rely solely upon the compasses. They thought they were sailing south; but in fact they were sailing west, directly towards the coast of Ireland. At about ten o'clock on Saturday morning they sighted land – but not where it was supposed to be. It was the island of Lambay, thirteen miles from Dublin.

The captain threw the helm to starboard, driving her in 'broadside' to the treacherous cliffs, but it was to no avail. Passengers had the perilous choice of jumping into the freezing winter seas, being dashed on the rocks, or clinging to whatever of the sinking wreck they could. The lifeboats were pointless in face of such treacherous conditions. The heavy weight of the women's clothing, especially in winter, dragged them down. Many clung vainly to the rope bridge, created as a temporary link to the shore, but they could not muster the strength against the pounding seas. Only three women out of 200 were saved. The crashing waves continued to drag the sinking ship further under water; and with each one that smashed upon the ship, scores of passengers, by now desperately clinging to the broken hull, were dragged into the churning seas. By the time it was over, 370 lives were lost. Like the *Titanic*, another White Star Line vessel, the location of the *Tayleur* remained undetected for many years. She was eventually found in 1959 some thirty miles off the south-east corner of Lambay Island in the first bay below the falling rocks, about 120 feet out and in only fifty or sixty feet of water.

The *Tayleur* was the largest and supposedly safest merchant ship afloat. The compasses had been adjusted in Liverpool before leaving, using Airy's method. Who, then, was to blame? The recriminations were swift, in an attempt to determine who, or what, was at fault. The culprit, it seemed, was the adjustment of the ship's compasses. The verdict of the Dublin County Coroner, for example, was that:

> This deplorable accident occurred in consequence of the highly culpable neglect of the owners in permitting the vessel to leave port without the compasses being properly adjusted or a sufficient trial having taken place to learn whether she was under control of the helm or not.

The issue of whether they were or not opened a chasm of divided opinion in the nautical world and it was once more to bring Janet into the orbit of the Astronomer Royal, George Airy.

The steering compass of the *Tayleur* had been adjusted at Liverpool using Airy's method immediately prior to her departure. The judgment prompted the Reverend Dr William Scorseby, for fifteen years highly critical of Airy's technique, to intensify his attack. In Liverpool in September 1854, at the twenty-fourth meeting of the British Association for the Advancement of Science, the Reverend Dr took the opportunity to express his views in his paper, 'On the loss of the *Tayleur* and the changes in the Compass in Iron Ships'. The Association was established in 1831, 'a Low Church version of the High Church Royal Society', and Scoresby was a founding member. Once more he asserted his view that Airy's mechanical system of adjustment by fixed and permanent magnets was 'not only delusive, but calculated to become the occasion of serious danger'. In particular he suggested that the magnetic signature of a ship, established during its building, was essentially unstable and could change at sea under the pounding of the waves or the effect of the ship's engines, and, if the magnetic signature could change, fixed magnets (according to Airy's method) could be a danger. In the case of the *Tayleur*, Scoresby concluded, *this* was the major contributory cause of her loss. In short, Airy was to blame:

> This ship's magnetism did obviously change, and the permanent magnets seriously augmented the new errors produced on the compasses. And, though in this instance the direction of operation of the adjusting magnets was but incidental, the effect, so far as the authorized reports may guide us, was fatal; – so that had there been no adjusting magnets the captain would have been guarded against the delusion that he was making a fair course down the [Irish] Channel, and would have been in a very different position as to safety ... By attempting to adjust a changeable influence by a permanent influence, they were liable to produce an aggravation of error.

This lecture caused serious alarm. One 'gallant officer' present for the lecture cried out, pleadingly, and with evident frustration, 'Why, you have upset all our plans; you have told us compasses cannot be trusted. How are our iron ships to be navigated? Show us the remedy!'. Ripples of nervousness flashed around the community of underwriters and shippers in Liverpool and, for a time, they refused to allow their cargoes to be loaded in iron ships. The lecture ignited a public and acrimonious dispute between Airy and Scoresby and opened the door to the sceptics, who saw the whole art of compass adjusting as akin to sorcery, or a 'black art' as it has been described, then and since.

In the May 1854 edition of the *Mercantile Marine Magazine and Nautical Record*, a lengthy letter to the editor was published under the pseudonym, 'An Old Salt', on 'Compass Adjustments'. He described himself as 'one, once connected with a command in the Merchant Service and still interested in its welfare from old recollections and prepossessions'. He opened with a pleading question: 'why do masters of iron vessels leave to others a duty (affecting the lives of all on board) of such importance as the swinging of the ships they command?'. It was, essentially, a rhetorical one: they shouldn't. He then went on to criticise compass makers and adjusters – 'the opticians', or 'the landsmen', as he called them – for thrusting 'their peculiar qualifications into notice':

> Have the opticians any interest in arriving at a solution of the subject? or would it not rather spoil the nice little annuity now made by some of them? Are they (landsmen) more capable of reducing a theory into practice – a theory that must first be developed from the observations of those in charge of ships? Why cannot shipmasters give their attention to the subject a little, instead of being led by the nose by quack-doctors, whose interest lies in continuing a system of scientific mystery, so that the poor dupes have nothing else left but to pay for their gullibility.
>
> I have given a little attention for some time past to the compass-adjusting process, and have been surprised to find how easily Owners and Captains are gulled by a sort of specious or bouncing mannerism, exhibited by some of our scientific adjusters to the Merchant Service – with their infallible dodges warranted to bother a compass against its will and against all rules laid down by scientific men who *really* understand the subject ...
>
> Really Mr Editor, you must for the benefit of the class you represent (the Merchant Captains) give a detailed account of all the various mysterious methods of 'compass adjusting' so that those in charge of iron ships may be better able to perceive what these patent manoeuverers *really* do for the benefit of those poor devils at present led by the nose by them. Leaving you to overhaul the subject as you think best.

As one of the leaders in the compass making and adjusting business, the 'quack-doctors' that the 'Old Salt' had in his sights, Janet was highly affronted by his remarks and she was not going simply to let them pass. She immediately wrote a sharp retort to the editor, with the same heading, 'Adjustment of Compasses', describing herself as 'an Adjuster'. It was published in July 1854 and showed that she was not only a leader but an eloquent spokesperson in her field:

> SIR, – In reply to old Mr Salt's query, in your May number, 'Why do Masters of iron vessels leave to others a duty (affecting the lives of all on board) of such importance as the swinging of the ships they command?' I will take the liberty of saying that it cannot proceed from want of sufficient interest in, or knowledge of the subject, for with the intelligence now abroad, and the various works on magnetism,

no man can be *ignorant* of the principles on which the adjustments of his compass are made, nor *indifferent* to a matter so all-important in navigating an iron ship.

Commanders will tell old Mr Salt, that at the time a vessel is to be swung, they are overwhelmed with the cares of getting ready for sea – their minds are distracted by the variety of duties devolving on them, and therefore they gladly cede into more efficient hands so important and all-absorbing a responsibility as adjusting their compasses.

It is difficult to imagine how the whole rank and file of opticians can have so offended old Mr Salt as to call forth comments so depreciatory of their talents and capabilities. Surely it must be admitted by the unprejudiced, that those who devote so much time and attention to the construction of the compass, must know something about the laws which govern, and the disturbing causes which affect its action; and if old Mr Salt will try back only a little, he will find that most of the improvements made in that and other instruments used on board ship, have been made by landsmen.

No doubt, in old Mr Salt's seagoing days, he knew much less about the compass, (and had besides a very different kind of instrument to deal with,) than the Commanders of the present day, who are too much enlightened to allow themselves to be either 'humbugged' or 'bounced' out of knowledge, so important to them, by old Mr Salt's adjusting jugglers – the simple principle adopted to counteract the influence of the mighty floating mass or iron, which surrounds the little guardian of the ship is self-evident, and although so easy in application, old Mr Salt might not find the office quite so much of a sinecure, nor so profitable, as he would lead the public to believe.

Were he to take a turn amongst some of the opticians, he might find that they are not only 'up to a thing or two,' but are possessed of scientific knowledge which they are daily developing for the benefit of the seagoing public, and, if we may judge from the broad fact of *our fleet of iron vessels having been able to navigate in safety for some years past the most intricate passages both at home and abroad*, that they are likewise capable of applying their scientific knowledge to effecting the nice adjustment of the compass on board iron ships, whatever means they may please to adopt. In this enlightened period there can be no mystery about the compass beyond its own mysterious workings, and the best energies of those employed in manufacturing an instrument of so much importance in this iron age, are taxed to the utmost to make it a good and efficient guide under all the adverse circumstances by which it is surrounded.

The *slap-dash* manner in which old Mr Salt's 'old recollections and prepossessions' induce him to dispose of the subject, is not only unjust towards those who have proved by what they had done *that he knows nothing about them or their qualifications*, but is unsuited to the discussion of grave and scientific matters, while at the same time it is apt to carry away and mislead those who have no opportunity of judging for themselves, and I therefore trust you will allow me to take up the gauntlet so unceremoniously thrown down by old Mr Salt, and to subscribe myself, with sincere wishes for the success of your periodical.

Airy's method had a worthy champion and no more was heard from the 'Old Salt'. As Airy had been unable to attend the Liverpool meeting and to express any views face-to-face with Scoresby, the dispute between them was played out in another quarter, and publicly, in correspondence in the *Athenaeum*. In letters to the editor on 17 and 28 October 1854, Airy vigorously defended his system of compass correction. While acknowledging the 'beauty and importance' of Scoresby's extensive experiments, he thought it likely that the experiments produced an impression of applicability to iron ships far greater than was warranted. Using the *Tayleur* disaster as the 'text for the principal discussion' was, moreover, likely to inflame rather than solve the problem:

> When the feelings are excited, the judgement of the speaker, as well as the hearers, is very likely to be perverted.

Airy was firmly convinced that the magnetism of the ship could not have been disturbed as a result of her labouring in heavy seas to anything like the extent that Scoresby claimed. Acknowledging that there could be change, Airy therefore suggested that the 'permanent' magnetism be better described as 'sub-permanent' magnetism, rather than Scoresby's description of 'retentive' magnetism, but was absolutely convinced that the magnetic signature of the ship could not change in such a short time as claimed of the *Tayleur*, and decried 'the alarmist doctrines of Dr Scoresby'.

The dispute once more brought into sharp relief the mechanical versus the tabular schools of dealing with magnetic deviation. Airy's method was of the former kind, using compensating magnets to counteract deviation, while the Admiralty worked on the tabular principle, keeping a record of deviations in a log for each ship. Merchant ships preferred the mechanical, correcting with magnets along the Airy method. The jury was still very much 'out' on the best way of dealing with the very serious problems of distortions on compasses. As for the real cause of the *Tayleur* disaster, another suggestion was made by John Thomas Townson, the Secretary to the Local Marine Board in Liverpool, that it was due to 'heeling error', the distorting effect when a ship tilts over, which she would surely do in heavy seas under strong winds.

In the interests of speedily resolving the continuing doubts, the Liverpool shipowners set up the Liverpool Compass Committee to see what further light could be thrown on the subject. Over the next four years they set about their task with great seriousness and diligence, producing, in all, three reports. The conclusions of the Committee were broadly in favour of Airy, not accepting Scoresby's argument for sudden changes in the sub-permanent magnetism of a ship. As a result, Airy's method was also gradually accepted by the Compass Department of the Admiralty; but Scoresby also had some vindication in that his recommendation for a masthead or 'pole compass' was also adopted and was used on merchant ships well into the beginning of the twentieth century. As far as the lunar distance method of finding longitude was concerned, as late as 1881 it was still high on Airy's agenda. After his retirement that year on 15 August, he published yet another book outlining his method of clearing the lunar distance, in the hope of encouraging a greater use of this method of finding longitude at sea.

But, for the moment, the attack of Scorseby was deeply unsettling for Airy. It was a time when he needed serious allies and he found one in Janet Taylor. Opening his post on the morning of 30 November 1854, he received an extensive, and surprising, letter from her, written from her home. It had been fully eight years since her last communication with him on the subject of compass adjustment on iron vessels. This had been the spirited exchange in February 1846 regarding the vessel *Duke of Oporto*. While Airy did not warm to her suggestions at the time for 'improvements' in his method, he acknowledged then that she had established credentials in the adjusting world and was happy to recommend her firm, given that she utilised his method of compass adjustment. Now she wrote at a time when endorsement of his method was most timely:

Sir,

I have long wished to address you on the subject of adjusting compasses, and only delayed fearing that during your experiments in the north such an interruption would be troublesome. Since my last communication with you on this subject (I think 1846) we have had some hundreds of iron vessels of all sizes through our hands. We have swung them and adjusted their compasses according to the valuable directions you then gave me, and we *have not had one failure*, and I can name amongst the entire fleet nearly all the largest steam ships and sailing vessels which have left the Thames.

I have seen with much regret the efforts made to do away with your system of magnets, knowing the difficulties and *accidents* that *must* arise if a 'Table of Errors' is alone to be relied on, perfectly agreeing with you that it is liable to the same errors in the event of a change in the ship's sub-permanent magnetism as the mechanical correctors and leading moreover to greater risk, and not having progressed in our Merchant Service as those interested in its advancement could have wished.

The scientific lines and principles which produce in iron ships the disturbance of the compass have been too ably discussed to need comment from me. I have only to do with the practical application of a correction, – a point sometimes too much overlooked by the philosophers – in no instance requiring greater consideration than the present. We have reswung many vessels after 6 or 8 months voyages and found no greater deviations on the compass made by the magnets, than would in all probability have arisen from the change undergone in the magnetism of the ship itself, which would have affected a 'Table of Errors' in a like proportion.

I have carefully made my own Magnets according to Dr Scoresby's directions and before placing them I have tried by means of shifting the compasses elevating them to all imaginable heights to discover very great original errors we have sometimes met with. Some who adjust compasses by the *Government principle* have endeavoured to influence public opinion in their favour. I rejoice at the present investigation which must lead to a better understanding of the subject, and I trust no innovations will be allowed on your system until a decidedly better one is properly tried. Captain Fitzroy suggests that 'observations on a few well (chosen) points of the compass are sufficient'.

My long experience proves this to be a very dangerous expedient and one which I believe has led our northern Liverpool contemporaries to make frequent mistakes, and I think we could produce observations made on board various ships, that would shew the necessity of a vessel being swung entirely round.

In a little vessel we swung this week, the 'Waverley', she had a compass elevated about 18 feet, and it shewed the same error as one placed immediately under it about 6 feet from the deck – for it unfortunately happens on board Merchant ships that where a neutral point might be found, it would be impossible to place a compass and the little time generally allowed for correcting compasses, precludes the (proving) of experiment, and I think some consideration is due to those who have under every disadvantage (for instance the haste with which such nice operations are obliged to be made, the *most trying* positions in which compasses are placed oftentimes, the inconvenient nature of swinging etc etc) sets forth whole fleets of iron vessels to navigate the passages in our Northern hemisphere.

I could communicate many interesting facts which almost daily fall to our notice and to which, many, who talk learnedly about disturbing forces are utter strangers, but I should be taking too much of your valuable time. In the heeling over of ships, I do not think we have ever met with of more than 2 or 3 degrees in compasses placed in the ordinary binnacles standing about 2½ feet from the deck, but in skylight compasses and those placed low for *convenience*, a *grave* consideration in Merchant ships, serious errors have arisen from the needles being brought in close contact either with iron (beams), or the magnets used to correct original errors on the horizontal, but the subject is one so complicated that it appears to me impossible to arrive at any general rule for finding local deviation. But your principle of adjustment for correction has worked so well, where carefully applied, that I hope you will resist any attempt to abolish it, until experience has proved the existence of a better.

We adjusted all the large Iron Steamers that made the first voyages Round the World, and to India and back – no fault was found with the compasses and Captain Hyde of the 'Argo' expressed himself much satisfied with their working both out and home. I have endeavoured to obtain reliable information on the subject of adjustments on the other side the line, but the reports are so unsatisfactorily made that I am afraid to rely on them.

Apologising for so long a letter.

I am Sir

Yours obediently
Janet Taylor

Airy was quite taken aback. He was aware of her business in the field, but that it was so extensive he had not appreciated at all. Here he now had a ringing endorsement of his method by someone who claimed to have adjusted 'hundreds of iron vessels of all sizes' and '*all* the large Iron Steamers'! Just how many ships had been overseen by Janet and her men? What wealth of practical detail they could provide! He responded immediately, declaring that her letter 'may prove of considerable value'. First, he sent it to Beaufort at the Admiralty, requesting that it be returned as soon as he had read it. On 6 December he then wrote to the eminent marine surveyor Rear Admiral Frederick William Beechey, the first Superintendent of the Marine Department of the Board of Trade since

1850, again forwarding Janet's unsolicited correspondence as an indication of the level of support he was evidently receiving for his technique:

> My dear Sir,
> I enclose a letter which I have just received from Mrs Taylor, and I send it because I think that it may repay you the trouble of reading. At any convenient time would you have the kindness to return it to me.
>
> I do not know Mrs Taylor, and I do not know who is her working man in the matter of correction, and (as you will see) I have not written to her or applied to her in any way. But the statements which she makes are entirely in accord with those which I have received from others.
>
> The present panic regarding iron ships is, I really believe, one of the most ridiculous that ever occurred. For one ship that has sensible error, I believe that 100 are free from sensible error. The case of the 'Tayleur' which has been made the stalking-horse, I do not doubt to be a case of *dishonesty*, not Doctor Scoresby's ...
>
> I am, my dear Sir,
>
> > Yours very truly
> > G. B. Airy

Beechey's response made it clear that he already held Janet in high regard:

> My dear Sir,
> ... Mrs Janet Taylor's letter must be gratifying. I rejoice, she is a very sensible person. She has her work executed by a man who she keeps in her employ for this purpose.
>
> The panic in Liverpool is very great but I think it will have a good effect and I wish to take advantage of it to impress upon Captains the propriety of observing daily the variation at sea by azimuth compass and comparing it with the Binnacle compass.
>
> It will give me much pleasure to go into this matter as far as I am able but you know I am quite unequal to any mathematical investigation of the question.
>
> I return Mrs Taylor's note and am
>
> > Yours very truly
> > F. W. Beechey

For his part, Scoresby fanned the flames of the panic by publishing lengthy articles on 9 and 16 December 1846, 'On the Correction of the Compass in Iron Ships', again attacking Airy: 'The question is whether Mr Airy's mode of compass adjustment is essentially wrong in principle, and so may delude and endanger the navigator by confiding in it?'. The orderly, oracular and almost obsessional Airy would certainly not let this rest. He needed to retaliate – and with hard evidence. Janet's letter had intrigued him. Just how much experience had she, or her 'working man' had with his method? It suggested it could be considerable, but just how much was to astonish him.

After the first article appeared in the *Athenaeum*, Airy wrote to Janet as well as to John Gray, a nautical optician and compass adjuster in Liverpool (and one to whom William Reynolds had been apprenticed), seeking their assistance in providing a response to Scoresby's attacks based on real evidence and from those whose clear practical understanding had obviously impressed him. To Janet he wrote on 11 December 1854:

Madam,

In the present state of discussions on Iron Ships, I should be very much assisted by the information which is asked for in the enclosed questions. Perhaps you could transmit answers to me (if you see no objection) in three or four days. And perhaps you would allow me to publish the substance of your answers – at least in proportion to the whole number of ships, without mentioning the whole number and also without giving your name. But it would be valuable to me that every number should be given to me as taken from your lists.

I presume to adding this request to you, as I gather from your letter lately received, that it would be agreeable to you to promote, from authentic information, a better understanding on this matter than that which possesses the public mind at present.

I am, Madam,

Your obedient servant
G. B. Airy

Airy included a detailed questionnaire. His questions were not for the simple shopkeeper, but were from one initiate to another – one who truly understood the problems and challenges of correcting compasses for magnetic deviation. Honoured by this acknowledgment, and enthusiastic to participate as best she could, Janet dropped all non-urgent business and devoted the next five days to the task, filling page after page of her large blue writing pad. On 16 December, the very same day that Scoresby's second article appeared, she despatched her reply:

Sir,

I have now forwarded the replies to your queries, and hope I have not been too lengthy. My remarks are quite at your service to do with them what you please. If, without interfering with your private views, you could render them serviceable to me in my professional capacity, of course I should be obliged, but I give them to you unconditionally, being too happy to render any service I can to benefit a cause I have had so much and long at heart.

I remain Sir,

Yours obediently
Janet Taylor

Her comprehensive and candid answers to his questions were enclosed, along with various 'Deviation papers' of ships as indicated. She confirmed that she had been adjusting ships by his method since 1845. Airy was astonished at the detail, the knowledge and the experience revealed, and from the very first question:

In how many steam ships have you corrected the compass? In how many sailing ships?

To which Janet replied:

We have only kept the registers of the last 100 vessels we have adjusted – previously we kept no particulars. Out of that number 12 have been Iron sailing vessels.

'The *last* 100 vessels!' He was now utterly astounded, particularly when he learned in response to another question that twenty-five to thirty of these had been 'long voyage ships' (voyages longer than to the Baltic, the Mediterranean, or Halifax).

He eagerly read her responses to his other questions:

When ships have not been reswung, is it presumed that they do not need it? Or have you in many instances received positive information that they do not need it?

To which she responded:

Generally so – in few cases Commanders have known the amount of any trifling increase in the error that has arisen and allowed for it, but in 9 cases out of 10 although vessels have been adjusted with magnets 2, 3 and 4 years, the Captains have assured me that their compasses were quite correct.

All the large screw steamers belonging to the General Screw Steam Shipping Company which have made voyages to Australia and home round Cape Horn – and to India and back, had their compasses adjusted when first built, and *have not been reswung since because they have not required it*. Our not having reswung others is likewise because they have not required it.

More reassurance, here – that they have *not required* reswinging – and she was talking about 'all the large screw steamers' of a large firm. She also reported that:

We have the care of all the Dover and Folkestone boats, all the English and Irish steamers which trade backwards and forwards, and in fact of nearly all the little steamers that sail out of London to the various Northern ports and never have any to reswing, *that* have been properly done in the first instance ....

As each question followed, the response added to his sense of vindication of his method and its effect in compensating for the sub-permanent magnetism of the ship; it also increased his respect for the woman who had written the responses. Such extensive business could only have been obtained through experience and the significant confidence of her clientele; and such detail in her reply could be provided only by someone who had both a deep theoretical *and* practical understanding of the subject.

Airy was particularly interested in one matter that was specifically involved in the brawl with Scoresby:

Have you known any instance of a sudden change occurring in one or two days? What is the shortest you have known? To what amount?

Janet's response to this question was particularly important, given the claims made by Scoresby with respect to the sinking of the *Tayleur*. Her answer was unequivocal:

Never! Some years ago a vessel returned with the Poles of her compass *reversed* after a *thunderstorm*. The shortest period that we have known any changes to occur is from 2 to 3 years and then the error never exceeded a few degrees.

Two to three years, *not* two to three days as was the case of the *Tayleur*. Plus, the number of ships that did not require reswinging at all. More vindication. In addition, Janet was able to provide detail on practical matters, like the effect of rust:

> On many occasions when we have taken up magnets that have been enclosed in common wooden cases, we have found them covered with rust and the cases nearly full of water – the power of the magnets nearly gone. I first introduced the closed brass or copper cases – into which the magnets are put with sufficient Tallow to cover them, and then securely soldered in rendering it impossible for air or water to get at them. I likewise had many of my magnets numbered and their sustaining power registered, (so) that should the vessels have come again into our hands I could have ascertained exactly what power had been lost. This I hope yet to carry out, through the kindness of the Directors of the General S.S.S.

She also added some remarks that she provided confidentially – *not* for general consumption:

> We adjusted a vessel this week and found a fine azimuth compass kicking about the deck in a metal case, and on asking on board how it came there, the reply was that they thought it was only one of the *cooking utensils*, and in closing these remarks, I would briefly add that until the education of our Merchant Service is raised to a higher standard, all the care and attention now being bestowed on this subject will be of but little use – as we have daily instances of Masters not being able to apply the Deviations when they are given to them, but I would not like this opinion to go forth generally, as it might injure me.

Accompanying her answers were several documents. Of particular interest to Airy were the records of the actual adjustments undertaken, headed 'Records of Residual Deviations on the Steering and Standard Compasses on 32 points as follows', with every page including 'Adjusted by Mrs Janet Taylor, 104 Minories London' printed at the bottom.

(i) The Sailing Ship W.S. LINDSAY[21] – Captain Weston, adjusted at Greenhithe on 19th June 1854.
(ii) The Sailing Ship W.S. LINDSAY – Captain Weston, adjusted at East India Docks on 10th March 1853 (standard cabin and azimuth).
(iii) The screw steamer AUSTRALIAN – Captain Gilmore, adjusted at Greenhithe on 22nd September 1853 and swung at Greenhithe on 9th August 1854.

(iv) The steamship SYDNEY – Captain Askew, swung at Greenhithe on 7th August 1853 (steering & standard) and adjusted at Greenhithe on 17th May 1854 (steering & azimuth) and Captain Franklyn, adjusted at East India Docks on 20th July 1852 (steering only).

Also included were copies of letters from some of her captains: Commander Nathaniel Stewart of the *Lady Jocelyn*, a 1,325-ton iron steamer journeying around the Cape of Good Hope and to the islands of Mauritius in the Indian Ocean; Commander J. M. Mitchell of the Brazilian mailsteamer *Guanabara* written in Rio Harbour on 25 July 1853, advising that her compasses exhibited no deviation and performed brilliantly at night, being less than a mile out on each occasion; and Commander George Hyde of the *Argo*, a Royal Mail screw steamship of 2,000 tons, that had sailed from Southampton to Sydney and back, written at Southampton on 29 October 1853, saying that the compasses 'performed their duty much to [his] satisfaction'. She also promised to send a report on two vessels that she was in the process of reswinging, as soon as the results were available.

On a cold New Year's Day 1855, having completed the anticipated reswinging of the sailing ship *Typhoon*, a fast American clipper of 1,611 tons, Janet despatched her report. The *Typhoon* had returned from a second trip to Bombay and included with her letter were two pages of measurements she had completed on the *Typhoon* with Captain Bell, on both 24 November 1853 and 29 December 1854:

Sir,

I now have the pleasure of sending you for comparison the deviation papers of the sailing ship 'Typhoon'. She made a voyage to Bombay and back and the interval between corrections was, as you will see, a few days over 13 months. The Captain made great complaint of the compasses, which made me anxious to have the errors taken on them just as they came off the voyage. Time only permitted our taking them on the Cardinal Points and I have marked them in red ink.

I wish particularly to draw your attention to there being errors on the corrections. The comparison on the uncorrected errors speak for themselves. The compasses not being arranged on the two papers in the same succession, I have marked the corresponding ones with a red X.

We are now reswinging an Iron Screw and I will forward her papers when finished.

I remain Sir

Yours obediently
Janet Taylor

Not long afterwards she was also able to send the report on the *Sydney Hall*:

> We have just re-adjusted the compasses of the 'Sydney Hall' because she had had a house built under her bridge compass and great masses of iron placed near it.
>
> The steering compass had acquired an error of about ½ point on the North point, but all the other points remained the same. I think this error must have arisen from some other trifling alteration about the iron near the compass, as all the others and the intermediate points had not changed.

On reading Janet's lengthy responses, Airy was greatly pleased with the 'sheets of copious and most valuable information'.

Airy had also asked John Gray in Liverpool identical questions as those he had put to Janet. Gray had been a frequent correspondent with him for many years and was a keen supporter of Airy's theory, as well as being a fierce critic of Scoresby. The latter had written to the *Liverpool Journal* accusing Gray of being responsible for the wreck, on 9 September 1854, of the *City of Philadelphia*, on her maiden voyage, having sailed from Liverpool on Wednesday, 29 August. It was the third screw steamship of the Liverpool and Philadelphia Steam Ship Company. The weather was clear and for six days fine weather accompanied her. They had six compasses on board, all adjusted in Glasgow and Liverpool.

But once they were underway there were several problems, and the compasses didn't agree with each other. On 24 September the weather changed dramatically and when it was nearly midnight on the next day, she ran aground. Having reversed engines to get away from the rock that had entangled her, oakum and blankets were applied in an attempt to stop the hole, but it was not enough. Fortunately they were able to limp to shore in calm seas in a fog of the densest imaginable – a real 'pea-souper'. A fortuitous combination of adequate lifeboats, attention to duty, and propitious seas, meant that all passengers were rescued; but the accusation that the adjustment of the compasses was somehow to blame was stinging. In response, Gray wrote a letter to the editor:

> I beg to state that it was highly improper for the rev. gentleman to publish that which is not true ... I regret exceedingly that so much has been stated and calculated to mislead the public.

Once Airy had received all the required information from both Janet and Gray, he combined their results in a letter to the *Athenaeum* on 3 February 1855, quoting extensively from both his celebrated supporters. The evidence, he suggested, was overwhelming in favour of his view that the original magnetism of an iron ship, after slowly and gradually settling down, took on a permanent character which remained throughout the ship's life. Exceptions to this general rule could only arise from severe structural damage through grounding or collision, a fire, or the ship being struck by lightning. He felt confident that few who considered this evidence would support Dr Scoresby's 'alarmist doctrines'.

Having said this, Airy nonetheless frankly admitted that there were problems still to be solved. In addition to the issue of disagreement between Airy and Scoresby, a continuing challenge was the variation caused on ships sailing across magnetic latitudes. For example, ships whose compasses were adjusted in England and then sailed to the southern hemisphere found that their compasses were still in order on their return home. However, during the time that they were actually in the southern hemisphere, the state of the compasses varied greatly.

Airy, of an actively enquiring and scientific bent, was concerned about aspects of the application of his theory and concluded that compensating magnets should only be used to correct the sub-permanent magnetism of the ship. But how then to deal with transient induced magnetism in its vertical structures? One key suggestion was, rather than nailing corrector magnets in the vicinity of the compass, either to the deck or to the deckhead below, as had been the preferred method, a specially fitted housing, or purpose-designed binnacle, should be used, in which the correcting magnets could be placed and finely adjusted at the compass position. This had the effect of neutralising *both* the deviation caused by the ship's permanent magnetism and the transient-induced magnetism. John Gray developed and patented a binnacle according to the principles set out, in which the magnets could be moved in any direction and which included a vertical magnet to compensate for heeling error.

In his long letters published in the *Athenaeum*, Airy presented a detailed history of the progress of the science of ship magnetism from the time of his observations on the *Rainbow* and *Ironside*, in the late 1830s. But having said all this, and making his case, he ended by declaring, 'I now, therefore, terminate my part in this discussion'. Scoresby, however, had not. He was very much a man of 'the last word', responding with a long letter published in two parts on 10 and 17 March 1855, 'On the liability of the magnetic condition of iron ships to rapid or sudden changes'. It was, in part, conciliatory, expressing regret that anything he may have said may have 'interfered with a very long period of occasional pleasant and friendly intercommunication'. He also included cases in support of his claim that sudden changes could indeed occur in what he described as the 'retentive' magnetism of the ship.

Scoresby was also a practical and scientific man, of the self-taught applied manner of the day, and sought to add to his own list of experiments by undertaking a five-month voyage in 1856 on the *Royal Charter*, with his wife and her maidservant in tow. He was sixty-seven at the time and died not long after his return to Torquay. His findings were published posthumously in 1859, edited by Archibald Smith, who took the opportunity, in his forty-two page introduction, to add his own views on the subject – and clearly on the Scorseby side of the ledger against mechanical correction. Airy, having thought that the matter had been left as an 'agreement to disagree', was outraged, and penned another long letter to the editor of the *Athenaeum* on 12 November 1859. Like the fighter pilots of the First World War, many years later, Airy paid a respectful salute to his late antagonist:

> It is impossible in reading it not to be struck with the heroic self-devotion which could induce a man in advanced age to undertake such a voyage, for the sole purpose of ascertaining the truth of controversial points in his favourite science ...

But, as editor, Smith had overstepped his position to express his own views, Airy argued, especially when he criticised Airy in a way that was different even from Scoresby. And, as it turned out, the latter's experiments were inconclusive.

While Airy was reviewing the information provided by Janet and by Gray, another significant chapter in nautical history, and Janet's life, came to a close when Sir Francis Beaufort, Admiralty Hydrographer, retired at the age of eighty-one:

> Admiralty January 24/55
> Having been in HM Naval Service upwards of 67 years, 25 of which I have been employed in this laborious office, I feel that advancing age & severe infirmities make it my duty to retire, & leave its labours & responsibilities to younger and more active hands.
> F. Beaufort

Beaufort recommended, as his replacement in office, the surveying captain John Washington, Secretary of the Royal Geographical Society between

1836 and 1841, and a Fellow of the Royal Society from 1845. At his suggestion, Washington was duly appointed, serving as Hydrographer for the next eight years until his death, his legacy including a significant increase in the sale of Admiralty charts. Beaufort also asked that his 'excellent invaluable assistant', now Lieutenant Edward Hardy, be promoted to the rank of Commander. This was also done. For another month Beaufort continued his work on several charts, including those of the Norwegian and Swedish coasts, the White Sea and St Petersburg Bay. Meanwhile, Washington and others proposed a testimonial for him, an event to which, as a rather private and self-effacing man, he reluctantly agreed.

His diary entry on the matter read: 'there is sometimes more pride in supporting and adhering to one's humility than appearing to be guided by one's vanity'. In all, around 300 supporters raised a fund of £450 to commission a portrait and to endow a prize in Beaufort's name, awarded every year, to the officer gaining the highest marks for navigation and pilotage in the examination for the rank of lieutenant. Retirement was quite a shift for Beaufort, reflected poignantly in his diary comments at the end of that year:

> So ends ... a year that probably embraced the most trying period of my life, both bodily and mental... the sudden change from the exciting business of office to listless idleness.

There are many letters on record of Janet's complaints about Robert Bate, but only once in six years did she write about charts under Betty's headship. This was in late 1849 when seeking copies of the Falkland Islands chart, and even this was of a far different tone from her letters when Betty's husband was at the helm – and none when she was, in turn, replaced by Potter. Clearly Robert's personal animosity to Janet had coloured all his dealings where she was concerned. His widow, a businesswoman on his demise, perhaps understood things far better than her late husband.

While the Airy–Scoresby war was played out over the course of 1854 and early into 1855, another war was brewing: this one in the international domain, with Russia. In the autumn of 1853, the newspapers had been full of stories of Russia's designs on Turkey. Britain and France were of one mind to stop the Russian tide into the lands of the Ottoman. First, it was Turkish territory along the Danube, then Constantinople, leading the Ottomans to declare war late in 1853. But although the popular feeling was against Russia, Britain was hesitant at first.

There were some who laid this reluctance squarely at the feet of the queen's husband, Prince Albert, a German. Germany was pro-Prussian, and the Prussians were allied to Russia. How could Albert be a true Englishman? He must be a Russian spy – or so the papers said. Even though the prince had been the champion, indeed hero, of the Great Exhibition only a few years before, now people were quick to conclude that, surely, Britain's slowness to aid Turkey against Russia *must* be his fault. Perhaps, if he had lost his accent – so obvious when, at the moment that should have been his crowning glory, he opened the proceedings in 1851. One rumour even had it that the prince was imprisoned in the Tower of London, and the queen, of her own choice, had gone with him.

As the gossip and rumours of such doings ignited around London, crowds defied the January cold and filled the streets around the Tower. Minories was close by and the prattle below stairs was all about Albert. In mid-January the gossip in the nautical community gave way to the controversy triggered by the loss of the *Tayleur*. But the feeling of war was most definitely in the air, and, with it, tension about the prince.

And then, in March 1854, forty years of peace were broken when Britain and France at last declared war and troops were sent to the Crimean peninsula on the Black Sea. As is often the case at the outbreak of such international clashes, the public expected the war to be short and a resounding victory. But, as is also so regularly the case in the actuality of war, it was neither short, nor glorious. On 25 September 1854 allied troops set siege to Sebastopol, but it took nearly a whole year, until 8 September 1855, to take it. The troops suffered terribly from cholera and fever, despite the good efforts of Florence Nightingale and her team of nurses. In addition, they were forced to endure the ignominy of ineptitude of command and inadequate supplies. Then, in autumn the newspapers were full of the Charge of the Light Brigade of 25 October. An utterly foolish and useless military encounter, it was famously immortalised by Alfred Tennyson in writing 'Into the valley of Death/Rode the six hundred'.

The death toll in the war was indeed fearful. Nearly everyone had lost a friend or relative and, rather than being a great victory, the year of 1854 closed without Sebastopol taken and Russian power hardly dented. Lack of success abroad was deeply unsettling on the domestic front and, by the end of January 1855, another government had fallen: that of George Hamilton Gordon, 4th Earl of Aberdeen. The queen then called upon Henry John Temple, Viscount Palmerston to form a new one, shortly afterwards lamenting to her uncle Leopold that 'altogether, affairs are very unsettled and very unsatisfactory'.

For Janet, however, the issues of the nation were completely overshadowed when, in early December 1855, her chief compass adjuster, Frederick Wiggins, followed the lead of her head instrument maker, William Reynolds, of two years before and resigned. Wiggins had been with her for ten years, carrying out his adjustments under her watchful eye. He was her 'working man' in so many respects, developing his craft under her careful tutelage. As if his leaving wasn't bad enough, he didn't go very far: to set up a joint venture with Reynolds at No. 82 Minories, under the name of 'Reynolds and Wiggins, Opticians'.

Within two years Janet had lost her husband, then the head of her manufacturing operations in Reynolds, and now she was losing her principal protégé and professional associate. With England now at peace and the victor in the war, which ended in February 1856, Janet's standing had been vindicated by the acknowledgment of the Astronomer Royal, but she felt right at this moment as if her world were falling about her.

XXI

Mrs Janet Taylor & Co.

It was as if the world echoed Janet's spirits as the winter deepened. The river froze over for the first time since 1837/38, some eighteen years earlier. And then, to add insult to injury, when Wiggins went into partnership with Reynolds, they openly sought their previous clients. The new firm was announced in the *Mercantile Marine Magazine and Nautical Record* early in 1856, under the banner 'IRON SHIPS AND THEIR COMPASSES':

FREDERICK WIGGINS, (late Principal to Mrs Janet Taylor), in soliciting the patronage of Iron Shipbuilders, Shipowners, and Captains, begs to inform them that for the last TEN YEARS he has had the honour of FINDING THE DEVIATIONS AND ADJUSTING THE COMPASSES on board the LARGEST IRON VESSELS in the Port of London, during which period he has performed these important duties to the satisfaction of the principal STEAM-PACKET COMPANIES.

F. W. takes this opportunity of stating that he has entered into PARTNERSHIP with Mr. Wm. REYNOLDS, who has for the last TWENTY-FIVE YEARS manufactured every description of Nautical Instruments, and trusts by strict attention and economy to merit their support.

REYNOLDS & WIGGINS, OPTICIANS,
82, MINORIES, LONDON

While Wiggins empathised with Janet and what they had achieved together, he felt that it was time for him to make a new start, including a family. Janet had been an excellent mentor and teacher. She was a tough employer, being incredibly exacting and, at times, unforgiving, as there was no room for error in their work. Men's and women's lives were at stake, always, in what they did and an imperfect compass exacted its toll in disaster. Shipwreck waited in the wings to take its place on the stage whenever laxness entered into the compass adjuster's work, as in the loss of the *Tayleur*. But once George's mediating influence had gone, Wiggins had made up his mind. Janet took the news calmly, and, after she had reflected upon it for a while, a certain pride. After all, she didn't 'own' him, and his success was *her* triumph, too – the success of the good teacher.

Their reputation was such, now, that there was no shortage of candidates wanting to be taken under the wing of 'Mrs Janet Taylor'. Wiggins' sense of duty was somewhat alleviated when he was able to assist her in choosing her next apprentices in the compass-adjusting field. It was also a chance for her son Frederick to take a more active role, having shown some aptitude in this difficult craft. She was determined to take Frederick to Holland the first chance she had, to get some advanced tuition from her son-in-law Peter van Galen, now that she could no longer turn to Wiggins.

But Janet was not one to dwell too long on her troubles, and Wiggins' departure provided the catalyst to a renewal of energy in directions other than compass adjusting, which had kept her focused during the difficult period after George's death. To ensure her own fresh start, she now reinvented herself as 'Mrs Janet Taylor & Co' and in doing so picked up the threads of a number of creative projects in instrument design that had been simmering for some time. Just two months after Wiggins had left, the February 1856 issue of the *Mercantile Marine Magazine and Nautical Record* carried the announcement of her 'new sea artificial horizon':

> SEVERAL attempts have been made of late years to supply an artificial horizon of such a character as to be adapted for use on board ship. It is probable that nothing will be found so effectual for the purpose as the simple contrivance to which we here draw attention, and which has been brought out by Mrs Janet Taylor, 104, Minories, London.

This was an ingenious device, using the mercury principle and intended for use with either quadrants or sextants. A later issue of the magazine reported extremely positively on the invention and its development in the intervening time. 'Janet Taylor's Artificial Horizon for sea use has been so far improved upon as to render such an addition to the quadrant and sextant highly beneficial for the purposes of navigation'. Adding that 'the

Artificial Horizon has been well spoken of by several Masters', the article was followed by a letter from a ship-master, J. R. Luckes, the Master of the iron barque *Rosario*, who had sent an unsolicited testimonial on its great benefits, even to the beginner, or, in contemporary terms, a 'tyro':

> Sir
>
> As I believe you take a great interest in whatever benefits the Mercantile Marine, I would beg to call your attention to the Artificial Horizon, lately brought out by Mrs Janet Taylor. I have used it and found it of the greatest advantage in Navigation; indeed I prefer it to any other instrument of the kind, as I believe it to be (from experience) more accurate.
>
> Mrs Taylor's Artificial Horizon can always be used and that by the merest tyro in taking observations. I have no interest in recommending this instrument, further than, as being a ship-master, I am glad to see a really valuable addition to our instruments, taken proper care of. I have taken altitudes both by night and by day, using this Horizon, and have always found them correct, – the night altitudes much more so, than they could be taken with the real horizon on the clearest night – the simplicity of this instrument is one of its greatest recommendations.
>
> I remain etc etc
>
> J. R. Luckes

At the same time Janet was developing the next generation of compasses, progressing from the 'dry card' model to the 'spirit compass'. These contained a liquid such as alcohol and water to support the graduated card that pivoted around its centre. The great advantage of the liquid compass was the reduction of pivot friction and vibrations of the card caused by the motion of the vessel. It wasn't long before she sought permission for it to be tested on a Navy ship, writing to the Secretary of the Admiralty on 25 March 1856:

> Sir,
>
> Having made a special Compass either for screw vessels or boat binnacles, I am desirous of having it tested on board one of Her Majesty's ships, and reported on. May I therefore beg you will obtain permission for it to be sent to Woolwich.
>
> I remain Sir
>
> Yours obediently
> Janet Taylor

On 5 April, the new Admiralty Hydrographer, John Washington, replied. He readily agreed to her request and asking that she send her new compass to the Compass Observatory in Woolwich, 'where the Supt. will report on board which vessel it should be tried'. After rigorous testing, her device was duly tested and found to be satisfactory in all respects.

Her manufacturing business now included a wide range of nautical and scientific instruments – compasses, barometers, telescopes, octants, sextants, binnacles, chronometers, air and water thermometers, aerometers (instruments for determining the mass or density of a gas, especially air) and hygrometers (instruments for measuring humidity). She was also an agent for 'sounding machines', a device in which a glass ball with a weight was dropped over the side of a ship. The ball disengaged when its weight hit the bottom and from the known rate of descent and ascent, the depth of the water could then be derived. And then there was the exclusive agency for Macrow's patented 'alarm lock and bolt':

> This lock cannot be picked, and if by any means an entrance is effected the alarm is given some seconds beforehand. They are beautiful in appearance and the key very small.

Such new interests led Janet to lease additional premises at No. 146 Leadenhall Street, the home of the East India Company and an important business location for maritime retailers. It was a risk to take on the liability of another lease, and £160 a year at that, but Janet sought to overreach her recent disappointments by expanding her business assertively, as 'Mrs Janet Taylor & Co'.

At the same time, Janet renewed her attention to her publishing enterprises and she continued to publish her own books as well as those of others. The year following George's death she published the seventh edition of her *Luni-Solar and Horary Tables*; the tenth edition of her *Epitome of Navigation and Nautical Astronomy*; the seventh edition of her *Diurnal Register for Barometer, Sympiesometer, Thermometer and Hygrometer*; and, in 1855, the third edition of her *Handbook to the Local Marine Board Examination for Officers of the British Mercantile Marine Board*, described by the *Mercantile Marine Magazine* as 'Without any pretensions, the best book of the kind that has yet been published'. (So much so, it is still in print today.) And then there was an English edition of *A Guide to Lieutenant Maury's Wind and Current Charts*.

With each publication Janet took the opportunity to promote the various arms of the business, as well as proudly displaying testimonials from reviewers, one example being a statement from the *Liverpool Mail* regarding her *Tables*:

> Mrs Taylor indeed merits high praise, and may we add national gratitude; she has removed the chief difficulties which obscured the science of Navigation. We have no hesitation in saying that here is the most complete treatise on Navigation which has ever been published.

She had every reason to be very proud of what she had achieved, both with George as her business partner, and now on her own. She could rightly claim as fact, and not as puffery, 'that her firm had the honour of being selected for recommendation by Professor Airy (the Astronomer Royal)' and to assert that she was:

> By Special Appointment
> Mrs JANET TAYLOR
> 104 Minories E. London
>> (Patronised by nearly all the various governments in the World and the principal Ocean Steam Navigation Companies at Home and Abroad)
>> Manufacturer of every description of Nautical and Mathematical Instruments
>> Improved Compasses for Iron Ships
>> The Deviations in the Compasses of Iron Ships Found and corrected

Janet continued to report to John Washington on problems in Admiralty charts that came to her attention and he always welcomed her doing so. Having drawn attention to an error with respect to a light on the South Pier Head at Torbay, near Torquay, in the south of England, he responded warmly:

> I am much obliged to you for pointing out the mistake in the chart of Torbay. The light in question is on the South Pier Head as you will see by a new chart of Torbay recently published, a copy of which I have the pleasure of forwarding to you by this post. The old chart has been cancelled and should you have any copies of it remaining on hand, Mr Potter the Admiralty Agent has instructions to exchange them for the new charts. You may like to know there are several light corrections in Lunca and Banka Strait which will be published in 2 or 3 days.

And so, it seemed for the time being, that business continued satisfactorily. Meanwhile, the rhythm of London was punctuated by the marking of wars, the celebration of births and the mourning of the deaths of its monarchs, and around 2 a.m. on 14 April 1857 the guns fired again from the Tower of London when the queen, just a month shy of her twenty-eigth birthday, gave birth to a fifth daughter, Beatrice. But then, in the following autumn, the Indian Rebellion brought horror to the nation in the reported atrocities on British people following the mutiny of native Indian troops, or 'sepoys', of the British East India Company.

They killed soldiers and civilians alike, starting in Bengal and spreading into Delhi and surrounding towns. On each telling, in fortnightly instalments as the mail ships arrived from the subcontinent with news, and as the stories rapidly passed around, with many recounted in the *Times*, the scale of the horror against Europeans and Christians escalated. Nightmare upon nightmare was brought home to Britain. The reported attacks on women and children – of English women raped, husbands killed in front of their families, even parents forced to eat their children's flesh – galvanised the retaliation and made the retribution extreme over the following year, as reflected in the words of the popular poet, Martin Tupper:

And England, now avenge their wrongs by vengeance deep and dire,
 Cut out their canker with the sword, and burn it out with fire;
  Destroy those traitor regions, hang every pariah hound,
 And hunt them down to death, in all hills and cities 'round.

The violence of the whole rebellion also led to the end of the East India Company's monopoly of India when the mutiny was finally quelled the following year in 1858 and the queen assumed direct political control.

For Janet, however, the year of 1857 brought sadness to her door on a personal level again, when her eldest sister, Isabella, took gravely ill during the last days of the summer. In a moment Janet dropped everything to be by her side, in Rotterdam, the place where Isabella had settled with her husband Robert in 1829 and raised their three children. Isabella had been virtually a mother to her after their own had died when Janet was only seven. Accompanying her on this trip was Frederick, now twenty-three, to learn more of compass adjusting from Peter van Galen and to add to his developing skills. Janet was at her side in Rotterdam when, on 13 October, Isabella died, aged sixty-two. Isabella had been their father's right-hand woman and taken charge of their youngest brother, Frederick, in turn. And then, after she had returned to London and as the winter once more set upon the City, Janet received the news that, on 17 December, the man whom she admired so much, Francis Beaufort, had died.

Since his retirement three years before, Beaufort's physical abilities had diminished and he was at times either chair or bed-bound. Despite these setbacks, his mind was actively engaged to the end, his last months being spent in a cottage at Brighton where he could be wheeled along the promenade or take in the sun on the terraces. In the afternoon of the day before he passed away at the age of eighty-three, Beaufort spoke with his doctor on the necessary requirements to be a good historian and, according to a family letter by his daughter Rosalind, his family doctor was amazed by his 'wonderful clearness, memory, spirit and animation in the discussion of a book he was reading'. Survived by all of his six children, he was buried in the graveyard at Hackney Church, where, two months later, his beloved second wife Honora was also interred. In the county of Kent in the south of England, a small church at Gravesend was dedicated to his memory.

With the opening of the year 1858, the attention of the maritime world of Britain focused upon the launch of Isambard Kingdom Brunel's monster iron ship, the *Great Eastern*. As the world's largest ship, a 23,000-ton vessel, she was quickly dubbed the 'Leviathan' and her launch was eagerly anticipated. But the tides had not delivered their expected winter highs and the launch at Millwall degenerated into a debacle, some even said a disgrace, accomplished only after several attempts, following which the great vessel was towed to Deptford to be completed. The unusually low winter tides had ramifications in other directions as well, triggering the 'year of the great stink'. As the waters receded, the banks of the Thames, and everything that lay there, were exposed.

And as London's sanitation arrangements were much the same in the first half of the nineteenth century as they had been for the previous 400 years, the consequence was quite disgusting. All privy refuse went almost directly into the Thames and by 1858 the great river had become virtually an open sewer. All the fish died; and by the early summer the stench was unbearable. Where the windows of Parliament had used rose petals to hide the growing smell in previous years, by August of this summer only sheets soaked in chlorine were powerful enough to ward it off.

As London's water supply was drawn from the river, cholera was also prevalent, although at the time the connection between water and the disease had not yet been fully realised. It was thought, rather, that 'miasma', or unhealthy vapour, was to blame. But it wasn't the odour, borne in the air, but its source, faecal matter, intermingled in the water supply, that was the problem. And when it came to sewage, if you got rid of the source of the smell, you also got rid of the source of the contamination. In 1855 the Metropolitan Board of Works had been established to find a remedy, and in 1858 Joseph Balzagette began his masterful scheme to divert all of the sewage from the Thames through great sewer lines along its banks, enclosed in what was to become the modern Embankment promenade as a triumph of Victorian architecture and civil engineering. It was the unbearable stench resulting from the abnormally low tides that was the final catalyst for the approval of Balzagette's plans.

For those living near the river, like Janet in Minories, it was too much to endure. Year after year she had suffered the increasingly nauseating odour from the Thames in the summers and the suffocating dirty fogs of winter, and now it was overpowering. So she moved her residence from No. 1 Hammet Street to No. 1 Grove Park Terrace in the south London suburb of Camberwell, well away from the putrid river, although it meant a daily commute of two miles to Minories. Even having moved this far, as the summer began Janet was very glad to be leaving London completely when she left for Holland. Her son Frederick was to be married in Holland on 21 July to Elizabeth Badon-Glybon, an unexpected but delightful outcome of her sad journey the year before. Janet's stepdaughter Emily had done a bit of match-making and introduced Frederick to Elizabeth.

For Janet, it was an excellent excuse also to escape the London stench and assist the young couple in the wedding preparations as well as to take Ada, now fourteen, and Alfred, thirteen, to meet their cousins in Holland. Frederick and Elizabeth returned to England and, in the following autumn, on 14 October 1859, Elizabeth gave birth to their first child, Esther Janet Taylor. Although this was Janet's first grandchild, she was very anxious for the young couple during the baby's first year, as the death of her stepgrandchild, Emily's first, in July 1842 was still very much in her mind.

The times in Holland always gave Janet time for reflection. Without George by her side anymore she found the comfort and conversation in the household of Emily and Peter greatly consoling – particularly after the death of Isabella. She was alarmed that the firm of Reynolds and Wiggins had recently decided to team up with the rival firm of James Imray at No. 102 Minories, forming formidable business rivals as 'Imray, Reynolds and Wiggins', describing themselves as nautical instrument makers and chartsellers. Janet had turned fifty-five in May and with her advanced years it was becoming increasingly difficult to run her diverse business operations virtually single-handedly. She realised by now, if she hadn't fully appreciated it before, how important a role George had really played in the business, not on the intellectual side much, or ever, but in all the day-to-day side of managing people and, dealing with the daily demands of cash flow, he had played a real part. And she missed him.

Despite her best efforts, none of her children had really wanted to take over the business. Dite's interest in the compass-adjusting activities of Wiggins didn't last and although Frederick showed more promise, his interest too was limited despite her encouragement, being more intent on starting a family of his own and establishing himself in life. And now her eldest son, Herbert, had decided to emigrate to Australia, where he was to become an engine driver.

After Esther's birth, the winter that settled on the country was another bitterly cold one. The snows fell deep in the north, where Janet's sister Joyce and many others of her family still lived, and the frosts sat heavily on London, aggravating the condition of her lungs that had plagued her since she was a girl. How ironic, she reflected, as the weather seemed yet again to know her innermost thoughts and feelings and to play them out before her.

XXII

The End of an Era

It had always grated that Mrs Somerville secured a civil list pension, and as much as £300, but Janet had received nothing. Had *she* been recognised through an award, award*s*, such as Janet had been accorded by other sovereigns? Surely, after Janet's acknowledgment by those like the Astronomer Royal, and the kings of other nations, her time had come. And indeed it finally did, some sixteen years after her correspondence with Sir Robert Peel, and after another successful decade of publishing, producing instruments, and running her business, when a civil list pension of £50 per year was finally granted to her on 10 January 1860.

A paltry £50 per year: the lowest amount that could have been awarded, and this, now twenty-two years after her first attempt. The intriguing 'official' reason was 'the death of her husband', and yet it had already been six years since George had passed away. But her financial circumstances were now less than satisfactory and she was grateful for anything. The departure of Reynolds and Wiggins to set up in opposition to her had had a significant impact on her business, notwithstanding her reluctant acceptance, and it formed the basis of her latest application.

Announced in a report on the civil list pensions granted in the year between June 1859 and June 1860, there were six of £50 per year, seven of £100, one of £125, one of £150, and one of £25, topping up an award the prior year of £75. They were awarded for a mixture of straitened circumstances and contributions – some, of the awardees; some, of their relatives. The awards reflected the tension between merit and need that had featured in the discussion, covering both aspects in the language of the grants. The six spinster sisters of Dr Dionysiuis Lardner, for example, were awarded £125 in equal proportions, to be held on trust,

'In consideration of their late brother's labours in the cause of science, and of their scanty means'. Mrs Helen Gallwey, the daughter of John Hoppner the portrait painter, 'In consideration of the long services of her husband, as British Consul at Naples'.

Those who were awarded pensions in their own right included the £100 awarded to Dr Robert Blakey, 'In consideration of his exertions to aid and promote the study of philosophy, and of his straitened circumstances'; a similar award to Miss Julia Pardoe, 'In consideration of 30 years' toil in the field of literature, by which she has contributed both to cultivate the public taste, and to support a number of helpless relations'; and to the Reverend Henry Logan, 'In consideration of his contributions to the mathematical and scientific literature, and his present state of destitution, in consequence of the loss of his eyesight'. When it came to contributions to the maritime community, there were only two awards.

One was the pension of £100 awarded, on trust, for Mrs Sarah Jane le Blane, 'In consideration of the great benefits conferred on naval science by her father, the late Sir Samuel Bentham'; and the £50, in trust, for Mrs Janet Taylor, 'In consideration of her benevolent labours among the seafaring population of London, and of the circumstances of difficulty in which she is placed by the death of her husband'. The 'circumstances of difficulty' were true enough, but £50 was almost insulting.

Meanwhile the 'great counting' of the national census was repeated when, a decade after the prior one, a new census was recorded on the night of 7 April 1861. In capturing Janet's evening that Sunday, it provided a snapshot on her life at that moment, as it did of the whole nation. It revealed that 'Janet Taylor (widow) – authoress and instructress in Navigation and Nautical Astronomy', resided now at No. 1 Grove Park Terrace, Camberwell. Her (rounded) age was given as fifty, although in fact she was actually fifty-six at the time, using her continued liberality in rounding down as she had in earlier such moments, expressing perhaps a little private vanity. Also present on this evening were her son Alfred, now aged sixteen and employed as a clerk in the Peninsular Office (familiarly known as 'P & O'), and a domestic servant, Matilda Smith with a (rounded) age of twenty. Janet's only surviving daughter, Ada, having recently turned eighteen, was not with her mother that night but rather on her way to take up a position as governess with a cousin in Stockton, County Durham, for the family of Janet's niece, Jane Janson, the daughter of Janet's older sister Elizabeth.

Living in Camberwell, some way south of the river and westwards of Minories, had given Janet some relief from the odours of the Thames in summer, but the business address of 'Mrs Janet Taylor & Co' was still

No. 104 Minories and, on 22 June 1861, fire again came close to her door. It started in a warehouse in Tooley Street, near Guy's Hospital, just across the river from the Tower, a stone's throw from No. 104 and clearly visible from the upper windows from which she had watched time and London pass since 1845. The inferno developed into the largest blaze in the City since the Great Fire of 1666. Burning fat from the warehouse drifted down the river and threatened the wooden ships moored in the Pool, which were only rescued by being urgently towed out of harm's reach.

The London Fire Engine Establishment once more rallied to the cause, their fire vessels floating on the Thames, but they were unable to quell the fire. Three wharves and vast quantities of goods were damaged, and even the poor superintendent was killed when one of the warehouse walls fell on him. It took two days before it was brought under control and the consequences, both in insurance claims and public concern, were alarming; it also led, four years later, to the establishment of the Metropolitan Fire Brigade. And in the warmth of the early summer, the smoke and the smell of burning fat lingered in Minories for weeks and Janet was very glad to be clear of the worst of it.

In 1861 the national attention also became focused once more on the royal household. First, on 16 March, Victoria's mother, the elegant but overbearing Duchess of Kent, at last went to her rest, although she was not much lamented. Now it was Victoria's son Bertie, the Prince of Wales, who drew the people's attention in his continued philandering, with one mistress after another, being the gossip of all England, reminding some of the activities of his great-uncle, George IV. This distressed the prince's parents greatly, particularly his father, Prince Albert. Then the winter set upon the country, and it turned out to be another severe one. For those who were worn down by stress and worry, like Prince Albert, it did not take much for them to succumb, and the end of 1861 saw the country go into mourning with the death of Queen Victoria's beloved consort. He died of typhoid, a bacterial illness that struck king and commoner alike, at the age of forty-two. The very same disease that year had already killed Prince Ferdinand and King Pedro V of Portugal, cousins to the British royal family; and with the death of Prince Albert it came into the home and heart of the devastated queen. She went into deep mourning and did not emerge from it until 1874, thirteen years later.

Now to face a widowhood of forty years, she would wear black and remain unadorned by make-up for the rest of her life. For Victoria and all those who mourned at such times, it was only the improvement of sanitation in cities and the discovery of vaccination, antibiotics and penicillin that would salve the grief of nations, and grieving families.

And so, on 14 December 1861, the bells tolled again. Not the bells of the Tower, but those of St George's chapel, Windsor, to signal the prince's death. At Balmoral Castle, where she had spent so many happy times with her husband, the queen built a great cairn on the summit of a hill they had often visited together, inscribed:

To the Beloved Memory

OF

ALBERT, THE GREAT AND GOOD PRINCE CONSORT.

Raised by his Broken-Hearted Widow

VICTORIA R.

Through this long, sad, winter, Janet also had to confront her own personal dilemma. What should she do about her business? She still had things she wanted to accomplish, but knew that she could not keep it going for much longer. Cash flow was proving an increasing challenge. She had had to let her secretary William Bates go, and she had economised as much as she could on the domestic front, retaining only one servant at Camberwell. 'I will leave it for another day', she thought, as she had many times before, and decided to do what she knew best when challenges around her proved difficult. She focused on her writing, and publishing the work of others.

First, she produced the eleventh edition of her 350-page book, *An Epitome of Navigation and Nautical Astronomy: with improved Lunar Tables* to great acclaim, 'Mrs Taylor's rules' now having become the reference point for many others writing similar works, like Captain Charles F. A. Shadwell, RN, in his *Tables for Facilitating the Reduction of Lunar Observations*, published by J. D. Potter in 1860. Janet's *Handbook to the Local Marine Board Examination* came out every year and was the standard in the field. She also published a wide variety of works on a whole range of topics. *The Seamanship* included instructions for using Mortar and Rocket lines and the management of boats in open surf. Reehorst's *Mariner's Friend*, described in the Preface as:

> The mariner's friend, or polyglot indispensable and technical dictionary, containing upwards of five thousand modern nautical steam and shipbuilding terms, commercial and scientific expressions, denominations of art and an explanatory preface of requirements in ten different languages including English, Dutch, German, Swedish, French, Italian, Spanish, Portuguese and Russian.

The new year brought an opportunity for further recognition in the 1862 London International Exhibition of Industry and Art, again sponsored by the Royal Society for the Encouragement of the Arts, Manufactures and Commerce. Perhaps this would make amends for her contribution being overlooked or misunderstood in the Great Exhibition eleven years previously. (*Deliberately sabotaged* was something she had never wanted to acknowledge as a possibility.) This latest exhibition was planned to be in 1861, ten years after the one of 1851, but the Franco-Prussian War had intervened and led to a delay in the major international event by a year. Instead, it ran from 1 May until 15 November 1862. Again it was an astonishing sight, the building covering an area of about fifteen acres of the twenty-three acres of the Royal Horticultural Society gardens in South Kensington, with a massive display of 28,850 exhibits from thirty-seven countries.

In contrast to the opening of the Great Exhibition of 1851, where the queen had attended, she was absent from the opening of the 1862 exhibition, mourning Prince Albert's recent death. The throne sat empty and the busts of the queen and her prince were a sad reminder of his role in the early marvellous event, and the sadness of his passing. The exhibition nonetheless attracted over 6 million visitors, an even higher attendance than that of 1851, and ended with a profit. This time Janet decided to enter three of her inventions: a liquid compass that she called 'The Mariner's Compass', a sextant and a lantern.

Her compass, entered in Section C, 'Ships Tackle & Rigging', of Class XII, 'Naval Architecture including Ships' Tackle', appeared in the relevant Jury's Report as 'No. 2819'. With respect to the binnacles entered in this Section, and Janet's entry in particular, the jury commented:

> Much taste is displayed in some of the compass binnacles exhibited; their efficiency for iron ships is however impaired by being made so low. In any vessel with iron beams every compass should be at least 3'6" from the deck. Mrs J. Taylor (2819) exhibits a good liquid compass fitted in a low binnacle which latter will no doubt attract the attention of yachtsmen from the neatness and compactness of design.

Despite the overall favourable assessment of the jury, there was no award for her Mariner's Compass. 'Neatness and compactness' reminded her of the judgment of the embroidery of her fellow classmates at the Royal School. Where Janet had never achieved such qualities in her own needlework, perhaps Mrs Pawsey would be satisfied that now, some forty-nine years later, she was being recognised for 'neatness and compactness', but in another respect.

Her sextant and lantern were entered in the curious category of 'Philosophical Instruments and Processes Depending on their Use', which included sextants and other nautical instruments. The jury reported the entry of 'many novelties, the majority of which endeavour to effect an artificial horizon for use on shore or at sea if the horizon is obscured'. They did, however, make specific reference to her contribution:

> Among other improvements in sextants is a simple and effective contrivance by Mrs Janet Taylor by which a valuable increase is given to the extreme angle at which observations may be taken. This addition of 15° to the range of a sextant is very important to observers on shore who use the ordinary artificial reflecting horizons and can therefore take the altitude of no object which exceeds half the range of the sextant. No error or mechanical disadvantage attends this useful modification to the position of the index glass. Mrs Janet Taylor also exhibits a miniature lantern for night observations, which was found at Kew to burn with a sufficient steadiness in a fresh breeze.

Janet had achieved this important increase in angle by placing the face of the index glass over the axis of the instrument instead of the back. Her trials conducted at Kew Observatory indicated that, under favourable circumstances, angles of 145 degrees were perfectly practical. This was a significant breakthrough at the time. Did this qualify her entry for an award? An objective bystander may have thought so, but, coincidentally, or malevolently, Janet was deprived of such recognition in this category as revealed almost as an afterthought, in an asterisk at the end of the jury's report:

> *From the circumstances of these instruments being misplaced in the Exhibition, they were not duly considered by the Jury: any improvement in an instrument of such universal importance would undoubtedly have merited consideration.

'Misplaced'? Janet could not believe her eyes when she found the damning footnote. Echoes of prior disappointments flooded her mind: the anger, then dismay, she had felt when her first book was reviewed; the condescension in the assessment of her magnificent sextant in the Great Exhibition, the almost patronising award of a £50 pension, compared to that of Mrs Somerville. Once more she felt like it was time to let it all go.

Her health was suffering. Each winter the cloying smog of the City filled her lungs and made her feel like she was carrying great weights upon her shoulders and each summer the stench made her feel faint with every breath. Escapes to Holland and to the family of her stepdaughter Emily brought precious temporary relief, when she could manage it. Adding to her disquiet of mind was a court case when, towards the end of the London exhibition, she found herself embroiled in legal action.

The *Times* of 21 November 1862 carried a report from the Vice-Chancellor's courts of a suit in Chancery, Moses v. Taylor. Janet had found fairly rapidly that taking out the lease on 146 Leadenhall Street placed too much of a strain on her finances and she did not have the cash flow to sustain it. So she sublet the lower floors to a Mr Jones, who underlet part of the premises to Thomas Henry Dubbs. Mr Dubbs then engaged in certain activities of which his neighbours disapproved.

The lease to Janet contained a covenant that she, or her assignees:

Not carry on, nor permit to be carried on on the premises, during the continuance of the lease, any dangerous, noisy, noxious, or offensive trade, nor should she, her executors, administrators, or permitted assignees sell, assign, or underlet the same without the consent, in writing, of the plaintiffs.

Dubbs sought to conduct what was described as a 'mock auction' which attracted a large crowd and rather rough and ready passers-by. This caused much aggravation to the neighbours, in particular the Messrs Holder, shipbrokers, who occupied the upper floor of the premises. They didn't like what was going on, claiming that it was a 'noisy, noxious and offensive trade' and tended to the detriment of their business as the crowd 'deterred respectable persons from coming to them on business'. And so Janet, as the principal leaseholder, was drawn into the mess.

She needed legal representation when she was faced in Chancery by an application for an injunction to stop Dubbs' activities. Mr Toulmin appeared for her, in defence against the landlord, Mr Moses, represented by Mr Swanston. As reported in *The Times*, the Vice-Chancellor, Sir R. T. Kindersley, acknowledged Janet's standing in describing her as 'well known as a scientific nautical and mathematical instrument maker'. He decided that it was not clear that the mock auction came within the terms of the lease restrictions. If it did, there may be a remedy in ejectment in another court. If not, it may be a matter for the police. Meanwhile, Janet expressed her regret to the Messrs Holder and promised to do what she could to stop the noise and nuisance of Mr Dubbs, sympathising with them for the impact it may have been having on their business. While she won her case, and was awarded costs, she was still considerably out of pocket. Moreover, the stress of the court case, on top of everything else, brought her to breaking point.

In 1863, Janet published the sixth edition of her *Directions to the Planisphere of the Stars*. Her 'Introduction' read as her own swansong, of her aspirations and passions expressed over a lifetime – an escape from the mundane round of having to maintain a business:

> The science of Astronomy offers to the reflective mind, a wide field for study and contemplation, and tends much to raise the heart and feelings beyond the scenes of the world to that Almighty Being, who has spangled the heavens with innumerable orbs, each rolling in infinite space, and all maintaining the same beautiful order and harmony of motion as when they first issued forth from the hand of their Creator.
>
> To this sublimity of feeling is added, by the strictness of mathematical reasoning, a confidence of mind, of the Navigator especially, from the facility with which the places, magnitudes and motions of the heavenly bodies can be calculated; and from these again are deduced rules and by which the exact position of vessels on the boundless ocean, as well as places on land, may be estimated with the greatest precision. These reflections cannot fail to produce sentiments of deep humility, for our little world, although beautiful and wonderful in formation, and of surpassing loveliness in sea, earth and sky, is but a mere speck in the universe when compared with the immense bodies which revolve in boundless space beyond our orbit.
>
> The magnificence and extent of the starry regions, increase as improvements in the telescope enable the observer to fathom further into the depths of space, but after all the mind of man has done in this science, he seems still only to rest on the threshold of this part of Creation, for it would almost appear to say to the most advanced of our Astronomers 'so far shalt thou go and no further'.[22]

In writing these words, she wanted to escape 'the scenes of the world' that she had to face at that moment. Her thoughts were drawn very much to her childhood in Durham and her walks with her father. It was the reference point that gave her a sense of stability when her own world seemed to be falling in upon itself, piece by piece. Mathematical reasoning was the 'sublimity' which connected her with her God and her father.

And then, towards the end of the year, it looked as if Britain might be at war again. The duchies of Schleswig and Holstein, adjoining Denmark and under Danish rule, but largely German to the core, were coveted by the Prussian-dominated German Confederation. When German troops occupied Holstein and sights were set on Schleswig, Britain's sense of honour and duty were galvanised. The Princess of Wales (Princess Alexandra having married the errant Bertie on 10 March 1863) was a Danish princess after all, and the German Confederation's actions, as an affront to her father who had inherited the throne of Denmark in November, were also an affront to Britain.

The queen was beside herself and was without her beloved Albert to guide her. Her daughter, Vicky, was married to the Crown Prince of Prussia and in the midst of Prussia's military manoeuvring against Denmark, and her son was married to its princess. Using whatever influence she had, and in the interests of averting all-out war with Britain entangled, the queen breathed a sigh of some relief when, in April 1864, an armistice was reached, although the result was a triumph for Prussia and Austria, which had wrested the territories from Danish rule.

Janet continued to pay the land tax of £4 3s 4d each year as the occupier of No. 104 Minories as her business premises, but her home in Camberwell was about to vanish. Where the construction of the Blackwall railway had stopped at her doorstep in Minories, the building of the London underground railway system was to claim her residence in Grove Park Terrace. On 10 January 1863, the first section of the London Underground from Paddington to Farrington Street had opened. Some 30,000 people travelled on the little steam trains to commemorate this event, and thereafter 25,000 commuters regularly used the line daily. London's growth also led to a number of the properties in Grove Park Terrace, Camberwell, earmarked for demolition for railways, including her own.

By the beginning of 1864, Janet's concerns about her business could be avoided no longer. After mounting pressure from her creditors, proceedings for bankruptcy were initiated. Having turned sixty on 4 May, the *London Gazette* a week later published a notice of adjudications and first meetings of creditors, amongst them listing, for 11 a.m. on 31 May, 'Janet Taylor, The Grove, Camberwell'. Under the Bankruptcy Act (1571), Commissioners of bankrupts could be appointed to allow a bankrupt to legally discharge their debts to creditors by an equitable and independent distribution of assets and then begin trading again with outstanding debts wiped out. The notices in the *London Gazette* were published by the commissioners to inform creditors.

Janet could no longer side-step reality by thinking upon the heavens. She had no choice but to sell up everything she could, rescuing only a few small things to preserve for her children: her furnishings, that she had chosen with such care, and her precious piano, were all sold. With the demolition of Grove Park Terrace she moved to No. 156 Camberwell Grove, but she realised it would only be temporary. Illness seemed to be a daily fact of her life as the stress of the collapse of her world took an increasing toll on her health. Over the next year, she clung to whatever relationships she could with her children, who by now were increasingly far flung across the globe. Herbert had emigrated to Australia in 1858, Dite soon after, and in 1865 their younger brother Alfred joined them.

By 1865 her son Frederick and his wife Elizabeth had five children: four daughters, then a son. He had followed his mother's path to some extent, becoming, as recorded in the 1861 census, an optician and mathematical instrument maker. But he, too, found this business difficult in the coming years and was thinking of alternative careers, perhaps as a clerk in some financial capacity, as he had shown himself adept at numbers. By the next census in 1871 he had indeed changed careers and listed himself as 'Accountant's clerk' and the family no longer could afford to maintain any servants.

And while Janet had a special and enduring relationship with her stepdaughter Emily, she had become somewhat distanced from her only daughter Ada, who had married a coachman with the name of King, someone of whom Janet did not approve. Janet was very conscious of matters concerning class, having worked so hard to earn her place in the respectable middle class ranks of London and anxious to distance herself from the rapidly expanding 'lower' middle classes. This is also what irked her about the disparity in her civil list award and the award to Mrs Somerville, that perhaps Mrs Somerville got the award because she was more 'high class' than Janet. She was pleased when Dite married well in Australia. He had worked as overseer on a sheep station, 'Exmoor', in Southern Queensland and married Rachel Henning, the sister of the owner Biddulph, in March 1866. In writing to Dite in Australia, after he married Rachel, she was interested in hearing about 'the class' of people around them. Ada's 'unsuitable' marriage pained her greatly.

As she began to unravel the threads of her life, Janet packed up the few precious things she had rescued from her creditors and, one by one, sent them to her family. It broke her heart to think of her once beautifully furnished and decorated house and how all had to be sacrificed. But she could not allow herself to dwell on such matters for long.

In 1866 she finally gave up her business operations completely and sold the business premises at No. 104 Minories to John Bryer. After an apprenticeship with Edward Dent, Bryer had gone into the business of watch and chronometer making in Clerkenwell and later at Barbican. Like Frederick Wiggins had been to her, Bryer was to Dent, and Janet noted the irony when, where she had been the 'sole agent for Dent's Chronometers', now his former apprentice was taking over her business. In a strange twist of events, No. 104 Minories was sold in 1896 to Tresillian Wiggins, the son of Frederick. Janet also published the twenty-seventh edition of her *Handbook to the Local Marine Board Examination for Officers of the British Marine*. It sold for 7s 6d and was the last edition of this work and the last publication in her name.

And then, as the winter of 1866 brought with it the usual aggravation of Janet's bronchial condition, on top of all her financial woes, she decided, after much soul searching, to leave London altogether. Although the Christmas had been mild, the period immediately following was very severe. Janet's much loved niece, Jane Chester, was ill, and as spring turned into summer in 1867 her condition was worsening. Jane's mother, Janet's sister Joyce, begged Janet to come. Joyce's husband, Canon Matthew Chester, had been the incumbent at St Helen Auckland for over forty-five years, and there was plenty of room at the Vicarage, a short way down the road from his church, for Janet to join them indefinitely.

Joyce was despairing; and Janet at last was able just to leave London without any concern as to what she was leaving behind. The pull of Durham was strong and now she could give heed to it. She was there to see her niece's suffering end when she passed away on 20 June 1867, aged forty-two, the same age as Joyce's and Janet's mother and their dear sister, Elizabeth.

The wheel had turned full circle. After fifty years of the frenetic pace of London, Janet was now back in the part of the country where she had begun her life's journey.

XXIII

Return to Durham

The summer of 1867 came to a sad end when Janet's niece, Jane Margaret Chester, was laid to rest in the graveyard of the parish church of St Helen Auckland. It reminded Janet of so many other deaths and made her conscious of her own mortality. But, for now, her sister's grief at her daughter's death was overwhelming, and it cast a pall over the household. When their younger brother, Frederick, now living in Newcastle, and his six-year-old son, also named Frederick Peter, like his father, made their annual trip for a few days in August to see 'Aunt Chester' and 'Uncle Canon', from the perspective of young Frederick it was a very dull visit. As the months passed, the sadness at the Vicarage still clung to everyone and everything around it.

For a young boy, the company of his cousins was not the entertaining company of others of his age. In addition to Aunt Chester and Uncle Canon, both in their seventies, there was their unmarried son, George, aged thirty-six; Uncle Canon's sister Barbara, in her late fifties; and now Aunt Janet, sixty-four – hardly lively company for a child, with not even any younger servants to relieve the oppressing feeling of the elderly, let alone the weight of the sadness of cousin Jane's passing. His father was the youngest sibling of a large family, and the displacement of generations was felt at its keenest that summer at St Helen.

By the end of the year, Janet was relieved to find some escape herself when, with an old friend from her girlhood, she was able to spend some time in Edinburgh, further north, but always with a milder climate. Her health was an increasing worry. The Vicarage was somewhat sombre at the best of times, but now it was positively cloying under the weight of the sadness, and the winter's chill was taking its toll again with her lungs.

It was not just the smog of London that aggravated her affliction. Cold, damp, smoke, just about anything would trigger an increasingly lengthy period of suffering. One of the many Durham cousins took her place at the Vicarage to see to her sister Joyce, and Janet left for a month's welcome respite with her old friend. They stayed in a guest house on Princes Street from which they could enjoy a view of Castle Rock, rising perpendicularly before them and the gardens nestling at its base. The majestic and imposing rock was the remnant of an ancient volcano upon which had been built a fortress of one kind or another, and a royal castle, at least since the twelfth century until 1603 when James VI of Scotland became James I of England, the first of the house of Stuart to sit on that throne.

Janet enjoyed the order and Georgian elegance of Edinburgh's 'New Town', built in the second half of the eighteenth century. The fine public buildings gave, as she wrote to her children, 'a noble appearance to the City', and she imagined 'that in summer it will deserve the name of the modern Athens'. Its streets and squares were named after the Hanoverian rulers at the time of its construction: George III and Queen Charlotte – Janet's benefactor of all those years ago, and the reason that she had left Durham as a girl to take that long southwards journey to Queen Charlotte's school at Ampthill ('The Royal School for Embroidering Females', she reflected pensively).

The time in Edinburgh made Janet rather nostalgic, for all the things she had held dear over her lifetime. She wanted to maintain contact with her children, but it was not always easy, especially as three of her sons were now in Australia. The cycle of letters was always a long one, and often disjointed. While she wrote every month to Dite and Rachel, her letters could take a much longer journey, and theirs in return. But always they gave her an opportunity for much musing, and on 21 January 1868 she wrote from Edinburgh to their new home, 'The Peach Trees', in Stroud, northern New South Wales:

My very dear children
I have just received your letter dear Rachel here of the 19 Novr and very pleased I am to find *at last* you are happily and comfortably settled in your new home – God grant you happiness, health and prosperity in It – I can fancy all your bother and bustle in getting things in order and can well understand dear Dite's anxiety to get some part in tolerable order before you saw it – but you would be too well pleased to return to your bush life to care much about the trouble of getting your house in order – you say dear Rachel that you have just received my letter of July!!

I am only here for a month, staying with a cousin, a widow like myself, with whom I spent much time in our girlhood, but from whom I have been separated since our marriages. She became a Roman Catholic, tho' her father, husband, besides 2 cousins were Protestants. I see lots of Priests & find them very agreeable, amusing and very gentlemanly. The society here is very good so that I am enjoying myself much after the extreme dullness & monotony of St Helens ...

I have consulted a Physician since I came, and he speaks very cheeringly of me and says my lungs are but little affected, but that there is great delicacy and I require great care. I hope to get some rules for managing myself and then I hope I shall be set up, besides which this opinion is heartening and gives me spirit to go on ...

I can well imagine dear Dite's delight with the piano and musick. I hope you too dear Rachel are an enthusiast or you will be tired out, for believe me, Dite, could never tire. I hope to be able to send out some of the old musick but no doubt you will have many of my old things already. I am very glad to find Bishop's songs are again coming into fashion for some, nay, most of his compositions are very beautiful and so thoroughly English that we ought to be proud of them as a national style of musick. I have heard a little good musick and singing since I came here, but it is now many months since I heard a *feast* ...

You are better off, dear Rachel, than I am to be in range of a circulating library, for you will scarcely believe it, there is not a thing on the facts of Bishop Auckland, the nearest town. When I am at St. Helens, I am quite dependent on my friends lending me books, for I would not get on without learning. Mr Chester has a very fine collection of books, but they are generally of too sombre and heavy a character for me, altho' there is much I delight in and am glad to meet with, but when one wants the spirits lifted, we require lighter reading.

By the time you receive this your garden will be in progress, and that will be a great charm and delight to you both, for I find you dear Dite are becoming quite a lover of country life & all its belonging. I was showing your sketch of Exmoor to some friends here last night and they were delighted with it being so artistically done & so interesting as representing a country one hears so much about just now. I am sorry you are having a bad season just as you begin your new life, but as it will only affect you in the shape of dearer food, it will not matter much. Thank you for your information, dear Rachel, about the creeks and gulleys – I shall try to recollect ...

Have you any snakes in your part of the country? I find some of the Australian species are very venomous, so pray take care ...

I hope you will like your clergyman. Remember to tell me what sort of man he turns out to be, & whether he tries to do his duty energetically and judiciously. What class of people are the inhabitants of Stroud? Any educated, genteel folks amongst them etc, for it would be pleasant to find you could have a few friends at such a distance – too far off to bother as morning callers, but near enough to ride over to take tea with once and again. Such changes are agreeable without being *laborious* or inconvenient.

I cannot, dear Dite, tell you anything about Fred for we have very little communication – but I fear he is not doing so well as he might be. I am looking forward with much delight to going South in the Spring, but I shall not stay with them.

Poor Emily & her family have all been laid up with scarlet fever, but by their last letter all were doing well and she said I was to give her love to both of you & say she would write next mail. I sent her your new address.

Now my very dear children adieu. This will reach you just after you have passed your second anniversary of your marriage. God bless you both, spare you to be blessings to each other for many years to come. I shall think of you on the day and I congratulate you in my heart. Dear Dite you will remember *many* such happy days at *home*. Accept best love and kisses from your affectionate Mother

Janet Taylor

PS – Do not forget to tell me if you hear anything of Herbert and Alfred. I have heard nothing.

Janet's letters always contained such a mixture of personal interest, family matters, even science. In Edinburgh she was intrigued by the coal:

The coal here is very remarkable, it seems as if the wood were only half converted into coal – for on first lighting it crackles just like wood, and in consuming leaves a cinder with the fibres of the wood distinctly visible, which cinder fully consumed leaves ashes just like wood ashes – it is very remarkable and very nice, for it lights up easily, and flourishes for hours until stirred up.

And she was acutely interested in politics, which had seemed so close to her door in Minories. The visit of the Duke of Edinburgh, twenty-three-year-old Prince Alfred, Victoria's second son and a captain in her Royal

Navy, to Her Majesty's Australian colonies between 1867 and 1868 was widely reported, both in Australia and in London. Janet was keen to learn how he would be received:

> Have you gone out of your way to see the Duke of Edinburgh. I hope he will behave properly when with you and *leave* a favourable impression. He has very much depreciated in public opinion here, and I can only hope he will see his errors and behave, for he was a great favourite previously – and promised to be a good sensible man. The Prince of Wales and he carried on sad games together. But it is to be hoped as they grow older, they will grow wiser.
>
> There is constant talk of war, and the Continent looks in a very troubled state. But I trust we shall escape – tho' America becomes inclined to be troublesome. The Fenian movement has been very alarming, but I hope now we are fairly aroused to look these matters firmly in the face and things will settle down again. I think it would all have been stamped out too long ago but for the Americans. You will be well up in all European affairs, having so many papers & periodicals, so it is no use saying much about these things. Happily you are far away out of such troubles & may quietly look on at a distance.

The distance was not as far as Janet may have supposed, as sectarian unrest between Irish Catholic and Protestant factions, fighting over Irish independence from England, also showed its face in the colonies. On 12 March, while the Duke was visiting Sydney, the Fenian Henry James O'Farrell shot and seriously wounded him. O'Farrell was hanged for the sin of his failed assassination attempt, and the duke, having recovered from his injuries, dedicated hospitals in Sydney and Melbourne celebrating his near escape from death; they are still known as 'Royal Prince Alfred' hospitals. Janet pored over the newspapers to learn of events at home and abroad. While on one level welcoming her return to the familiar county of her childhood, on another she felt so constrained, indeed frustrated, by the Vicarage and the circle of events at St Helen. Minories seemed a million miles, even years, away.

Janet was much relieved, and very pleased when, at the end of summer, in September 1868, younger brother Frederick again visited St Helen. Like the van Galens, the previous winter had hit his family hard, with coughs and scarlet fever striking them low for weeks. Janet was delighted to see them well again. She had always had a soft spot for her youngest sibling, especially since their time at No. 44 Oxford Street, and in each other they found some light relief from the seriousness that pervaded the Vicarage.

Poor Frederick had been quite dislocated over his life and she truly believed that the death of their mother, so soon after he was born, affected him profoundly as he never knew her. Janet's older sisters, and she in her turn, had done what they could to step into the yawning gap left by their mother's death – and they each also felt it terribly – but Frederick was the youngest and always left behind in so many ways. His second marriage to Elizabeth Heap was clearly not a happy one, and evidently more by way of 'convenience', as Frederick had fallen on hard times and had three daughters to support. When the widow Heap 'crossed his path', he knew, as he said, 'it had to be', but he acknowledged privately that 'troubles and misfortune followed quite too much for me'.

But by September there were also some happier times. Joyce's son, George, drove them to see their niece Jane Janson, their sister Elizabeth's daughter, near Heighington, and Janet was delighted to join the outing. The afternoons spent in the fields after harvest brought back so many memories of their childhood with grandfather Seymour Deighton and family members at Dr Pasture in Wolsingham, the sight, the smell and the sound of it. Young Frederick was quite astonished at his seemingly aged relatives' antics, but he was also very moved when they took him to see his grandfather Peter Ionn's grave in Wolsingham – the 'Peter' after whom he and his father were given their middle names – and the plaque in the church in his honour. It located him amongst a universe of otherwise ancient family and gave him something very tangible to remember.

After spending the remainder of 1868 at the Vicarage, and the winter again in the cold of Durham, Janet was excited to spend an extended time over the following summer in Rotterdam with the van Galens. Janet enjoyed so much her six weeks in Rotterdam, but it also reinforced her sense of her own mortality and propelled her sending her remaining treasured and personal items to her family – a package here, a box there, with music, especially of the composer Rowley Bishop whom she loved so much, or other 'trifles'. In particular, she packed up the pastel portrait of herself that George had had drawn early in their marriage. She even managed to cobble together £60 for Dite to help him with his new home, an amount representing her whole pension for the year and a little bit besides. While in Rotterdam she also wrote to Rachel and Dite with news as ever of her family, her surroundings, and her aspirations. Emily's home was called 'Kennis', or 'knowledge' in English – and she wrote from there on 17 August:

My dear children
I write this, but do not know when you will receive it as I can find no one to tell me about the mails ... I am determined to take the benefit of

the doubt and start supposing that you will get it sometime this year. I have just received your June letter and delighted I am to find the box has at last reached you and that you were pleased with the contents ...

I have fixed going back at the end of the month or the beginning of next when I hope to get you another box of trifles off. By then, dear Dite, I shall have settled all my little anxieties about the poor remains of my once beautifully furnished and decorated house. It almost breaks my heart to think *how they* have all been sacrificed.

I know exactly where you have hung the painting, and just where I can look down upon you. You, dear Rachel, make me quite long to see your beautiful country, and were I 10 years younger I would start off to lay my bones besides you.

By this time you will have received *the Bishop* and may perhaps have seen the original that followed by the next mail. Mind you tell me how he is liked, & all about his reception ...

Poor Ada has married a man quite unsuited to her *in every way*. But he is good & kind to her and really she seems very happy. She has a pretty dear little baby, called 'Zoë Janet'. The first name after some good French woman who was kind to her when she was in France. Ada's name is King. Of course she is devoted to her baby & thinks there never was such another. I quite long to get back to see it!! ...

There is certainly a complete change here from anything in England. And I think I have noticed more the great difference in manners, character and habits of the people. The town is very much improved, but they still keep up the same style of houses with their miserable staircases ...

Goodbye and God bless you both. Accept lots of love from the household of the van Galen family and loving kisses

From your affectionate mother.

At the top of the letter was a coloured-in sketched map, about two inches square, of Rotterdam. Next to it was a brief note written by two of her grandchildren: 'Emily's and Frank's performance – to decorate Uncle Dite's paper.' By the time this letter made its way to Dite and Rachel, Janet would be dead.

At the end of summer Janet caught a ship from the Hook of Holland, south of Rotterdam, to Harwich, then by coach to the north road to Durham, rather than going back to London and from there north. She so wanted to see Ada's baby, Zoë, but could not face such a long journey on top of the passage from Holland. When she returned to St Helen in the autumn, the winter brought its familiar, but dreaded, companion to her in the form of bronchitis, and as the cold etched its way into the corners of the Vicarage, she became increasingly limited in her ability to move around. By early January it took all her effort just to sit in the deep armchair near the window – her last link to the sky and the world beyond.

The days were now short and the nights ate into her bones. Her body ached just with the effort of breathing. She sensed now that her time was short, as she struggled for breath, and once more wanted to seek the reassurance of God's wonders in the heavens. As she felt her strength ebb, little by little, she pulled her shawl tightly around her and begged her sister to open the curtains. Painfully lifting her face to the window, Janet could see the stars spread out like a tapestry before her. Her eyes searched frantically across the familiar jigsaw of the sky. Then she found it: Polaris, the Pole Star. Her star.

On Wednesday, 26 January 1870, Janet saw Polaris for the last time and passed away of 'bronchitis'. For the modern ear, 'bronchitis' sounds transitory, eminently treatable, but for so many at this time, it was a chronic, and debilitating condition, often with complications that we would now call asthma, or worse, pneumonia, which, before penicillin, was usually a death sentence, particularly for the young or elderly. And so it was for Janet Taylor.

Her death certificate recorded her occupation simply as 'Teacher of Navigation'. Four days later she was buried, the ceremony performed by her brother-in-law, Canon Matthew Chester. An announcement in the 'Deaths' section of *The Times* of Saturday, 29 January, reported that:

> On Wednesday, 26th at the Parsonage, St Helen's Auckland, the residence of her sister, Mrs Janet Taylor, formerly of 104 Minories and The Grove, Camberwell, after a few days illness. Friends will kindly accept this intimation. Australian papers, please copy.

It was only through the copying in Australian papers that her sons in Australia learned of their mother's death, many months later.

And then, on 4 February, Janet's nephew, the Reverend Canon Thomas Henry Chester, Rector of Easingham, and Joyce's son, posted another announcement in the *Durham County Advertiser*, providing only a little more detail:

> At the vicarage, St Helen's Auckland, at the house of her brother-in- law, 21st ult,. Mrs Janet Taylor, fourth daughter of the late Rev Peter lonn, vicar of Sately in this county. She was the authoress of several books on Navigation and Astronomy and a few years ago a pension was granted to her for her services by the Government.

Such things to mark her life, 'fourth daughter of the Reverend Peter Ionn', her rank and station amongst a list of later father's progeny, and the simple, but telling summation of her life's work, 'authoress of several books on Navigation and Astronomy', and that she had been acknowledged by the government. One paragraph for a life's work. But a life's work can be summed up even more simply, and poignantly, than that, as in the words of her youngest brother Frederick, recorded in some surviving family papers:

Poor Janet.
RIP

XXIV

Remembering Janet

Memory is a funny thing. There are the kinds of memories that one can record as 'posterity'. First there are family records, noted in family Bibles and other such things of old. Then there is a scrap here; a scrap there – a pastiche of formal and informal memory. Remembering Janet starts with a headstone.

The Chesters did what they could to honour her passing, as she had few worldly goods of her own, notwithstanding a lifetime of hard work. Her brother Frederick had fallen on hard times and could offer nothing. Janet's nephew, the Reverend Thomas Henry Chester, sought to enlist the Admiralty to make a contribution towards a suitable memorial to his extraordinary aunt. When the then Hydrographer, Captain George Henry Richards, read this request, his response was brief, and to the point:

> As to the contribution of the late Mrs Janet Taylor, of the Minories, on the advice of the Rev T. H. Chester of August 19th. I cannot understand why the Admiralty should be asked to contribute towards a Memorial to the late Mrs Janet Taylor unless they are prepared to do the same for any Teacher of Navigation who may die.
>
> G. H. R. 26 August 1870

It was dismissive, even disdainful, and Richards had profoundly missed the point. Teaching navigation was probably the one thing on which Janet spent the *least* time. What would her ally and friend Rear Admiral Sir Francis Beaufort have thought? A 'Teacher of Navigation'? Hardly.

Thomas's father, Canon Matthew Chester had a family plot in the graveyard adjacent to the church. It was a worthy plot for the Canon, measuring about eight feet by ten feet. Surrounded by a low looped iron railing, it also sat among eminent company: in particular, the family of the Eden baronetcy of West Auckland, one of whom, Sir Anthony Eden, was Prime Minister of the United Kingdom, 1955–57. Having failed to gain any support from the Admiralty for a memorial, Thomas suggested that something simple, but enduring, would be appropriate. And so it was: a plain granite cross and plinth, placed on a sandstone base, with a simple inscription

IN MEMORY OF
JANET TAYLOR
BORN 13th MAY AD 1804
DIED JANUARY 26th AD 1870

Dominating the plot was a grand and imposing column of about eight feet, on which the burials of the assembled members of the Chester family were recorded in turn. When Janet was buried she joined other members of her sister's family. Her niece:

In memory of Jane Margaret only daughter of the
Rev Matthew and Joyce Deighton Chester, of St Helen's Auckland
Died June 20th 1867 aged 42 years

Her younger nephews, the Chesters' two sons, who had died in childhood:

Also their son Matthew Ionn aged 19 days and Charles aged 9 years

Only the very next year, after Janet's passing, Canon Matthew Chester joined his sister-in-law in the family grave, and his death, too, was duly entered on the sandstone column:

The Rev Matthew Chester for 50 years of this Parish
Died on the 18th July AD 1871

There is also a stained glass window in the church in his memory. Janet's sister, Joyce Deighton Chester, meanwhile outlived her husband for almost twelve years, before she too joined them:

Joyce Deighton wife of the above Rev Matthew Chester who died
10 May AD 1883 aged 86 years

And, in time, their son George Heber Chester also found his way there:

George Heber son of the Rev. Matthew Chester
who died 3rd September 1911 aged 79 years

Such is the abbreviated way of historical record in graveyards.

She was not forgotten by the nautical world as evidenced by an entry in Volume 63, p. 417, of the 1894 of the *Nautical Magazine*. It refers to 'Mrs Janet Taylor' as 'a lady of some mathematical distinction who wrote upon nautical astronomy in the early part of this century. By making use of an auxiliary angle she obtains the following formula'. It then went on to describe a complex trigonometric equation that appeared in one of her books, a formula that was clearly considered advanced and still useful. It read

$$E = d \ p \cot h \ \mathrm{cosec}\theta \ \mathrm{cosec} \ p \ \sin(p - \theta)$$

and proceeded to explain the meaning of each term.

As the years passed Janet Taylor's story was soon condensed into perfunctory biographical entries like that in Fredrick Boase's *Modern English Biography* published in 1965:

Taylor, Janet – married George Taylor, lecturer of the nautical academy and mathematical instrument maker at 104 Minories, London, who died 1845. Carried on business from 1845 to 1858. Granted Civil List pension of £50 on 16th January, 1860 in consideration of her benevolent labours among the seafaring population of London. Author of Luni-Solar and Horary Tables with their application to nautical astronomy in 1833; An Epitome of Navigation and Nautical Astronomy in 1842; A Planisphere of the Fixed Stars, accompanied by a book of directions in 1846; A Guidebook to Lieut. Maury's Wind and Current Charts in 1855; Handbook to the local marine board examination for the officers of the British Mercantile Marine 25 ed. 1865.

d. January or February 1870.

At least this gave her more credit than being merely a 'teacher of navigation'.

Nearly 100 years later, another account was provided by Professor E. G. R. Taylor (no relation of Janet's) in her renowned treatise, *The Mathematical Practitioners of Hanoverian England 1714–1840*. This massive work includes over 2,000 mathematicians who contributed to the profession in the designated period and Janet was singled out for special mention, even though her life's work continued for many decades after 1840. Her entry ran to almost a full page, while many other biographies spanned only a couple of lines. The lengthy description of her read, in part:

> One of the most socially interesting warehouses, that of Mrs Janet Taylor, has disappeared completely. It was unique in that it was run by a woman who was herself a competent nautical writer and not simply a widow carrying on her husband's business. Indeed her husband George Taylor was still alive and appears to have worked with her. That Janet Taylor was so much talked about at the time arose from her publication in 1833 of a new set of Lunar Tables compiled by herself.

The impact of Janet's work, acknowledged clearly by Professor Taylor, was seen best, perhaps, by those at sea. In 1881, some eleven years after her death, Lieutenant S. T. S. Lecky wrote, in his quaintly titled, *Wrinkles in Practical Navigation*, that:

> Youngsters frequently display no little aptitude in becoming acquainted with the stars and the planets. They should always be encouraged. A material help in the practical part (that is in locating and identifying stars) will be found in the Planisphere published by Mrs Janet Taylor, which is one of the best of its kind.

Lecky was referring to Janet's *A Planisphere of the Fixed Stars and Directions for Use* which first appeared nearly fifty years before. His simple words of tribute would have brought a smile to her face: 'one of the best of its kind'.

The goodwill of her business was another testimonial to her success: years after her death, the entries in the Post Office Directories for both 1872 and 1876 read '104 Minories Mrs Janet Taylor, Nautical Academy'. The goodwill of the business that John Bryer had purchased was still making an impact. And in the Great International Fisheries Exhibition that was held in London from 12 May 1883 to 30 October 1883, Bryer entered an instrument, a chronometer with unusual technical features. It had won a first prize. Bryer had kept the name of 'Mrs Janet Taylor & Co.' in his business title and it bore the following inscription:

J Bryer & Son
Late: Mrs Janet Taylor & Co.

Gold Medal and Diploma 1883
　　International Fisheries Exhibition
　　　　By appointment to Nautical Academy, 104 Minories, London
(opposite Railroad).

By the end of the decade, however, her name was no longer listed, and
in 1883 the occupants were 'Dobson & Jones, Solicitors' and 'Bryer &
Sons, Nautical Academy'. Bryer continued to pay the land tax on No.
104 Minories until his death in 1895 when it was left to his daughter
Susannah, who sold it the following year to Tresillian Wiggins. The
firm of Imray, Reynolds and Wiggins continued to operate at No. 102
Minories after Janet retired in 1868. It did not take long for Wiggins to
break away from the partnership to branch out on his own, going into
business with his son at No. 10 King Street.

By 1884 Imray had gone and the London Post Office Directory
shows that they were associated with the manufacture of talc and
mica and in 1890 they moved into her old premises at Nos 102–104
Minories. During the 1930s, Frederick's grandson Harold P. Wiggins
presented to the National Maritime Museum in Greenwich an octant
bearing the name of 'Mrs Janet Taylor' on the arc. The gift was made
in memory of his grandfather whom he acknowledged as being one of
her apprentices.

In 1933, nearly sixty-five years after her death, an article appeared
again in the *Nautical Magazine*, singling Janet out for special mention.
This was a two-part treatise on the beginning of organised instruction in
navigation. It began:

> To record the innumerable private 'coaches' of the nineteenth century
> is outside the range of this account, but we cannot conclude our brief
> survey without mention of Mrs Janet Taylor.
>
> Her Nautical Academy at 103 Minories, London, was much patronised
> by officers of the East India Company and of the Navy in the early part
> of the last century. She was a most competent astronomer and published
> stellar and lunar tables, and indeed exhibited a sextant as late as the
> Great Exhibition in 1851.

'A most competent astronomer' – a fair remark; and she did exhibit at the
Great Exhibition, although her entry was not appreciated at all.

Apparently she moved to 104 Minories and little is known about her. However, 'crammers' of lesser magnitude were always plentiful.

This simply implied that she was clearly a cut above the 'crammers'.

In December 1977, some 107 years after her death, there was still a mention of Janet in the *Nautical Magazine*, referring to the critical review of her book and her feisty response to it in 1835, and indirectly acknowledging the quality of her work:

> From that broadside, it becomes evident that contributors to the Magazine in those days were just plain rotten chauvinistic pigs. And PEEVISH ones withal. Change, change, all is change. Nowadays a proportion of our contributors is of the fairer sex and none of our contributors is peevish – well, not often, and not very. But conversely, none of our lady contributors has produced any top grade navigational text-books recently. It's a matter of swings and roundabouts.

All of this is about her public self – her books, her instruments, her school. But who remembers Janet, as a person? As mother? As sister?

Her youngest brother, Frederick, did; and some of his jottings survive. In 1869, Frederick had set down his 'Mems', or memories, of his family, an exercise to fill the time when constrained to home 'by tight boots', with the added warning inscribed: 'Never get Tight Boots'. He laid out before him a large piece of parchment, with a linen backing, and divided it into four rows of five shields in which he set about recording his memories and stories of his family. And over the ensuing days and weeks he filled in seventeen of those shields, with three blank shields for additions in time, although they still remain blank. In time, thus inspired, he also constructed a much larger chart of family history, drawing in all manner of family records in the way of the amateur and oral genealogist of time past, adding to the family Bible a rich tapestry of kinship and anecdote. It is from his memories that many of the singular details in this story have been drawn. For his 'Mems' of his sister Janet, or Jane Ann as he knew her, he allocated two shields, joined by '='. This is what he wrote:

Jane Ann, As I may say was the Great Gun of our family. When very young was through the Interest of Michael Angelo Taylor MP. Durham City, got an appointment for her to Queen Charlotte's School at Ampthill Bedford = shire where there were only a few first class ladies she being much younger than any of them became a great favourite and she got instructions in music Languages &tc her forte seemed to be figures Queen Charlotte died soon after her appoint^t and Govern^t gave up the school, she was then sent to a Ladies School at Hendon n^r London a assistant & finish her Education she then went as governess to a Rev^d Mr Huntly of Kimbolton

My Bro^r Seymour wanting a Housekeeper she returned to London and then got acquainted with George Taylor who was a widower with 2 Boys & a Girl he having early in life been at sea gave her the Idea of puting her figures to work at Navigation she published her Book call^d Navigation Simplified and Lunar Tables opened a school for the instruction of young & old students in navigation, she was introduced to King William & Queen Adelaide and afterwards had an offer as reader to our Queen Victoria, she receiv^d a gold medal from the Pope and complimentary letters from other Crown^d Heads in Europe and got a pension of 50 per year from the Country had a large family who are now distributed over the 49th of the Globe

Beneath the right-hand shield was also penned a note, written in two instalments:

She still living (1869) at St Helens Auck^d with the Rev^d M Chester
Lived at St Helens Auckland
January 26th 1870 died 65
and was buried in the Family vault of M Chester in St Helens Churchyard.
Poor Janet. RIP

What of Janet as a mother? Nothing remains, or is evident. Rachel Taylor's letters survive, but her reflections are as a daughter-in-law – and a distant one, at that, who had never met her mother-in-law. Her judgment was that Janet thought more of the stars than her sons, as she wrote in a letter of 19 May 1865. Janet's son Frederick had more to say and was also obviously the principal informant for William Anderson, when in 1871, the year following her death, the second edition of his book, *Model Women*, appeared. Reverend William Anderson, a Doctor of Divinity whose hobby was biographical collections, selected 'only a few of the actors and thinkers who have attained extensive celebrity, of those eminent women no longer living'.

In his section, for example, on 'Literary Women', he included amongst the seven writers selected, Hannah More and Elizabeth Barrett Browning, but in 'Scientific Women', he included but two – 'Caroline Lucretia Herschel' and 'Jane Anne Taylor [Janet Taylor]'. Anderson included a fair amount of detail of Janet's early life, and the narrative, being written so close to the time of her death, bears the hallmarks of family informants, with some of the inaccuracies, or slippage in detail, that often comes from such sources. But Anderson also had some insights as to her physical appearance that only someone who had met her or had spoken to someone who had, could say. Anderson wrote of her 'lack of vigour' in describing a physical weakness, which he identified as a general characteristic in the female sex, attributable, perhaps, to the condition of universal Eve:

Mrs Taylor was rather tall, somewhat slender, and a little defective in muscular development. For many years she was subject to a disease of very common occurrence in Great Britain. Her head was large, and in perfect harmony with all its component parts. The brow broad, smooth, and high, gave the face a pyriform appearance, which diminished gradually as it descended, till it terminated in the delicate outline of the chin.

In holding up Janet as one of his 'Model Women', Anderson provided a uniquely powerful contemporary tribute:

Intellect was the constitutional guide of her entire being. An active temperament and strong and evenly-balanced mental powers enabled her to awaken the minds of her pupils, and to write what was worth perusal and re-perusal. She spent much time and money and care on science. Her quick perceptive faculties ranged the heavens, explored the earth, and fathomed the sea, in search of facts, which her prominent reflective powers enabled her to explain and apply, so as to accomplish innumerable ends otherwise unattainable. A more quiet and singular union of rare powers in a woman, than hers, does not occur to us.

Many an officer now in the mercantile marine owes his present position to the teaching he received in her classes. As an instructor, she was without equal in her day; and we doubt whether more modern teachers have surpassed her in the system she adopted.

Mrs Taylor had not only a well-cultivated head, but what was better, a healthy, affectionate, and loving heart. She had a lively moral sense for perceiving right and wrong. Perhaps the greatest of her moral attributes was charity. Enjoying only a moderate competence, and obliged to make a decent appearance in life, she nevertheless gave large sums to those from whom lover and friend were put far away, whose harp was turned into mourning, and their organ into the voice of them that weep.

There is also an excellent entry on Janet by Dr Gloria Clifton, Emeritus Curator of the National Maritime Museum and Royal Observatory, Greenwich, in her landmark 1995 book *Directory of British Scientific Instrument Makers 1550–1851*. But there is also much misinformation published, even in recent times, in understating the achievements of Janet. One such example is the book *The Biographical Dictionary of Women in Science: L-Z* by Marilyn Bailey Ogilvie and Joy Dorothy Harvey, published by Routlege in 2000. The entry on page 1270, produced in part below, diminishes the role played by her and gives undue credit to George. For example, it was Janet who founded the Academy (it is why only her name is on it) and it was she who designed the nautical instruments. She did not simply 'edit a series of books' in 1833 but she wrote many of them over a period of nearly three decades. And George never had a teaching role at the Academy while Janet was instrumental in this. Moreover, George died in 1853, not 1845:

> Janet Taylor was married to George Taylor, founder of the Nautical and Mathematical Academy located in London's east End. Her husband also made nautical instruments there. Beginning in 1833, Janet Taylor demonstrated her mathematical skills by editing a series of books on nautical astronomy and navigation.
>
> After her husband died in 1845, she took over his teaching as well as his instrument making firm. She was called the 'Mrs Somerville of the marine world' in recognition of her mathematical abilities.

Between 1855 and 1866 Janet published twenty-seven editions of her book 'A Handbook to the Local Marine Board Examinations for Officers of the British Mercantile Marine Board'. The sheer number of editions speaks for itself, but in August 2008 the very same book was again published by *BiblioLife*, based in the US. It states, 'We believe this work is culturally important and have elected to bring the book back into print.' It is astonishing to think that a work of this nature would still be relevant 140 years after the last edition appeared. Indeed, it is still available to purchase today.

And so, from a combination of sources such as these, and the more formal records as remain here and there, her story as told in this book has been woven. To end this narrative it is perhaps fitting to record the obituary published in the *Athenaeum*, on 5 February 1870, just ten days after her death:

MRS JANET TAYLOR

The past week's obituary records the departure of a remarkable person. Mrs Janet Taylor was a mathematician of the first class: as such to be commemorated by the side of Mrs Somerville; less universally cultivated but no less admirable in exposition than the latter named lady. In any event, little is known of her in the outside world. But her logarithmic tables we have been assured on fair authority, are correct and complete in no ordinary degree. And it was her singular occupation to prepare young men for the sea, by her tuition in the higher branches of mathematics.

A more quiet, a more singular union of rare powers of will and knowledge, especially in a woman, than her do not occur to us. She lived at the extreme east end of London, among her pupils and clients. We believe that she was as gentle and simple in herself as she was deeply versed in the abstract sciences which she professed. Perhaps some surviving relative or friend may be able to throw light on the life and labours of one who was as extraordinary from her acquirements of knowledge as from her social reticence.

It was, indeed, her singular occupation to prepare young men for the sea. It was her wish for all mariners to be guided, and safe, at sea. It was her passion, her singular occupation, and her enduring wish, that they – all women's husbands and sons – should be safe.

That prescient obituary recognised that it would, indeed, fall to a relative to take up the cause. In 1995, one such relative, her great-great-great-great nephew, John Croucher, descended from her eldest brother, William Ionn, began a search to throw that light. John is a mathematician and a teacher too, and it was a long journey which ended, and began, in a much neglected part of the graveyard of St Helen's. By then, a large ash tree had grown through Janet's grave, dislodging the granite cross from the sandstone base of her monument. The cross was lying face down, and her name was buried in the soil. By 2004, the tree had gone and the fence demolished in the process. The plot by then had also become seriously overgrown with weeds, blackberry bushes and more small trees. It was unrecognisable as the once proud resting place of the Chesters.

But in June that year, John and his wife Rosalind Croucher had the gravesite professionally restored, including the refixing of the cross to the base and the construction of a new plaque affixed to the base of the granite plinth, with the following inscription:

DEDICATED TO JANET TAYLOR (BORN JANE ANN IONN), MATHEMATICIAN, ASTRONOMER, AUTHOR, INSTRUMENT MAKER, INVENTOR AND FOUNDER OF HER OWN NAUTICAL ACADEMY. RESTORED BY HER DESCENDANT PROFESSOR JOHN S. CROUCHER AND HIS WIFE ROSALIND, AUSTRALIA, 2004, IN HONOUR OF THE 200TH ANNIVERSARY OF HER BIRTH.

In the constraints of a headstone, we sought to give, for posterity, a summation of her life's work. And together we completed this book in the hope that, in a small way, her story may now be seen in the light it deserves: the story of the extraordinary Janet Taylor.

Testing the Mariner's Calculator

A remaining question in the legacy of Janet Taylor is whether her Mariner's Calculator, in which she had placed so much faith, and which she had patented, was given a fair assessment. As recounted in this story, Sir Francis Beaufort was given the task to assess it, but, given his personal circumstances at the time, he was hardly in a position to evaluate it fully. Or was his judgment fair?[23]

To test this, the author John Croucher obtained a research grant from Macquarie University in Sydney, Australia, and the willing involvement of one of Britain's leading compass adjusters and nautical antique dealers, Ron Robinson of Hamble, in the south-east of England. Using the details set out in the patent, and the ingenuity of his skilled instrument restorer, a replica was produced, combining antique elements to give as faithful a rendition of the original as could be achieved. It was a challenging brief, as the patent gave only partial information and the assessment was to be undertaken knowing that Beaufort's report had been unfavourable but without the specific detail of it. But Ron felt a real affinity for what Janet had accomplished. A strange journey of purpose and happenstance led the author to Ron's door.

John and his wife, Rosalind, met him when they went looking for instruments that bore her name. When Rosalind contacted him, seeking to find an instrument for John's birthday, Ron responded with the eloquence and humour that they came to learn was characteristic of him, that it was like 'finding a Canaletto in the cupboard', and, yes, he had one – a dry card compass in a wooden box.

After this fateful meeting, Ron was their guide and facilitator in locating and buying a number of other instruments that bore the distinctive hallmark: 'Mrs Janet Taylor, 103 Minories'; or 'Mrs Janet

Taylor & Co, 104 Minories'. When they wanted to test her instrument, Ron was the obvious choice. After several months he had completed his assignment and John and Rosalind again made the journey to his door to learn first-hand of his findings.

In the reconstruction of the Mariner's Calculator, Robinson noted that the patent was helpful, but only to a limited extent: 'The drawings were technically inadequate to produce an exact instrument since in parts they were verging on the sketch and were barely sufficient'. Consistent with other patents of the period, not all details were revealed – to avoid replication by other craftsmen. However, what provided a very useful adjunct to the patent was the photo Robinson obtained of the only surviving original Mariner's Calculator, in the Sotheby's catalogue which had included the instrument for sale.

The reconstruction was undertaken by an experienced craftsman, specialising in the restoration of period instruments, mainly nautical instruments. Tools and techniques of the era were familiar, and period elements from other instruments were able to be incorporated into the construction, such as a wooden handle from another sextant of those times:

It's an original handle, quite distinctive of the period, with a nice patina of age. With respect to the mirrors: the frame, i.e. the mirror holder of the index mirror, together with the frame of the horizon mirror, are both originals from a sextant of the same period as the Mariner's Calculator. Indeed the mirrors where the silvering has somewhat aged are original – more commensurate with the spirit and period of the instrument. It's child's play to put in new mirrors. But using original components gives the reconstruction the age and patina it deserves.

When asked were there any problems in the construction process, apart from some slight deviation in constructional details, Robinson reported that:

The main difficulty from day one, having looked at the drawings, and trying to grasp tasks which the calculator set itself, involved scales which departed from the norm. It is straightforward to engrave in degrees, similarly in parts divided into minutes, as was the norm for most sextants. Indeed on what we call the top sextant arc the engraving is limited, simply to demonstrate angular division. It doesn't encompass the whole 180 degrees of division, but only a part thereof. As regards the additional scale originally placed on the top arc, this referred to distance.

I do not consider it possible to engrave this distance scale where it would accurately or sensibly reflect the scale design by Janet Taylor.

There were limitations as to division of the scale in the patent. The distance scales were there, but not sufficient information on the drawing to project the scales and duplicate them. Early on we decided to run with what we could produce – the same construction and style as the original, but with the proviso that there would be shortcomings on the scale in order to produce precise measurements. My goal was that the replica would look almost exactly as the original.

When it came to the central question prompting the reconstruction of the instrument – namely, does it work – Robinson prefaced his conclusions by saying that:

I cannot give an unqualified answer to that. It has to be qualified, in the context of several things. If one follows Janet Taylor's instructions for use and her statements as to what it was capable of doing, there is a very sound factual and logical progression in her work. *In theory* it should have done exactly what she said it would do.

When pressed as to whether one could prove or disprove her claims, he responded:

There is no part of her written instructions that is fundamentally flawed. She followed the laws of geometry absolutely. It's clear to me that she had an absolute and clear grasp of her subject: total – sufficient to write competently about it. I am unaware of any serious holes that were poked in her theory. But she dug a small hole for herself in terms of this being the machine that was going to do all things for the navigator.

The fundamental problem that Robinson identified, in terms of the 'small hole', was the sheer intricacy of the instrument. It was, he concluded, 'a very complex machine', and while 'what it was setting out to do was correct in principle', it lacked 'practicality'. He greatly respected, indeed admired, Mrs Taylor's 'appetite and zest to produce the "do-all" machine', and acknowledged that the Mariner's Calculator was built 'with delicacy and charm'. But as to practicality, 'that was another matter':

It is one of those clever ideas. Any person of her talent – extraordinary talent – is likely to wish to produce *something*. It may be that she took her eye off what its likely practical use would be.

If I were to have the original Mariner's Calculator before me today, I would find it an instrument awkward, to say the least, in use. I would expect to find it requiring a degree of delicacy and dexterity which would be trying under normal seagoing conditions – especially at her time. With the arrival of steamships, apart from the ship rolling and pitching, you have a reasonable platform from which to make your observations. But with a sailing ship – when the sails are full – it's a different matter, and you don't have the advantage of electric light. Conditions were not snug. They were thoroughly uncomfortable – like an agricultural worker having to work on a bad day. You can never separate the instrument from the conditions prevailing and the operator's state of mind at the time. You have to consider field conditions.

Was Beaufort the right person to test the instrument? Robinson reflected upon this and responded:

The Hydrographer is not the right person to test most things. He would have got someone else to do it for him. He would have sought an opinion around him, in-house. But whether they were qualified or not is another question.

He would have wanted to give her good advice. I am convinced that had he given it the thumbs up, and the Admiralty bought, say, three, I still believe it wouldn't have succeeded. I don't think the world of mercantile navigation missed an opportunity. It was an awkward and complicated thing that would have required a dexterity of fingers and a dexterity of brains that the seamen of the day would not have had – even today.

Some 100 years after the invention, Lieutenant Commander Ken Alger, a teacher of navigation and a keen amateur historian fascinated by the story of Mrs Taylor, hypothesised that Beaufort was being cruel to be kind.[24] Robinson had some sympathy for this suggestion:

Beaufort was blunt. What was called for was a blunt opinion from someone that was sympathetic to you. Such an opinion from a friend, someone you admired and respected, was more likely to be considered. It was the age of invention, when you could invent a machine to do almost anything. But to get a true sense of it, imagine giving something like the Mariner's Calculator to someone like a coal miner, with fingers like sausages, in poor light and under seagoing conditions.

There is a striking similarity between the succinct report to the Admiralty by Beaufort and the reflective observations of Robinson. The 'clumsy fingers of seamen' noted by Beaufort, were the 'fingers like sausages' for Robinson. The science was sound, but the instrument would be unworkable in practice by men with hands like these. In 1983, in his *History of the Navigator's Sextant*, Charles H Cotter, had expressed reservations about Janet's instrument, describing it as 'clumsy, yet ingenious'. In other words, Cotter viewed it as exceptionally clever, but totally impractical. But where Cotter suggested that the instrument was 'clumsy, yet ingenious', perhaps it would be fairer to say that the instrument was ingenious but impractical in the 'clumsy' hands of its potential users.

And so it remains, it seems, an inspired, curious, white elephant of the history of nautical invention.

APPENDIX A

Miscellaneous Information

Table A.1 Janet Taylor's children

Name	Date of birth	Janet Taylor's age
Herbert Peter	30 December 1831	27
Henry Frederick	4 October 1833	29
Seymour John	18 February 1835	30
Deighton	16 September 1836	32
Jon Justinian	16 April 1839	34
Janet	2 May 1841	36
Ada Marian	29 January 1843	38
Alfred Robert	9 August 1844	40

Table A.2 Janet Taylor and her siblings

Name	Date of birth	Date of death	Spouse
Elizabeth	26 March 1790	24 March 1876	George Dixon
William	15 August 1791	6 July 1877	Ann Vickers (1) Ann Craddock (2)

(Continued)

Table A.2 (*Continued*)

Name	Date of birth	Date of death	Spouse
Isabella	18 June 1795	13 October 1857	Robert Taylor
Joyce Deighton	6 February 1797	10 May 1883	Matthew Chester
Matthew Seymour	1 August 1802	20 November 1844	Emma Corbett Ross
Jane Ann	*13 May 1804*	*26 January 1870*	*George Taylor*
Emeline	1 February 1806	1865	James Hardy
Frederick	30 May 1811	7 February 1884	Elizabeth Heap

Table A.3 Other Janet Taylor relatives

Name	Relationship	Date of birth
William Deighton	Great-grandfather	1686
Margaret Deighton (Allinson)	Great-grandmother	1687
Seymour Deighton	Grandfather	29 March 1718
Joyce Deighton (Thompson)	Grandmother	1736
Matthew Ionn	Grandfather	1721
Elizabeth Ionn (Chester)	Grandmother	1722
Peter Ionn	Father	8 March 1762
Jane Ionn (Deighton)	Mother	20 January 1769
George Taylor Jane	Husband	20 March 1792
Peter Van Galen	Son-in-law	20 September 1805
George Taylor Jane Jr	Stepson	17 May 1817
Emily Taylor Jane	Stepdaughter	15 August 1818
Charles Frank Jane	Stepson	22 March 1822

Table A.4 Prime Ministers of England during Janet Taylor's lifetime

Name	Begin	Finish	Party
William Pitt	10 May 1804	23 January 1806	Tory
William Wyndham Grenville (Lord Grenville)	11 February 1806	25 March 1807	Whig
Duke of Portland	31 March 1807	4 October 1809	Whig
Spencer Percival	4 October 1809	11 May 1812	Tory
Robert Banks Jenkinson (Earl of Liverpool)	8 June 1812	9 April 1827	Tory
George Canning	12 April 1827	8 August 1827	Whig/Tory coalition
Frederick Robinson (Viscount Goderich)	31 August 1827	8 January 1828	Whig/Tory coalition
Arthur Wellesley (Duke of Wellington)	22 January 1828	16 November 1830	Tory
Charles Earl Grey	22 November 1830	9 July 1834	Whig
William Lamb (2nd Viscount Melbourne)	16 July 1834	14 November 1834	Whig
Sir Robert Peel	10 December 1834	8 April 1835	Tory/ Conservative

(Continued)

Table A.4 (*Continued*)

Name	Begin	Finish	Party
Lord Melbourne	18 April 1835	30 August 1841	Whig
Sir Robert Peel	30 August 1841	29 June 1846	Conservative
Lord John Russell	30 June 1846	21 February 1852	Whig
Edward George Geoffrey Smith Stanley (Lord Derby)	23 February 1852	17 December 1853	Tory
George Hamilton-Gordon (4th Earl of Aberdeen)	19 December 1852	30 January 1855	Conservative/Peelite
Henry John Temple (Viscount Palmerston)	6 February 1855	19 February 1858	Whig
Lord Derby	20 February 1858	11 June 1859	Tory
Lord Palmerston	12 June 1859	18 October 1865	Whig
Lord John Russell	29 October 1865	26 June 1866	Whig
Lord Derby	28 June 1866	25 February 1868	Tory
Benjamin Disraeli	27 February 1868	1 December 1868	Tory
William Gladstone	3 December 1868	17 February 1874	Liberal

Table A.5 Reigning Monarchs of England during Janet Taylor's lifetime

Name	Reigned	Spouse
George III	25 October 1760–29 January 1820	Charlotte
George IV	29 January 1820–26 June 1830	Caroline
William IV	26 June 1830–20 June 1837	Adelaide
Victoria	20 June 1837–22 January 1901	Albert

Table A.6 Books written by Janet Taylor with years of known editions

Year	Title	Edition
1833	Luni-Solar and Horary Tables	1st
1834	Lunar Tables	1st
1835	"	2nd
1836	"	3rd
1844	Lunar and Horary Tables	4th
1847	"	5th
1849	"	6th
1851	"	7th
1854	"	7th
1834	The Principles of Navigation Simplified	1st
1837	"	3rd
1842	An Epitome of Navigation and Nautical Astronomy	1st
1843	"	2nd
1844	"	3rd

(*Continued*)

Table A.6 (*Continued*)

Year	Title	Edition
1851	"	9th
1854	"	10th
1858	"	11th
1859	"	12th
1846	Planisphere of the Fixed Stars with Book of Directions	1st
1847	"	2nd
1853	"	4th
1863	"	6th
1846	Diurnal Register for Barometer, Sympiesometer, Thermometer and Hygrometer	1st
1852	"	6th
1854	"	7th
1855	A Guide Book to Lt. Maury's Wind and Current Charts	1st
1855	Handbook to the Local Marine Board Examinations for Officers of the British Mercantile Marine Board	3rd
1865	"	25th
1866	"	27th

Table A.7 Home and business addresses of Janet Taylor since her marriage and the approximate dates she took up residence

Date	Home address	Date	Business address
February 1830	6 East Street, Red Lion Square London	February 1830	1 Fen Court, Fenchurch Street, London
August 1835	103 Minories, London	August 1835	103 Minories, London
February 1845	1 Hammet Street, London	January 1845	104 Minories, London
January 1858	1 Grove Park Terrace, Camberwell		
January 1864	165 Camberwell Grove, Camberwell		
January 1868	The Vicarage, St Helen's Auckland, County Durham		

Glossary of Terms

Many of the following nautical terms and other items appear in this book. Those marked with an asterisk are provided by Janet Taylor herself in the many editions of her book *Epitome of Navigation and Nautical Astronomy*.

Admiralty: Early in the eighteenth century the office in charge of England's Navy was placed in the hands of the *Lords Commissioners* known as the 'Board of Admiralty' or simply 'Admiralty'. The board derived its powers from the royal prerogative and no act of Parliament defined or constrained them.

Admiralty law: The 'law of the sea'.

Altitude: Measures the position of an object above the Earth and is the angular elevation (up to 90°) above the *horizon*.

Amidships: In the centre of the boat.

Astronomer Royal: The Director of the Royal Greenwich Observatory in London.

Astronomical latitude: The angular distance of a heavenly body from the ecliptic – i.e. from the great circle formed by the intersection of the plane of the Earth's orbit with the *celestial sphere*.

*Axis: Of the celestial sphere is an imaginary line passing through the earth's centre and produced to the heavens about which the heavenly bodies appear to have a diurnal motion.

Azimuth: The arc of the horizon from the *celestial meridian* to the foot of the great circle passing through the *zenith*, the *nadir*, and the point of the *celestial sphere* in question. In navigation it is reckoned from the north point of the horizon towards the east point.

Barleycorn: A measure equal to one-third of an inch (or about 0.8 centimetres).

Bearing: The direction of an object from the observer.

Binnacle: A cylindrical pedestal with provision for illuminating the compass face from below. Each binnacle contains specially placed magnets and pieces of steel that cancel the magnetic effects of the metal of the ship.

Blueback chart: A chart usually having a blue paper backing and published by a private commercial publisher.

Buoy: A floating device used as a navigational aid by marking channels, hazards and prohibited areas.

Celestial: Pertaining to the sky or visible heaven.

Celestial equator: The great circle in which the plane of the (terrestrial) equator intersects the *celestial sphere*; it is therefore equidistant from the *celestial poles*.

Celestial meridian: The great circle of the *celestial sphere* which passes through its poles and the observer's zenith.

Celestial navigation: A method of using the stars, sun and moon to determine one's position. Position is determined by measuring the apparent altitude of one of these objects above the horizon using a sextant and recording the times of these sightings with an accurate clock. That information is then used with tables in the Nautical Almanac to determine one's position.

Celestial pole: The 'North' Celestial Pole is the point in the sky about which all the stars seen from the northern hemisphere rotate.

Celestial sphere: The imaginary spherical shell formed by the sky, usually represented as an infinite *sphere* of which the observer's position is at the centre. That vast apparent concave in which all the heavenly bodies seem to be situated.

Chronometer: A timekeeping device with a special mechanism for ensuring accuracy when used for determining longitude at sea.

Clearing the lunar distance: To clear the apparent distance between both the sun and the moon, or between the stars and the moon, of the effects of refraction and parallax error, thereby obtaining the true distance.

Compass: In navigation or surveying, the primary device for direction-finding on the surface of the Earth. Compasses may operate on magnetic or gyroscopic principles or by determining the direction of the sun or a star.

Declination: In astronomy, the angular distance of a body north or south of the *celestial equator*. Of a celestial body, it is that portion of the celestial meridian between the equinoctial and the centre of the object, or its angular distance from the equinoctial line, reckoned either northward or southward.

Diurnal: Pertaining to each day.

Equator: An imaginary line around the centre of the world at Latitude 0°.

Equinoctial: Sometimes called the *celestial equator*, it is a great circle coincident with the terrestrial equator and divides the heavens into two hemispheres, the northern and southern. It is called the equinoctial because when the sun appears on it, the days and nights are of an equal length all over the world – twelve hours each. This happens twice a year, about 21 March which is called the 'vernal equinox' and 23 September which is called the 'autumnal equinox'.

East India Company: Established in 1600 to challenge the Dutch-Portuguese monopoly of the spice trade. Queen Elizabeth granted the company monopoly rights to bring goods from India and with the approval of local Indian rulers, the East India Company established trading posts in Madras, Bombay and Calcutta. It ceased trading in 1834 and instead acted as a managing agency for the government. The company finally came to an end in 1873.

Ecliptic: A great circle traced out by an imaginary plane supposed to pass through the earth's orbit, and to be extended in every direction to the sphere of the heavens. It cuts the equinoctial in an angle of 23° 28' which is called the 'obliquity of the ecliptic'.

Epitome: A summary or condensed account.

Equator: The great circle around the Earth that is everywhere equidistant from the geographic poles and lies in a plane perpendicular to the Earth's axis.

Geocentric latitude: The angular distance of a heavenly body as measured from the centre of the Earth.

Great Circle: A circle drawn around the Earth such that the centre of the circle is at the centre of the Earth. Following such a circle plots the shortest distance between any two points on the surface of the Earth.

Heeling: When a boat tilts away from the wind, caused by wind blowing on the sails and pushing the top of the mast over. Some heel is normal when under sail.

Horizon: In astronomy, the boundary where the sky seems to meet the ground or sea. Also defined as the intersection on the *celestial sphere* of a plane perpendicular to a *plumb line*.

Hydrographer: Before the 1900s this was the compiler of charts and who worked in an office. They were not necessarily a marine surveyor of mariner. The Hydrographer of the Navy was responsible for the compilation and publication of Admiralty charts.

Latitude: Imaginary lines drawn around the world and used to measure distance north and south of the Equator. The North Pole is 90° north, the South Pole is 90° south, and the Equator is at 0°.

Lighthouse: A structure, usually with a tower, built onshore or on the seabed to serve as an aid to maritime coastal navigation, warning the mariner of hazards, establishing their position, and guiding them to his destination.

Log: A written record of a boat's condition, usually including items such as boat position, boat speed, wind speed and direction, course and other information.

Longitude: Imaginary lines drawn through the North and South poles on the globe, used to measure distance east and west. Greenwich, England, is designated as 0°, with other distances being measured in degrees east and west of Greenwich.

Lords Commissioners: The governing body of the *Admiralty*.

Lunar: Pertaining to the moon.

Lunar distance: The angular distance of the moon from the sun, a star, or a planet, employed for determining longitude by the lunar method.

Lunar method: The method of finding a ship's longitude by comparing the local time of taking (by means of a sextant or circle) a given lunar distance, with the Greenwich time corresponding to the same distance as ascertained from a nautical almanac, the difference of these times being the longitude.

Luni-solar: Based on the relations or joint action of the moon and the sun.

Merchant navy: A non-combatant commercial fleet that that engages in transporting mainly cargo but sometimes people.

Merchant ship: A cargo ship often involved in overseas trade.

Meridian: A great circle of the earth passing through the poles and any given point on the earth's surface. (See also *prime meridian*.)

Nadir: The point 180° opposite the *zenith*, directly underfoot. The point directly under the feet.

Navigation: The science of directing a craft by determining its position, course and distance travelled.

North star: See *Pole star*.

Occultation: The passage of one celestial body in front of a second, thus hiding the second from view. It especially applies to the moon's coming between an observer and a star or a planet.

Octant: Similar to a *sextant*, but with only a 45° arc. They were first used to calculate latitude but were replaced by sextants with a 60° arc in the latter half of the eighteenth century.

Parallel sailing: Sailing in which the course is along a parallel and departure is the product of cosine latitude times the difference of longitude

Plane (or plain) sailing: An approximate method of navigation over small ranges of latitude and longitude. That is, on a course plotted without reference to the curvature of the earth.

Pilot: A collection of charts bound in an atlas. A term also used by the British Admiralty in the titles of their sailing directions from 1855.

Piloting: The act of guiding a vessel through a waterway.

Plumb line: A light line with a weight (plumb bob) at one end that, when suspended, defines a vertical line.

Polar distance: Of a heavenly body is its distance from that pole nearest the zenith of the observer.

Pole star: The brightest star in Ursa Minor; at the end of the handle of the little dipper. The northern axis of the earth points toward it. Also known as *Polaris* or *North star*.

Prime meridian: The imaginary line used to indicate 0° longitude that passes through Greenwich, a borough of London, and terminates at the North and South poles. Also known as *Greenwich meridian*.

Quadrant: An instrument containing a graduated arc of 90° used in astronomy and navigation.

Refraction: The change in direction of a wave passing from one medium to another caused by its change in speed.

Rhumb line: A line that passes through all meridians at the same angle. When drawn on a Mercator chart, the rhumb line is a straight line, because the Mercator chart is a distortion of a spherical globe on a flat surface. The rhumb line results in a longer course than a great circle route.

Right ascension: Of a heavenly body is its distance from the first point in Aries, reckoned on the equinoctial line, in degrees, minutes etc from 0° to 360°, and in hours, minutes and seconds from 0 h to 24.

Run aground: To take a boat into water that is too shallow for it to float in; the bottom of the boat is resting on the ground.

Sailing directions: Nautical information on coasts and islands and the passages between them.

Sextant: An instrument for determining the angle between the horizon and a celestial body such as the sun, the moon, or a star, used in celestial navigation to determine latitude and longitude. The device consists of an arc of a circle, marked off in degrees, and a movable radial arm pivoted at the centre of the circle. A telescope, mounted rigidly to the framework, is lined up with the horizon. The name comes from the Latin sextus, or 'one-sixth', for the sextant's arc spans 60°, or one-sixth of a circle. Sextants were first developed with wider arcs for calculating longitude from lunar observations, and they replaced octants by the second half of the eighteenth century.

Screw: A propeller with several angled blades that rotates to push against water or air.

Screw ship: A propeller-driven vessel.

Siderial day: The period of time between two successive transits of any star over the meridian.

Sideral time: To which a sideral clock is set, begins when the first point of Aries comes to the meridian and is counted through the twenty-four hours until the same point returns again to the meridian.

Solar: Pertaining to the sun.

Sounding: The depth of the water as marked on a chart.

Sphere: A solid of revolution of a semi-circle about its diameter.

Spheroid: A solid of revolution by rotating an ellipse about one of its two axes.

Swing: To determine the deviation of compass errors on all points and make appropriate adjustments.

Trinity House: A corporation decreed by the Royal Charter and given the responsibility of dealing with all matters concerning navigation in England.

Wake: Waves generated in the water by a moving vessel.

Zenith: The point on the celestial sphere vertically above any place or observer. The vertical point immediately over the head of the observer. The point diametrically opposite to the zenith, vertically beneath any place or observer, is called the *nadir*.

Zenith distance: The distance of an object from the zenith, or the complement of its altitude.

Documents Relating to the Death of George Taylor

The will of George Taylor, husband of Janet Taylor, is contained in the Grant of Probate dated 25 March 1854 (Public Record Office, London, Cat. Ref. PROB 11/2188). The will itself was made on 1 July 1853 when George would have known he was gravely ill. He passed away on 12 September 1853. The death certificate showed that he had suffered from chronic bronchitis for two years and abdominal dropsy for three months prior to his death.

A copy of the will is shown below. This has been deciphered by the authors and the lines correspond exactly to those in the Grant of Probate document. The names in italics are signatures of both George and the two witnesses *Sarah Maria Hobson* and *Fred Harrison*, the latter being a London solicitor.

Grant of Probate for George Taylor dated 1 July 1853

This is the last Will and Testament
of me George Taylor of Hammet Street America Square in the
City of London Gentlemen I give devise and bequeath to my dear wife
Janet all my real and Personal Estate and Effects whatsoever and
wheresoever to hold to her and her heirs executors administrators and
assigns absolutely And I appoint my said wife Executrix of this my
will in witness whereof I have executed to set my hand this first day of
July one thousand eight hundred and fifty three (sgd.) *George Taylor*
did [?] and [?] by the said George Taylor the testator as and for his
last Will and Testament in our presence and in the presence of each other
and in his presence and at his request who accept to subscribe our
names as witnesses (sgd.) *Sarah Maria Hobson* (sgd.) *Fred Harrison*
Solicitor 628 Bloomsbury Square.

At the bottom of the Grant of Probate, following the will itself, is the part of the document that relates to the probate. This took place on 25 March 1854, just over six months following the death. Once again for ease of comparison, the lines correspond exactly to those in the original document:

Proved at London 25th March 1854 before the worshipful George
Edward Sayers Doctor of Laws and Surrogate by the oath of Janet Taylor
widow the relict the sole Executrix to which administration was
granted having been first sworn duly to administer.

Peter Ionn's Last Will and Testament

Below is the last will and testament of Janet Taylor's father, Peter Ionn who was born on 8 March 1762 and died at Wolsingham on 2 May 1821 at the age of fifty-nine. At the time of making this will on 14 April 1818, Peter was a fifty-six year-old widower, his wife Jane having passed away on 30 May 1811. The three executrices at the time of making the will were his three eldest (and unmarried) daughters Elizabeth (then aged twenty-seven), Isabella (aged twenty-two) and Joyce (aged twenty-one). His adult sons, named in the will, were William (aged twenty-six) and Seymour Deighton (aged twenty-four). The remaining four children were all aged under eighteen, these being Matthew Seymour (aged sixteen), Jane Ann (aged thirteen), Emeline (aged twelve) and Frederick Peter (aged six). None of this latter group is specifically mentioned by name.

At this time it is almost certain that his daughter Jane Ann was still at Queen Charlotte's School in Ampthill. William was working as a solicitor in Bishop Auckland at the time.

I, P. Ionn of Wolsingham in the Co. of Durham, do make this my last will and testament in that is I appoint Elizabeth, Isabella and Joyce my three eldest daughters Executrices to this my last will and testament. I give my son William all the furniture and plate which he has at Bishop Auckland and which was borrowed of me. I give to my five daughters living at the time of my death all the rest of the household furniture, Linen, Plate etc. to be equally divided amongst them, my books papers prints and manuscripts I give to my executrices to dispose of and give such of them as they think proper to any of my children. All my real and personal estate at Dr Pasture and Parkwall, also Bail H House I give bequeath share and share alike as tenants in common to my two sons Seymour and Frederick and my five daughters, them to their executors, administrators and assigns. A power left to my executors to sell Bail H House and pay just debts and funeral expenses. My house, Garth, Gardens and outbuildings, maltery etc I give and bequeath for the use and occupation of all my children who live in as long as they remain unmarried without rent to anyone, as soon as anyone marries then his order right dies and the aforesaid premises at Wolsingham remains the property of the unmarried as long as they are unmarried wish to live in the premises then the said premises are their own and to occupy a part and let the rest for their own use when they all marry or remove from these premises to dwell in other places for more than two years then these said premises shall go to my son William and his heirs for ever – revoking all other wills I declare this my last will and testament duly signed this 14th day of April 1818.

P. Ionn (signed)

Witness to the above
   Thos Whitfield (signed)
   Mary Ann Hodgson (signed)
   Hannah Marquis X (her mark)

Attached to the will, and written on the same day, there was a brief note as to why William was not getting a share of the properties, at least until all the other children had either married or moved out.

Explanation of the will dated April 14th 1818.
   My reason for leaving William no share is because in his education and other expenses he has got more than his share – and now stands indebted to me above that share £200 to be paid to my Executrices – if any of my children who are entitled by this will to occupy any part they please, letting the other and appropriating the rent to the rest who are unmarried and may live from home – my funeral must be very private with the utmost economy.

The probate document of the will, granted nearly twelve months after Peter's death, concerned the swearing of two of the executrices, daughters Elizabeth and Joyce who were present and Isabella who was absent.

Covering note to the will
The will of Peter Ionn of Wolsingham in the Co. of Durham.

On the second day of April 1822 Elizabeth Ionn and Joyce Deighton Ionn both of Wolsingham in the Co. of Durham spinster daughters of the Testator and two of the executrices named in the within written will were sworn as usual (under £1000) a power being reserved for granting a probate of the said will to Isabella Ionn spinster the other executrix when she shall apply for the same.

Before me
Philip Brownrigg, Surrogate

APPENDIX E

Janet Taylor's Children

At the time of her death Janet Taylor had six surviving children. Here is what is known of their lives.

Herbert Peter
Herbert, the eldest child, was born on 30 December 1831. In 1858, he emigrated to Australia where he made contact there with his younger brother Deighton in 1865. He lived in Sydney and worked as an engine driver, but little else is known of his activities.

(Henry) Frederick
Frederick was born on 5 October 1833 and married Elizabeth Badon-Glyben (born 5 October 1833) at S'Heerenberg in Holland on 21 July 1858. They had seven children:

Esther Janet, born in London on 14 October 1859 and died at Bexley Heath in Kent on 15 March 1938. She married Frank Allchin (born 1 March 1851, died 23 February 1903) on 14 October 1893. They had two children, being Marian Esther (born 28 Oct. 1894) and Florence Violet (born 25 Nov. 1895).

Theodora Johanna (known as Dora), born on 6 May 1860 and died on 27 January 1915. She married Walter Frederick Mieville (born 1855) on 26 March 1882, who in 1902 was created a Knight Commander of St Michael and St George. In doing so, Theodora became Lady Dora Mieville.

Janet, born on 15 August 1861 in London and died 2 February 1923 at Camberwell House in Peckham, Surrey.

Ada Johanna, born on 13 March 1863 and died 9 August 1863 in London.

Frederick Peter was born on 26 October 1865 in London.

Karl Johann Robert, born on 6 November 1868 in London.

George Herbert Deighton, born 13 January 1876 and died 21 April 1876.

Frederick was listed in the 1861 census as an Optical and Mathematical Instrument Maker in London and was the only one of Janet Taylor's children to be involved in any way in her profession. He and wife Elizabeth emigrated to Egypt where he died in Cairo on 24 October 1879 at the age of forty-six years. His will was proved on 25 November that year and his entire estate, valued at under £450, was left to Elizabeth, who was also the sole executrix.

Deighton (Dite)

Deighton was born on 18 September 1836 and took a trip to Australia in 1862. Having arrived in Sydney he reportedly 'rode off into the bush instead of reporting back on board'. He made his way to Queensland where he obtained a position as sheep overseer on Biddulph Henning's 250-square-mile property Exmoor Station in Queensland. Also living there was Biddulph's unmarried sister Rachel (born 29 April 1826), some ten years Deighton's senior.

Rachel and Deighton were secretly engaged on 7 November 1864 and on hearing the news, Biddulph fired him and he was made to leave. Nevertheless, although initially strongly opposed to the marriage, Biddulph eventually accepted it and the wedding took place on 3 March 1866 in Sydney.

They purchased 150 acres of land at Peach Trees near Stroud in New South Wales, building a house in which they lived until January 1872 when they advertised it for sale. It was finally sold for £150 on 11 May 1872 and they moved into their new home, Springfield, near Fig Tree on the New South Wales south coast on 31 July. At the age of thirty-eight years, on 26 November that year, Rachel's brother Biddulph Henning married Emily Tucker and they had three children.

Deighton became a chronic sufferer of asthma and as a result the couple had to leave Springfield in 1896. They then joined her sister Annie in renting a house called Lynwood in Terry Road, Ryde. It was there in November 1900 that Deighton passed away at the age of sixty-four, while Rachel died aged eighty-eight on 28 August 1914. She was buried alongside Deighton and over sixty years later was the subject of a play performed in November 1975 at All Saints Church in Hunters Hill. The couple did not have any children.

Jon Justinian

Jon was born on 16 April 1839 and later emigrated to the United States of America. There is a record of a Jon Taylor marrying Nellie Pendeana on 1 November 1875 in Carter, Tennessee, but despite the unusual spelling of his first name and the last name matching, it is unknown if it is the same person. It is reported that Jon did marry in the USA and had several children but details of his life otherwise remain a mystery.

Ada Marian

Ada, the only surviving daughter, was born on 29 January 1843 in the family home at No. 103 Minories. By 1868 she had married a coachman by the name of King, a union of which her mother strongly disapproved. The 1871 census revealed that they had two children, Zoë Janet, aged two, and Charles aged six months. For reasons unknown the marriage did not survive much past that point and on 15 May 1873 Ada married the laundryman John George Janson. By this time, with her parents both deceased and all of her brothers overseas, she mistakenly wrote down her father's name as 'John' Taylor on her marriage certificate. She was only ten years old when her father George Taylor passed away. The year following their marriage, Ada and John had a son George, the first of six boys, the others being Harold, Herbert, Frank, Philip and John. By 1895 Ada and her husband John ran a small laundry business at Tottenham in North London. At the age of fifty-nine, Ada passed away during the last three months of 1902 at the age of fifty-nine, while John survived a further twenty-six years and died in June 1928, aged eighty-two.

Alfred Robert

Alfred, the last child, was born on 9 August 1844 and emigrated to Australia in 1865. He obtained a temporary position as sheep overseer on 28 August 1865 on Biddulph Henning's property Exmoor Station in Queensland where he was looking for his brother Deighton. He turned out to be not very useful and was dismissed five weeks later on 6 October. At the time, his brother Deighton was engaged to Biddulph's sister Rachel, a match to which Biddulph was strongly opposed.

On June 4 1884 there is a record of Alfred visiting Rachel and Deighton in their home Springfield, staying until 2 October when he went to Cobar in western New South Wales. Three years later he again paid them a visit on 16 October 1887, this time only for the day, while they also ran into him while on a visit to the suburb of Burwood in Sydney on 18 May 1888. On 30 August the next year, Deighton went to Sydney and brought him back to stay with the couple for a week until 6 September. By this time Alfred was forty-three years old and still presumably unmarried.

Attempts to track his further movements have led to a record of an Alfred Taylor who was said to have been 'born in London in around 1840' and this certainly fits his description. This Alfred married Ann Smith on 10 March 1910 at 40 Munro Street, Ascot Vale, Victoria, and had as his profession 'poultry farmer'. He died less than two years later at the age of sixty-seven on 3 February 1912 at Deep Creek Road, Mitcham, Victoria, and on the February was buried in Brighton Cemetery, Brighton, Victoria.

This meant that Janet Taylor's five surviving sons were scattered in various parts of the world at the time of her death. Herbert, Deighton and Alfred were all in Australia, Jon was in America and Frederick was in Egypt, while only Ada remained in England. What is known, however, is that none of them followed in their mother's footsteps and took on a career in navigation.

Notes

1. The certified extract of his birth certificate, dated 8 August 1784, attesting to his baptism on 5 April. The year, however, is smudged, so that '1762' appears as '1761', the '2' being smudged into a '1'.

2. J. H. Lambert reported (somewhat quaintly and most likely an erroneous transcription from his source) that the queen supposedly said 'Let her come, not to work at tapestry, as at her age it would spoil her figure. But let her be educated with the four until she is of age to take the place of one of them' (J. H. Lambert, *Wolsingham from early times to 1938* (1960), held in the Durham County Records Office, Durham, p. 170). The *Ionn family papers*, held in private hands in France, include the following comment that 'her forte seemed to be figures', which is more accurate.

3. Reverend Huntley even had an orchid named after him '*Huntleya Bateman ex Lindley Orchidaceae*'.

4. 'To his coy mistress'.

5. Charles Manby Smith, *The Little World of London*, 1857, p. 128.

6. At this time Antwerp was part of the United Kingdom of the Netherlands, after tussles between Austria, Spain and France for control. The following year, in 1830, Belgian insurgents recovered Antwerp as part of a claim that led to Belgian independence on 20 January 1831.

7. Jane Ann's own family were at times 'I'onn', 'Ion', even 'Jon', and George's family name had at one time been 'Janet', suggestive of French Huguenot origins, and slipped from 'Jané' to 'Lane' in many of the records.

8. Contemporary satirist, Peter Pindar.

9. If Prince Charles, the Prince of Wales, succeeds his mother, Queen Elizabeth II, William IV's record will be overtaken.

10. From 1554 to 1924 copyright was usually protected by registration with the Stationers' Company in London, and designated in the flyleaves of a book

as 'entered at Stationers Hall'. However, because of the fees payable for registration and the number of complimentary copies required to be lodged at copyright libraries (eleven in 1801, reduced to five in 1836), the procedure of registration was often disregarded.

11. And like so many churches St Katherine Coleman is no longer there. It was demolished in 1925. Its bells found other homes – one at least is at St Catherine Westway White City Fulham, completed in 1923.

12. Addiscombe House, a military seminary of the East India Company.

13. The importance of accurate and readable charts for this region in particular became apparent just over 100 years later, when the Bay of Biscay, situated in the Atlantic Ocean off the north coast of Spain and west coast of France, was to earn itself the title of the 'Valley of Death' among the German U-Boat men from 1943 onwards during the Second World War with more than sixty-five of the craft lost at sea there.

14. In Hanover, Salic law prevented inheritance through the female line and so the dukedom passed to George III's fifth son, Ernest Augustus, Duke of Cumberland.

15. The Minories temporary terminus quickly lost importance and was shut permanently in October 1853.

16. This was a temporary station, which opened on 29 December 1836. It was replaced by a handsome station building, designed by George Smith, in April 1840, south-west of the town centre.

17. Albert's aunt, Victoria of Saxe-Coburg-Saalfeld, his father's younger sister, had married Edward Augustus, Duke of Kent, the fourth son of George III, so they were first cousins.

18. As a flat-bottomed vessel it was best suited for river travel and spent its life on the Seine and Loire rivers in France and was eventually broken up in 1855.

19. The instrument is now in the collection of the Royal Observatory, Greenwich. It indicates that it was used by the Royal Navy in 1847 and was later displayed at the Admiralty Compass Observatory at Slough.

20. The vessel itself was later purchased by the Admiralty and used as a troop ship.

21. Named after the Member of Parliament for Tynemouth, William Schaw Lindsay.

22. The words of Palmerston reflecting on what he would have said to Russia to prevent the Crimean War.

23. See J. S. and R. F. Croucher, 'Mrs Janet Taylor's "Mariner's Calculator": Assessment and Re-assessment' (2011), 44 *British Journal for the History of Science*, pp. 493–507.

24. K. Alger, *Mrs Janet Taylor – 'Authoress and Instructress in Navigation and Nautical Astronomy' (1804–1870)*, Fawcett Library Papers No. 6, L. L. R. S. Publications, London, 1982, p. 9.

Further Reading and References

Over 1,000 references were used in researching this book and this section outlines some important examples of them. They include all available correspondence between Janet Taylor and the UK Hydrographic Office, the Admiralty, the Astronomer Royal Sir George Airy and numerous others. Many of these are letters and manuscripts that can only be found by an inspection of the original copies since they are not available any other way.

The primary sources are those that contained material that could generally be obtained only by a personal inspection of the original documents. The books listed below are separate from the material referenced above and are divided into the two relevant categories; namely, the environment in which Janet Taylor lived and the development of sea navigation with emphasis on the period until her death.

Primary Sources
Admiralty Library, Portsmouth
Airy papers, Cambridge University Library, Cambridge
Atlas magazine
Athenaeum magazine
British Census Household records 1841–1881
British Library (including the Peel collection), London
British Science Museum, London
Burial Records, Parish of St Helen Auckland, County Durham
Clergy List for London, 1866
Court Minutes, Trinity House, London
Durham University Library, Durham

Durham County Advertiser
Durham County Records Office, Durham
Durham Diocesan Records
Family Record Centre, London
General Register Office (Births, Deaths and Marriages), London
Great Exhibition 1851, catalogue
Guildhall Library, London, manuscripts Section
Headstones, cemetery in the churchyard of St Helen Auckland, Durham
Henning Collection of documents, Mitchell Library, Sydney
Liverpool Mail
Mercantile Marine Magazine and Nautical Record
National Maritime Museum, Greenwich
Nautical Magazine
National Almanac and Astronomical Ephemeris
Patent Office, London
Post Office Street Directories, London
Public Record Office, Kew
Royal Archives, Windsor Castle
St Katherine Coleman Church Baptism and Burial records, London
Sydney Morning Herald, Sydney
The *Times* newspaper
UK Hydrographic Office Archives (Minute Books), Taunton, Somerset
United Service Journal and Military Magazine

Selected Books and Articles

English life during the time of Janet Taylor

Adams, S. et al, *The Illustrated History of the 19th Century* (Rochester, Kent: Grange Books, 2000)

Atkinson, A., *A Further History of Wolsingham Grammar School* (UK, 2014)

Bevington, M. M., *The Saturday Review, 1855–1868: Representative Educated Opinion in Victorian England* (London: Periodical Publications, 1941)

Briggs, A., *The Age of Improvement, 1783–1867* (London: Longman, 1979)

Brundage, A., *The Making of the New Poor Law: the Politics of Inquiry, Enactment and Implementation, 1832–39* (London: Hutchinson, 1978)

Christopher, J., *The London & Blackwall Railway – Docklands' First Railway* (Stroud, Gloucestershire: Amberley Publishing, 2013)

Cunnington, C. W., *English Women's Clothing in the Nineteenth Century: A Comprehensive Guide with 1,117 Illustrations* (London: Dover, 1990)

Daiches, J., *The Victorian Home* (London: Batsford, 1977)

Dawson, L. S., *Memoirs of Hydrography* (London: Cornmarket Press, 1969, reprint of the original 1885 edition)

Day, A., *Admiralty Hydrographic Service, 1795–1919* (London: HMSO, 1967)

Digby, A., *Children, School and Society in Nineteenth Century England* (London: Macmillan, 1981)

Emmerson, A., *The Underground Pioneers: Victorian London and its first underground railways* (Harrow Weald: Capital Transport Pub., 2000)

Finn, M. C., *After Chartism. Class and nation in English radical politics, 1848-1874* (Cambridge: Cambridge University Press, 1993)

Fletcher, S., *Feminists and bureaucrats: a study in the development of girls' education in the nineteenth century* (Cambridge: Cambridge University Press, 1980)

Gray, H., 'East End, West End: Science Education, Culture and Class in Mid-Victorian London' (1997), 32 *Canadian Journal of History*, pp. 153–183

Lane, P., *The Victorian Age 1830–1914* (London: B.T. Betsford, 1972)

Lasdun, S., *Victorians at Home* (London: Weidenfeld & Nicolson, 1981)

Margetson, S., *Fifty Years of Victorian London, from the Great Exhibition to the Queen's death* (London: MacDonald and Co., 1969)

Metcalf, P., *Victorian London* (London: Cassell, 1972)

Patterson, E. C., 'Mary Somerville' (1969) 4 (16) *British Journal for the History of Science*, pp. 311–339

Patterson, E. C., *Mary Somerville and the Cultivation of Science, 1815–1840* (The Hague: Martinus Nijhoff Publishers, 1983)

Roach, J., *A History of Secondary Education in England, 1800–1870* (London: Longman, 1986)

Robbins, K., *Nineteenth-Century Britain: Integration and Diversity* (Oxford: Oxford University, Press, 1988)

Rude, G., *Criminal and Victim: crime and society in early nineteenth-century England* (Oxford: Clarendon Press, 1985)

Seaman, L.C.B., *Life in Victorian London* (London: Batsford, 1973)

Somerville, M., *Personal Recollections, From Early Life to Old Age, of Mary Somerville* (Boston: Roberts Brothers, 1874)

Stamp, G., *Victorian Buildings of London 1837–1887, An Illustrated Guide.* (London: Architectural Press, 1980)

Tames, R., *Victorian London* (London: Batsford Academic and Educational, 1984)

Thrall, A., *The History of Adult Education in the 19th Century* (Doncaster. Metropolitan Borough Museums and Arts Service, South Yorkshire, 1977)

Wood, A., *Nineteenth century Britain 1815–1914* (London: Longman, 1960)

Wood, R., *A Victorian House* (Hove: Wayland, 1998)

Navigation covering to the end of the nineteenth century

Ageton, A. A., *Manual of Celestial Navigation* (New Jersey: D. Van Nostrand Co., Inc., second edition, 1961)

Airy, G. B., *Autobiography of Sir George Biddell Airy* (Cambridge: Cambridge University Press, 1896)

Albuquerque, Luís de, *Instruments of Navigation* (Lisbon: Comissão Nacional para as Comemoraçoes dos Descobrimentos Portugueses, 1988)

Alexander, W. C., *Modern Navigation: The Chronometers' Assistant (Great Circular Navigation, A Ship's Position)* (London: W. C. Alexander, 1855)

Allen, J., *The Navigation Laws of Great Britain, Historically and Practically Considered, with Reference to Commercial and National Defence* (London: Baily Bros & James Ridgway, 1849)

Armstrong, R. *The Early Mariners* (New York: F. A. Praeger Pub., 1967)

Astour, M.C., *Hellenosemitica. An Ethnic and Cultural Study in West Semetic Impact on Mycenaenn Greece* (Leiden: E. J. Brill, 1965)

Barham, W. H., *Theory and Practice of Navigation* (London & Glasgow, 1893)

Beazley C. R., *John and Sebastian Cabot: The Discovery of North America* (1964)

Becher, A., *Navigation of the Atlantic and Indian Oceans* (London, Potter, second edition, 1859)

Blance, A. G., *Norie's Nautical Tables with Explanations of their Use* (Cambridgeshire: Imray, Laurie, Norie and Wilson, 1983)

Brown, J., *The description and use of the triangular quadrant* (London: John Darby for John Wingfield, 1671)

Browne, J.H., *The Navigation Laws: their history and operation* (London: Smith, Elder & Co., 1847)

Bryant, Sir Arthur, *Pepys and the Revolution* (London: Collins, 1979)

Budlong, J. P., *Sky and sextant. practical celestial navigation* (New York: Van Nostrand Reinhold, 1975)

Calder, N. *How to Read a Nautical Chart* (2003)

Cardoza, Rod, *Evolution of the Sextant*, edited by A. N. Stimson, Head of Navigation Section, Department of Astronomy and Navigation, National Maritime Museum, Greenwich, England

Cohen, J. M., *The Four Voyages of Christopher Columbus* (1969)

Coldham, P. W., *Child Apprentices in America from Christ's Hospital, London, 1617–1778* (Baltimore: Genealogical Publishing, 1990)

Cook, M., *Cook's Sextant Tables* (Middlesex: Vega Instruments, 1980)

Cotter, C. H., *A history of the navigator's sextant* (Glasgow, 1983)

Cousins, F. W., *Sundials* (John Baker Pub., 1969)

Crane, N., *Mercator: the Man Who Mapped the Planet* (Orion, 2002)

Denne, W., *Magnetic Compass Deviation and Correction: A Manual of the Theory of the Deviations and Mechanical Correction of Magnetic Compasses in Ships* (Glasgow: Brown and Ferguson, 1979)

Forbes, E. G., *The Birth of Scientific Navigation: the Solving in the 18th Century of the Problem of Finding Longitude at Sea* (London: National Maritime Museum, 1974)

Foster, S. *The Description and Use of the Nocturnal* (London, *c.* 1685)

Frost, A. A., *The Principles and Practice of Navigation* (Glasgow: Brown and Ferguson, 1978)

Ganeri, A., *From Sextant to Sonar, the Story of Maps and Navigation* (London: Evans, 1998)

Goodman, N., *Polaris and All That (Navigational Expedients Using Elementary Astronomy* (London: British Astronomical Association, 1974)

Growhurst, R. P., *The Voyage of the* Pitt: *a Turning Point in East India Navigation.* Pamphlet (1969)

Green, Peter, *The Year of Salamis, 480–479 BC* (London: Weidenfeld and Nicolson, 1970)

Hakluyt, R., *Principall Navigations* (Pub. George Bishop and Ralph Newbery, 1587)

Hale, J. R., *Age of Exploration* (Amsterdam: Time-Life Intl, 1966)

Harden, Donald, *The Phoenicians* (Thames and Hudson, 1962)

Hawkes, C. F. C., *Pytheas: Europe and the Greek Explorers* (Oxford, 1977)

Herm, G., *The Phoenicians: the Purple Empire of the Ancient World* (London: Gollancz, 1975)

Hewson, J. B., *The History of the Practice of Navigation* (Glasgow: Brown, Son & Ferguson Ltd, second edition,1983)

Hogben, R., *A Sharp Lookout: One Hundred Years of Maritime History as Reported by 'Fairplay'* (London: Fairplay Pub. Ltd, 1983)

Hope, R., *A New History of British Shipping* (London: John Murray, 1990)

Howse, N., *Nevil Maskelyne: the seaman's astronomer* (Cambridge: Cambridge University Press, 1989)

Howse, D., *Greenwich Time and the Discovery of Longitude* (Oxford, 1980)

Hues, Robert, *Tractatus de Globis et eorum usu* (London: Hakluyt Society, 1889)

Huntingford, G. W. B. (trans.) *Periplus of the Erythraen Sea* (Hakluyt Society, 2nd series, No. 151, 1980)

Itzkowitz, N. and C. Imber, *The Ottoman Empire: the Classical Age, 1300–1600* (London: Weidenfeld and Nicolson, 1973)

Jerchow. Friedrich, *From Sextant to Satellite Navigation. 1837–1987, 150 years* (Hamburg: C. Plath, 1987)

Kennedy, G. (ed.), *The Merchant Marine in International Affairs, 1850–1950* (London: Frank Cass, 2000)

Laughton, J. K., Rev. Rodger, N. A. M., 'Sir Francis Beaufort', *Oxford DNB online*

Lenardon, Robert J., *The Saga of Themistocles* (London: Thames and Hudson, 1978)

Lewis, D., *The Voyaging Stars: Secrets of the Pacific Island Navigators* (Sydney: Collins, 1978)

Lindsay, W. S., *History of Merchant Shipping and Ancient Commerce* (London, 1876), Vol. III

Lloyd, C., *Sir Francis Drake* (London: Faber, 1979)

Markham, C. R., *The Journal of Christopher Columbus (During his First Voyage 1492–1493) and Documents Relating to the Voyages of John Cabot and Gas par Corte Real* (London: Hakluyt Society, 1893)

Markoe, Glenn E., *Phoenicians (Peoples of the Past)* (University of California Press, 2001)

Maunder, E. W., *The Royal Observatory, Greenwich: a Glance at its History and Work* (London: The Religious Tract Society, 1900)

May, W. E., *A History of Marine Navigation* (Henley on Thames: Foulis, 1973)

Mayer, H. E., *The Crusades* (second edition) (Oxford University Press, 1990)

McConnell, A., *R. B. Bate of the Poultry, 1782–1847: the Life and Times of a Scientific Instrument Maker* (London: Scientific Instrument Society, 1993)

McConnell, A., *No Sea Too Deep: The History of Oceanographic Instruments* (Bristol: Adam Hill Ltd, 1982)

McMurtie, F. E., *The Romance of Navigation* (London: Marsh & Co., Samson Row, 1925)

McPike, E. F., *Hevelius, Flamsteed and Halley* (1937)

Mennim, E., *Transit Circle: the Story of William Simms (1793–1860)* (York: William Sessions, 1992)

Mills, H. R., *Positional Astronomy and Astro-Navigation Made Easy: A New Approach Using the Pocket Calculator* (Cheltenham: Stanley Thornes Ltd, 1978)

Mörzer Bruyns, W. F. J., *The Cross-Staff: History and Development of a Navigational Instrument* (Amsterdam: Vereeniging Nederlandsch Historisch Scheepvaart Museum, 1994)

Nautical Almanac and Astronomical Ephemeris, founded and published by Nevil Maskelyne (1767–1811)

Nicolle, D., *Constantinople 1453: The End of Byzantium* (Osprey, 2001)

Parker, G., *Philip II* (London: Hutchinson, 1978)

Pigafetta, A., *Magellan's Voyage: A Narrative Account of the First Circumnavigation* (trans. R. A. Skelton) (New Haven and London: Yale University Press, 1969)

Pike, D. and O. M. Watts, *The Sextant Simplified*, seventh edition (2003)

Rajamanickam. G. and V. Gnanamanickam (eds), *History of Traditional Navigation* (Thanjavur: Tamil University, 1988)

Robertson, J., *The Elements of Navigation* (two volumes) (London, 1753)

Rutsala, D., *The Sea Route to Asia: The Adventures of the Portuguese Explorers, from Prince Henry the Navigator to Bartholomeu Dias and Vasco De Game (Exploration & Discovery)* (Mason Crest Pub., 2002)

Smith, A. M., *Ptolemy and the Foundations of Ancient Mathematical Optics: A Source-Based Guided Study* (Philadelphia American Philosophical Society, 1999)

Sobel, D., *Longitude* (Walker Pub., USA, 1995)

Starkey, H. F., *Iron Clipper* Tayleur: *The White Star Lines First* Titanic (Bebington, UK: Avid Publications, 1999)

Stefoff, Rebecca and William H. Goetzmann, *Vasco De Gama and the Portuguese Explorers* (Chelsea House, 1993)

Taylor, Eva Germaine Rimington, *Navigation in the Days of Captain Cook* (Greenwich, London: National Maritime Museum, 1974)

Taylor, Eva Germaine Rimington, *The Haven-Finding Art: A History of Navigation from Odysseus to Captain Cook* (London: Hollis and Carter, 1956)

The King George III Museum Collection, [1768-1970] K/MUS 1: Manuscript notebooks recording astronomical and meteorological observations compiled mainly at the Royal Observatory, Kew, with related notes on telescopic apparatus [1768-1840]. Ref. K/MUS 1/6 1772.

The Safegarde of Saylers or great Rutter, SAFEGUARD (London: Edward Allde, 1590)

Toghill, J., *Celestial Navigation for Beginners* (London: Ward Lock, 1980)

Thoren, Victor E., *The Lord of Uraniborg: A Biography of Tycho Brahe* (Cambridge: Cambridge University Press, 1990)

Turnbull, D., *Mapping the World in the Mind. An Investigation of the Unwritten Knowledge of the Micronesian Navigators* (Geelong, Victoria: Deakin University Press, 1991)

Villiers, A. J., *The Last of the Wind Ships, Introductory Text by Basil Greenhill, Extracts from Published Works by Alan Villiers* (London: Harvill Press, 2000)

Waters, D. W., *Science and the Techniques of Navigation in the Renaissance* (London: National Maritime Museum, 1976)

Williams, D. and A. White, *A Select Bibliography of British and Irish University Theses about Maritime History, 1792 to 1900* (International Maritime Economic History Association, 1991)

Williams, J. E. D., *From Sails to Satellites: the origin and development of navigational science* (Oxford University Press, 1992)

Biographical sources
On Janet

Alger, K. R., *Mrs Janet Taylor – 'Authoress and Instructress in Navigation and Nautical Astronomy' (1804–1870)* (Fawcett Library Papers No. 6, LLRS Publications, 1982)

Anderson, W., *Model Women*, Second Edition (London, 1871), pp. 228–240

Boase, F., *Modern English Biography* (London: Frank Cass, 1965)

Clifton, G. C., *Directory of British Scientific Instrument Makers 1550–1851* (London: Zwemmer in association with the National Maritime Museum), p. 275

Croucher, J. S. and R. F., 'Mrs Janet Taylor's "Mariner's Calculator": Assessment and Reassessment' (2011) 44 *British Journal for the History of Science* pp. 493–507

Croucher, R. F. and J. S., 'Mrs Janet Taylor and the Civil List Pension – a Claim to Recognition by Her Country' (2012) 21 (2), *Women's History Review*, pp. 253–280

Fisher, S., 'Taylor [*née* Ionn], Janet (1804–1870)', *Oxford Dictionary of National Biography online*

Haines, Catharine M. C., *International Women in Science: A Biographical Dictionary to 1950* (ABC–CLIO, 2001)

Taylor, E. G. R., *The Mathematical Practitioners of Hanoverian England 1714–1840* (Cambridge: The Institute of Navigation, Cambridge University Press, 1966), pp. 101–102, pp. 461–462.

On the family

Devey, T. V., *Records of Wolsingham* (Northumberland Press, 1926)

Lambert, J. H., *Wolsingham From Early Times to 1938* (Unpublished manuscript, 1960)

Surtees, H. C., *The History of the Parish of Wolsingham* (1929)

Family records held by the descendants of Frederick Peter Ionn, Janet's youngest brother.

Index

About the Authors

John S. Croucher is a Professor of Statistics at Macquarie University, Sydney. He has published over 130 research papers and 30 books, including the popular biography *The Kid from Norfolk Island*. He has been a Visiting Professor at the University of London (Birkbeck) and for eight years was a television presenter on football. John holds four PhDs and was the winner of the inaugural Distinguished Alumni Award at Macquarie University and in 2013 the prestigious Prime Minister's Award for Australian University Teacher of the Year, his five national outstanding teacher awards being the most of anyone in the country. He was the author of the column *Statistically Speaking* for the *Mail on Sunday* as well as *Number Crunch* in the *Sydney Morning Herald* for twelve years. A Fellow of both the Royal Society of Arts (RSA) and the Australian Mathematical Society, in 2015 John was made a Member of the Order of Australia (AM) for 'significant service to mathematical science in the field of statistics, as an academic, author and mentor and to professional organisations'.

Rosalind F. Croucher is an Adjunct Professor of Macquarie University and former Dean of Law at Macquarie and Sydney Universities. In 2011 she was recognised as one of the 40 'inspirational alumni' of UNSW, where she gained her PhD in legal history. In 2014 she was named as Australian Woman Lawyer of the Year and among the 100 most influential women in the country. She is also an author of a number of books and has published research in leading journals principally in the fields of equity, trusts, property, inheritance and legal history. A fellow of the Royal Society of Arts (RSA), and a Foundation Fellow of the Australian Academy of Law in 2007, Rosalind is an Honorary Fellow of both the Australian College of Legal Medicine and St Andrews' College in the University of Sydney. In 2015, she was made a Member of the Order of Australia (AM) for 'significant service to the law as an academic, to legal reform and education, to professional development, and to the arts'.

John S. Croucher photograph courtesy of Macquarie University. Rosalind F. Croucher photograph courtesy of Andy Baker.